DATA BASE

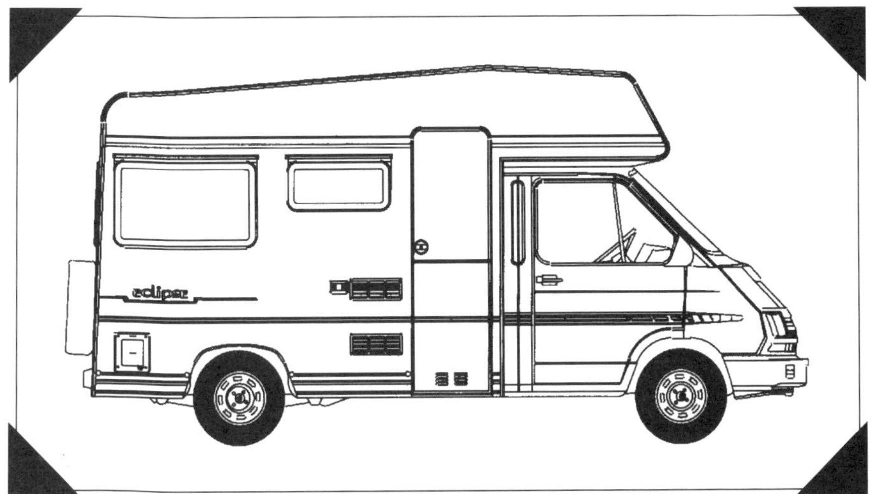

This page enables you to compile a list of useful data on your motor caravan, so that all the key information is easily within reach when you need it.

Make: ....

Model: ....

Body colour/s: ....

Paint code no./s (if known): ....

Year of manufacture: ....

VIN/Chassis number: ....

Unladen weight: ....

Maximum laden weight (MAM): ....

Maximum load capacity: ....

Overall length: ....

Overall width: ....

Overall height: ....

Fresh water capacity: ....

Waste tank capacity: ....

Tyre pressures

Front: ....

Rear: ....

Fridge model no.: ....

Heater model no.: ....

Oven model no.: ....

Cab door key number: ....

Other door key number/s: ....

Security lock number (if applicable): ....

Local dealership/s name and address:..

....

Telephone:...

Manufacturer's name and address:...

....

Telephone:...

Modifications:

....

Information that might be useful when you need to purchase parts: ....

....

....

(Illustration, courtesy Elddis Caravans)

First published in 1997 by Porter Publishing Ltd.

Porter Publishing Ltd.
The Storehouse
Little Hereford Street
Bromyard
Hereford HR7 4DE
England

British Library Cataloguing in Publication Data.

A catalogue record for this book is available from the British Library.

ISBN 1-899238-20-4

Series Editor: Lindsay Porter
Design: Martin Driscoll, Lindsay Porter and Lyndsay Berryman
Layout and Typesetting: Pineapple Publishing, Worcester
Cover photography: Jeremy Gale
Printed in England by The Trinity Press, Worcester.

Every care has been taken to ensure that the material contained in this Service Guide is correct. However, no liability can be accepted by the authors or publishers for damage, loss, accidents, or injury resulting from any omissions or errors in the information given.

Titles in this Series:

Absolute Beginners' Service Guide
Auto Electrics - DIY Service Manual
Caravan Owner's Manual & Service Guide
Classic 'Bike Service Guide
Diesel Car Engines Service Guide
Ford Escort (Front Wheel Drive) & Orion Service Guide
Ford Fiesta Service Guide
Ford Sierra (All models) Service Guide
Land Rover Series I, II, III Service Guide
Land Rover Defender, 90 & 110 Service Guide
Land Rover Discovery & Range Rover Service Guide
Metro (1980-1990) Service Guide
MG Midget & Austin-Healey Sprite Service Guide
Mini (all models 1959-1994) Service Guide
MGB (including MGC, MGB GT V8 and MG RV8) Service Guide
Peugeot 205 Service Guide
The Complete Trailer Manual
Vauxhall Astra & Belmont Service Guide
Vauxhall Cavalier Service Guide
Vauxhall Nova Service Guide
VW Beetle Service Guide

- With more titles in production -

The Complete Motor Caravan Manual

by

Lindsay Porter

Foreword

Motor caravanning has taken great strides over the last few decades both in terms of the appeal of this type of recreation and the technological advances in designs.

In today's competitive market place the motor caravanner has a bewildering choice of converters and conversions. From the lovingly individual DIY conversion to the sumptuous 40 ft American RV's, there is a motor caravan to suit all tastes and budgets.

Once the initial hurdle of purchasing the motor caravan has been overcome, then all that is left is to set off and enjoy this new found freedom...OR IS IT?

Visit any motor caravan rally on a Saturday afternoon and you will find groups of motor caravanners huddled round open tool boxes - "tinkering"! There always seems to be a need to modify, replace or update, or even just to show a fellow motor caravanner how something works. This need, has always been based on self taught skills or skills passed on by word of mouth. It has been difficult, until now, to come across a suitable publication that will guide the motor caravanner through all aspects of their hobby.

Here we have a publication that will help the novice with their first purchase and will also help all motor caravanners to update existing equipment, carry out modifications or servicing. "The Motor Caravan Manual" will not only be an invaluable reference item for all motor caravanners but will hopefully become an addition to the joys of motor caravanning.

Colin Reay
Executive Secretary
The Motor Caravanners' Club Ltd

Colin Reay

CONTENTS

	Data Base	***1***
CHAPTER 1:	***Safety First!***	***5***
	PART I: Important Points	5
	PART II: Servicing Hazards	6
	PART III: General Workshop Safety	8
	PART IV: General Motor Caravan Safety	8
CHAPTER 2:	***Buying Guide***	***9***
	PART I: Considering the Options	9
	PART II: Taking the Plunge	15
	PART III: Avoiding a Bad Buy	19
CHAPTER 3:	***Using Your Motor Caravan***	***21***
	PART I: On the Road	21
	PART II: Getting Ready to Go	23
	PART III: On Site	27
CHAPTER 4:	***Operating Instructions***	***31***
	PART I: The Base Vehicle	31
	PART II: The Living Accommodation	35
CHAPTER 5:	***Servicing the Living Accommodation***	***57***
	PART I: Preparing for the Start of the Season	57
	PART II: Before Every Long Journey	72
	PART III: Regular Checks	72
	PART IV: Every Three Months	76
	PART V: Once a Year	78
	PART VI: Preparing for Storage at End of Season	87
CHAPTER 6:	***Servicing & Maintenance***	***95***
	Engine Bay	95
	Around the Car	114
	Under the Car	120
	Longer Term Servicing	122
APPENDIX 1:	***Specialists and Suppliers***	***123***
APPENDIX 2:	***What to Take***	***124***
APPENDIX 3:	***Service Schedule***	***125***
	INDEX	***127***

Acknowledgments

So many people have assisted in the production of this book that it's difficult to know where to stop. Ivor Carroll contributed the 'words' for Chapter 6. My wife, Shan, took dozens of photographs for Chapter 5 and 6. Auto-Sleepers were extremely generous with their invaluable advice and support, as were Hayes Leisure, while Brownhills Motorcaravans also chipped in. The National Caravan Council also provided invaluable advice. A large number of manufacturers provided technical advice (see page 123) and at the fore were FIAT, Volkswagen and Mercedes Benz. Sincere and grateful thanks to all!

Lindsay Porter
Bromyard

CHAPTER 1 - SAFETY FIRST!

You must always ensure that safety is the first consideration in any job you carry out. A slight lack of concentration, or a rush to finish the job quickly can easily result in an accident, as can failure to follow the precautions outlined in this Chapter. Whereas skilled motor mechanics are trained in safe working practices you, the home mechanic, must find them out for yourself and act upon them.

Remember, accidents don't just happen, they are caused, and some of those causes are contained in the following list. Above all, ensure that whenever you work on your car you adopt a safety-minded approach at all times, and remain aware of the dangers that might be encountered.

Be sure to consult the suppliers of any materials and equipment you may use, and to obtain and read carefully any operating and health and safety instructions that may be available on packaging or from manufacturers and suppliers.

PART I: IMPORTANT POINTS

Vehicle Off Ground

ALWAYS ensure that the vehicle is properly supported when raised off the ground. Don't work on, around, or underneath a raised vehicle unless axle stands are positioned under secure, load bearing underbody areas, or the vehicle is driven onto ramps, with the wheels remaining on the ground securely chocked to prevent movement.

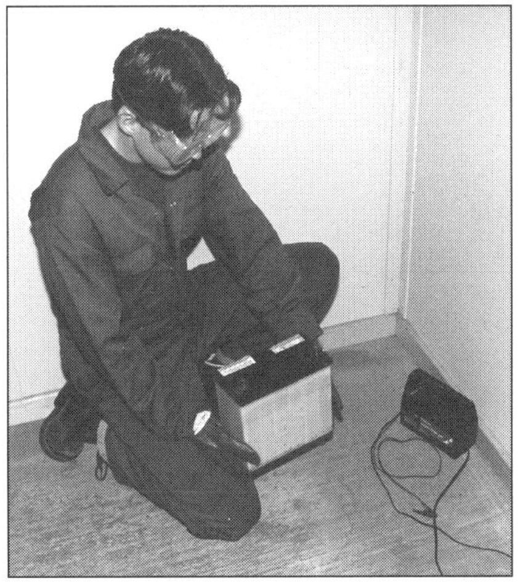

ALWAYS ensure that the safe working load rating of any jacks, hoists or lifting gear used is sufficient for the job, and that lifting gear is used only as recommended by the manufacturer.

NEVER attempt to loosen or tighten nuts that require a lot of force to turn (e.g. a tight oil drain plug) with the vehicle raised, unless it is safely supported. Take care not to pull the vehicle off its supports when applying force to a spanner. Wherever possible, initially slacken tight fastenings before raising the car off the ground.

ALWAYS wear eye protection when working under the vehicle and when using power tools.

Working On The Vehicle

ALWAYS seek specialist advice unless you are justifiably confident about carrying out each job. The safety of your vehicle affects you, your passengers and other road users.

DON'T lean over, or work on, a running engine unless it is strictly necessary, and keep long hair and loose clothing well out of the way of moving mechanical parts. Note that it is theoretically possible for fluorescent striplighting to make an engine fan appear to be stationary - double check whether it is spinning or not! This is the sort of error that happens when you're really tired and not thinking straight. So...

...DON'T work on your vehicle when you're over tired.

ALWAYS work in a well ventilated area and don't inhale dust - it may contain asbestos or other harmful substances.

REMOVE your wrist watch, rings and all other jewellery before doing any work on the vehicle - and especially when working on the electrical system.

DON'T remove the radiator or expansion tank filler cap when the cooling system is hot, or you may get scalded by escaping coolant or steam. Let the system cool down first and even then, if the engine is not completely cold, cover the cap with a cloth and gradually release the pressure.

NEVER drain oil, coolant or automatic transmission fluid when the engine is hot. Allow time for it to cool sufficiently to avoid scalding you.

ALWAYS keep antifreeze, brake and clutch fluid away from vehicle paintwork. Wash off any spills immediately.

TAKE CARE to avoid touching any engine or exhaust system component unless it is cool enough not to burn you.

Running The Vehicle

NEVER start the engine unless the gearbox is in neutral (or 'Park' in the case of automatic transmission) and the hand brake is fully applied.

NEVER run catalytic converter equipped vehicles without the exhaust system heat shields in place.

TAKE CARE when parking vehicles fitted with catalytic

converters. The 'cat' reaches extremely high temperatures and any combustible materials under the vehicle, such as long dry grass, could be ignited.

Personal Safety

NEVER siphon fuel, antifreeze, brake fluid or other such toxic liquids by mouth, or allow contact with your skin. There is an increasing awareness that they can damage your health. Best of all, use a suitable hand pump and wear gloves.

BEFORE undertaking dirty jobs, use a barrier cream on your hands as a protection against infection. Preferably, wear thin gloves, available from DIY outlets.

WEAR GLOVES for sure when there is a risk of used engine oil coming into contact with your skin. It can cause cancer.

WIPE UP any spilt oil, grease or water off the floor immediately, before there is an accident.

MAKE SURE that spanners and all other tools are the right size for the job and are not likely to slip. Never try to 'double-up' spanners to gain more leverage.

SEEK HELP if you need to lift something heavy which may be beyond your capability. Don't forget that when lifting a heavy weight, you should keep your back straight and bend your knees to avoid injuring your back.

NEVER take risky short-cuts or rush to finish a job. Plan ahead and allow plenty of time.

BE METICULOUS and keep the work area tidy - you'll avoid frustration, work better and lose less.

KEEP children and animals right-away from the work area and from unattended vehicles.

ALWAYS tell someone what you're doing and have them regularly check that all is well, especially when working alone on, or under, the vehicle.

PART II: SERVICING HAZARDS

Fire!

Petrol (gasoline) is a dangerous and highly flammable liquid requiring special precautions. When working on the fuel system, disconnect the vehicle battery earth (ground) terminal whenever possible and always work outside, or in a very well ventilated area. Any form of spark, such as that caused by an electrical fault, by two metal surfaces striking against each other, by a central heating boiler in the garage 'firing up', or even by static electricity built up in your clothing can, in a confined space, ignite petrol vapour causing an explosion. Take great care not to spill petrol on to the engine or exhaust system, never allow any naked flame anywhere near the work area and, above all, don't smoke.

Invest in a workshop-sized fire extinguisher. Choose the carbon dioxide type or preferably, dry powder but never a water type extinguisher for workshop use. Water conducts electricity and can make worse an oil or petrol-based fire, in certain circumstances.

DON'T disconnect any fuel pipes on a fuel injected engine while the ignition is switched on. The fuel in the line is under very high pressure - sufficient to cause serious injury. Remember that many injection systems have residual pressure in the pipes for days after switching off. Consult the workshop manual or seek specialist advice before carrying out any work.

Fumes

In addition to the fire dangers described previously, petrol (gasoline) vapour and the types of vapour given off by many solvents, thinners, and adhesives are highly toxic and under certain conditions can lead to unconsciousness or even death, if inhaled. The risks are increased if such fluids are used in a confined space so always ensure adequate ventilation when handling materials of this nature. Treat all such substances with care, always read the instructions and follow them with care.

Always ensure that the vehicle is out of doors and not in an enclosed space when the engine is running. Exhaust fumes contain poisonous carbon monoxide, even when the vehicle is fitted with a catalytic converter, since 'cats' sometimes fail and don't function when the engine is cold.

Never drain petrol (gasoline) or use solvents, thinners adhesives or other toxic substances in an inspection pit as the extremely confined space allows the highly toxic fumes to concentrate. Running the engine with the vehicle over the pit can have the same results. It is also dangerous to park a vehicle for any length of time over an inspection pit. The fumes from even a slight fuel leak can cause an explosion when the engine is started. Petrol fumes are heavier than air and will accumulate in the pit.

Mains Electricity

Best of all, avoid the use of mains electricity when working on the vehicle, whenever possible. For instance, you could use rechargeable tools and a DC inspection lamp, powered from a remote 12V battery - both are much safer. However, if you do use mains-powered equipment, ensure that the appliance is wired correctly to its plug, that where necessary it is properly earthed (grounded), and that the fuse is of the correct rating for the appliance is fitted. For instance, a 13 amp fuse in lead lamp's plug will not provide adequate protection. Do not use any mains powered equipment in damp conditions or in the vicinity of fuel, fuel vapour or the vehicle battery.

Also, before using any mains powered electrical equipment, take one more simple precaution - use an RCD (Residual Current Device) circuit breaker. Then, if there is a short, the RCD circuit breaker minimises the risk of electrocution by instantly cutting the power supply. Buy one from any electrical store or DIY centre. RCDs fit simply into your electrical socket before plugging in your electrical equipment.

The Ignition System

You should never work on a petrol engine's ignition system with the ignition switched on, or with the engine being turned over on the starter, or running.

Touching certain parts of the ignition system, such as the HT leads, distributor cap, ignition coil etc, can result in a severe electric shock. This is especially likely where the insulation on any of these components is weak, or if the components are dirty or damp. Note also that voltages produced by electronic ignition systems are much higher than those produced by conventional systems and could prove fatal, particularly to people with cardiac pacemaker implants. Consult your handbook or main dealer if in any doubt.

An additional risk of injury can arise while working on running engines, if the operator touches a high voltage lead and pulls his or her hand away on to a sharp, conductive or revolving part.

The Battery

Never cause a spark, smoke, or allow a naked light near the vehicle's battery, even in a well ventilated area. Highly explosive hydrogen gas will be given off as part of the charging process.

Battery terminals on the vehicle should be shielded, since a spark can be caused by any metal object which touches the battery's terminals or connecting straps.

Before working on the fuel or electrical systems, always disconnect the battery earth (ground) terminal. (But before doing so, read the relevant FACT FILE in *Chapter 5* regarding saving computer and radio settings.)

When using a battery charger, care should be taken to avoid causing a spark by switching off the power supply before the battery charger leads are connected or disconnected. Before charging the battery from an external source, disconnect both battery leads before connecting the charger. If the battery is not of the 'sealed-for-life' type, loosen the filler plugs or remove the cover before charging. For best results the battery should be given a low rate trickle charge overnight. Do not charge at an excessive rate or the battery may burst.

Always wear gloves and goggles when carrying or when topping up the battery. Even in diluted form (as it is in the battery) the acid electrolyte is extremely corrosive and must not be allowed to contact the eyes, skin or clothes.

Brakes and Asbestos

Obviously, any vehicle's brakes are among its most important safety related items. ONLY work on your vehicle's braking system if you are trained and competent to do so. If you have not been trained in this work, but wish to carry out the jobs described in this book, we strongly recommend that you have a garage or qualified mechanic check your work before using the vehicle.

Whenever you work on the braking system's mechanical components, or remove front or rear brake pads or shoes: i) wear an efficient particle mask; ii) wipe off all brake dust from the brakes after spraying on a proprietary brand of brake cleaner (never blow dust off with compressed air); iii) dispose of brake dust and discarded shoes or pads in a sealed plastic bag; iv) wash your hands thoroughly after you have finished working on the brakes and certainly before you eat or smoke; v) replace shoes and pads only with asbestos-free shoes or pads. Note that asbestos brake dust can cause cancer if inhaled.

Brake Fluid

Brake fluid absorbs moisture rapidly from the air and can become dangerous resulting in brake failure. We recommend that you should have your brake fluid tested at least once a year by a properly equipped garage with test equipment and you should change the fluid in accordance with your vehicle manufacturer's recommendations or as advised in this book if we recommend a shorter interval than the manufacturer. You should buy no more brake fluid than you need, in smaller rather than larger containers. Never store an opened container of brake fluid. Dispose of the remainder at your Local Authority Waste Disposal Site, in the designated disposal unit, not with general waste or with waste oil.

Engine Oils

Take care to observe the following precautions when working with used engine oil. Apart from the obvious risk of scalding when draining the oil from a hot engine, there is the danger from contamination contained in all used oil.

Always wear disposable plastic or rubber gloves when draining the oil from your engine. i) Note that the drain plug and the oil are often hotter than you expect. Wear gloves if the plug is too hot to touch and keep your hand to one side so that you are not scalded by the spurt of oil as the plug comes away; ii) There are very real health hazards associated with used engine oil. In the words of one manufacturer's handbook "Prolonged and repeated contact may cause serious skin disorders, including dermatitis and cancer." Use a barrier cream on your hands and try not to get oil on them. Always wear gloves and wash your hands with hand cleaner soon after carrying out the work. Keep oil out of the reach of children; iii) NEVER, EVER dispose of old engine oil into the ground or down a drain. In the UK, and in most EC countries, every local authority must provide a safe means of oil disposal. In the UK, try your local Environmental Health Department for advice on waste disposal facilities.

Plastic Materials

Work with plastic materials brings additional hazards into workshops. Many of the materials used (polymers, resins, adhesives and materials acting as catalysts and accelerators) contain dangers in the form of poisonous fumes, skin irritants, and the risk of fire and explosions. Do not allow resin or 2-pack adhesive hardener, or that supplied with filler or 2-pack stopper, to come into contact with skin or eyes. Read carefully the safety notes supplied on the can, tube or packaging and always wear impervious gloves and goggles when working with them.

Jacks and Axle Stands

Throughout this book you will see many references to the correct use of jacks, axle stands and similar equipment - and we make no apologies for being repetitive. This is one area where safety cannot be overstressed - your life could be at stake!

Special care must be taken when any type of lifting equipment is used. Jacks are made for lifting the vehicle only, not for supporting it while it is being worked on. Never work under the vehicle using only a jack to support the weight. Jacks must be supplemented by adequate additional means of support, positioned under secure load-bearing parts of the frame or underbody. Axle stands are available from most auto. parts stores. Drive-on ramps are limiting because of their design and size but they are simple to use, reliable and offer the most stable type of support. We strongly recommend their use.

Almost all motor caravans are heavier - sometimes considerably heavier - than cars. You MUST use raising equipment and ramps which are suitable for your motor caravan and NOT the car-weight versions sold in most auto-accessory shops.

Full details on jacking and supporting the vehicle will be found near the beginning of *Chapter 5.*

PART III: GENERAL WORKSHOP SAFETY

1. Always have a fire extinguisher of the correct type at arm's length when working on the fuel system.

If you do have a fire, DON'T PANIC. Use the extinguisher effectively by directing it at the base of the fire.

2. NEVER use a naked flame anywhere in the workplace.

3. KEEP your inspection lamp well away from any source of petrol (gasoline) such as when disconnecting a carburettor float bowl or fuel line.

4. NEVER use petrol (gasoline) to clean parts. Use paraffin (kerosene), white spirits, or, a proprietary degreaser.

5. NO SMOKING. There's a risk of fire or of transferring dangerous substances to your mouth and, in any case, ash falling into mechanical components is to be avoided.

6. BE METHODICAL in everything you do, use common sense, and think of safety at all time.

PART IV: GENERAL MOTOR CARAVAN SAFETY

1. In the interests of safety, replacement parts for an appliance should conform to the appliance manufacturer's specification and should be fitted by them or their authorised agent.

2. NEVER use portable heating equipment. It can be both a fire hazard and an asphyxiation hazard.

3. NEVER allow modification of electrical or LPG systems or appliances to be carried out, except by fully qualified specialists.

4. Water heaters fitted to motor caravans are of the 'room sealed' type. Any replacement must also be of the same 'room sealed' type.

5. Water heaters without a flue to the outside should not be used in your motor caravan, because they can be extremely hazardous.

6. Turn off all gas equipment and cylinders or tanks and any other heating appliances before travelling except heaters which are intended to be used while the vehicle is in motion.

IMPORTANT NOTE: Heaters intended for use while the vehicle is in motion MUST be turned OFF before refuelling the vehicle or changing its gas cylinders or refilling gas tanks, when fitted.

7. Ventilation openings are located below all the gas appliances, and in the base of the gas locker. These openings should be regularly checked and any mesh covering them cleaned with a stiff brush to prevent any risk of their becoming blocked.

8. Ensure that the refrigerator ignition is switched off before you start your journey. Otherwise, sparks will repeatedly be created. This would be particularly dangerous when visiting a petrol station or when gas bottles are being connected or disconnected.

9. When children, invalids or elderly people are left unattended in the motor caravan any locks or stable door catches that are out of their reach should be left in the open position.

10. Ensure that the child proof lock is not activated when the motor caravan is parked off the road.

11. Do not store aerosol cans in any areas in which they could be affected by heat, such as near to heaters, heating ducts, cookers etc.

Thanks are due to Auto Sleepers Ltd. for their assistance with Part IV.

CHAPTER 2 - BUYING GUIDE

In Part I of this Chapter, we concentrate on the fun part of buying a motor caravan: which type, which engine, where to buy; all that kind of thing. In Part II we concentrate on the nitty-gritty: getting the best deal and making certain that you're not buying a heap of trouble.

Just think about it. The holiday you want when you want it. The weekend away when you need it. Or the perfect day out. You could spend a day at the races or a month overseas. And all with the luxury and convenience of taking your own home on wheels wherever you go.

One enthusiastic couple called their motor caravan, "A Wendy House on wheels for grown ups!" and silly though it may sound, that's not far off the mark. Until you've actually experienced it, you can't imagine the sheer pleasure of taking a compact version of your own home around with you, enabling you to go wherever you want whenever you want.

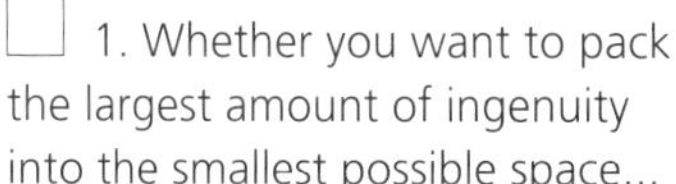

☐ 1. Whether you want to pack the largest amount of ingenuity into the smallest possible space...

☐ 2. ...or the maximum amount of luxury into something considerably bigger, motor caravanning is a recreational life style that can easily become a passion.

1

2

PART I: CONSIDERING THE OPTIONS

Shapes and Sizes

There is no answer to the question, "Which type of motor caravan is best?", because the right question to ask is, "Which type of motor caravan is best *for us*?" However, one excellent piece of advice we heard from a motor caravan salesman was, "Most people *think* they need a smaller motor caravan than they actually do!"

☐ 3. His advice - and it's sound! - is to get inside the living quarters with the seats in position, the door shut, preferably in the company of whoever you are going away with and imagine that outside, it's pouring down with rain for the second day running. Now, if you're the sort of person who insists on getting out and about no matter what the weather; if you're young, able bodied and determined to use your motor caravan as a warm, dry and infinitely more luxurious version of camping, the smallest vehicles may be fine for you.

3

Thanks are due to the Motor Caravan Information Service and the Caravan Club for some of the information supplied in connection with this Chapter.

If, on the other hand, you like having room to walk past your partner without having to sit down or (worse still!) have them tuck their knees up under their chin, you may want something a little larger.

For some, nothing less than a full scale American motorhome will do; for others the sheer convenience of being able to pop into the nearest town or use the vehicle as an everyday run-about are the most important features. As we said before, it's all a matter of what's right for you... But first of all, choose your weapon.

A-CLASS

4. Practically custom-built from the chassis up, these homes on wheels are definitely for the year-round, long distance motor caravanner. Although by far the most expensive option, (when new), any amount of equipment can be included for a truly luxurious home from home.

5. Main benefits: the wider cab often accommodates a drop-down roof bed which can be left made up ready for use...

6. ...and the cab seats usually swivel to form a part of the lounge area when on site. Space utilisation is, therefore, better than in a vehicle with a regular van cab.

COACHBUILT

7. With this type, a complete body section is built on to a chassis and cab, generally utilising the bonded construction favoured by trailer caravan manufacturers, which gives strength and rigidity and also offers a higher level of insulation than straightforward van conversions.

8. Alternatively, glass fibre reinforced plastic can be used for the complete shell or for roofs and end panels to allow rounded shapes.

9. With more space inside the interior than van conversions, coachbuilts can offer the type of facilities more often associated with a trailer caravan, including a permanent washroom/toilet compartment, and from two to six berth sleeping accommodation.

10. Over-cab coachbuilts, sometimes referred to as lutons, generally provide an extra double berth in the over-cab area while a low-profile coachbuilt is sometimes seen, with an elevating roof section over the main body.

HIGH-TOP

11. This consists of a permanently raised roof in place of the base vehicle's original roof (usually extending over the cab and sometimes plastic, though sometimes the van maker's optional steel high roof is used, for example Cockburn-Holdsworth Renaults which gives headroom generally between 6 ft. 6 in. and 6 ft. 9 in. The additional space means that two upper as well as two lower berths can often be provided and in some high-tops the rear portion can be sectioned off to provide a toilet/shower room. More insulation may be provided in the roof section although body insulation often remains fairly basic, with, usually, single-glazed windows in the van body. However, some now offer double-glazed plastic caravan-type windows (except windscreen and front doors). (Illustration, courtesy Auto-Sleepers)

ELEVATING ROOF

12. Basically the same as the fixed roof in terms of layout, but with the benefit of 'standing' headroom once the vehicle is stationary and the roof raised. On the road, the vehicle, like the fixed roof, can get under some height barriers that can pose problems for taller motor caravans, although check your measurements as the roof section does add a few inches to the basic van height.

13. Some elevating roof models offer room for extra sleeping accommodation in the roof section - generally canvas bunks and mainly suitable for children or lightweight/small adults. Some roof 'bellows' are flexible plastic, while some are insulated board. Plastic is prone to condensation overnight unless well ventilated and they are generally not as well insulated.

FIXED ROOF

14

14. These are perhaps the most restrictive of motor caravans, the roof height is that of the standard panel van and does not permit standing headroom. (Illustration, courtesy Murvi Motorcaravans)

Generally a two berth at most, additional space can be created by using an awning on the side or rear of the vehicle. Facilities and insulation are usually minimal with the exception of a few conversions that seem to be aimed at the away-from-home businessman rather than the average caravanner. Their raison d'entre is low overall height, allowing most of them to enter multi-storey car parks and domestic garages. Naturally they are also the cheapest type of conversion but many people add a fixed or elevating roof to them at a later date and as a result of their impracticality, this is the least commonly seen body type.

MICRO-MOTOR CARAVANS

15

15. These are smaller motor caravans, for those who perhaps need a dual-purpose vehicle for day to day motoring and weekend retreats. Space is limited but can always be augmented with an annexe. Small engines may give greater fuel economy, though at the expense of performance in some. Fixed or elevating roof models are available, together with small coachbuilts on this, the Bedford Rascal base van. Car derived van conversions - some now out of production - include the Citroen Visa, Peugeot 806 MPV, Austin Rover Maestro (out of production) and Seat Terra as base vehicles. The diesel engine options offer remarkable economy potential.

16

16. Interiors may be small-but-perfectly formed - but note how even the awning intrudes when packed away.

17

17. Even the driving room is minimal on the Bedford - and what about crash protection?

DISMOUNTABLE

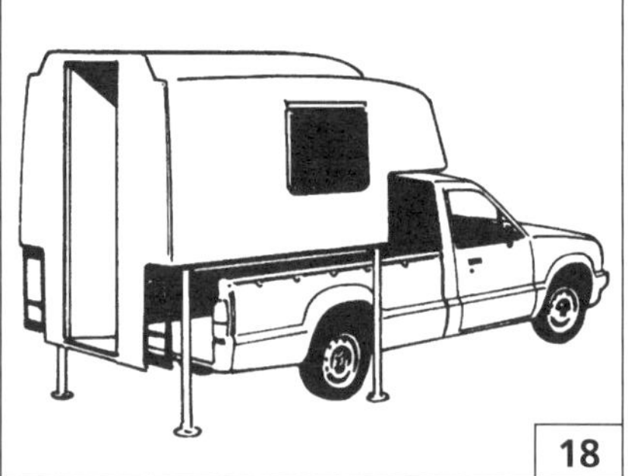

18

18. Consisting of a coachbuilt body which fits on to the back of a pick-up truck, these motor caravans offer considerable flexibility. The body may be left on site in much the same way as a trailer caravan thus retaining the pitch and freeing the pick-up for day to day motoring, although it can be quite a fiddle to mount and dismount the living section. Space is often limited, although the family can theoretically travel in the caravan section - although insulated from the driver and passenger, of course - and one wonders if they would be safe!

What to Consider

There are a number of key areas to consider before committing yourself to one style or another. Obviously, the depth of your pocket has a lot to do with it, but there are a number of other practical issues too:

VEHICLE SIZE

19

☐ 19. Coachbuilt and A-Class vehicles are usually 9 ft. (2.25 metres) and upwards in height while the length is frequently from around 18 ft. to 24 ft. (5.5 metres to 6.5 metres). Width is also an issue. Look up the width of your own car and then check the width of a number of motor caravans (including mirrors). Even if the difference alarms you, be assured that you very rapidly become used to the extra width - all those van and lorry drivers out there can't be wrong! - but it does make a difference if you want to visit a Cornish fishing village or some little nook in the Nook of Fife. You must also check that there are no bye-laws or covenants associated with your house which would prevent you from parking a large, caravan-style vehicle outside your house or even in your own drive. You should also consider your neighbours - it isn't really fair to wipe out the sky as seen through next door's kitchen window! (Illustration, courtesy Herald)

DAILY USE

Not only size must be considered if you're considering using the motor caravan as an everyday vehicle. There are also other practical matters, such as fuel economy, driver comfort, and so on - although insurance premiums are almost always a nice surprise!

20

☐ 20. If you intend carrying passengers in the back, you really *must* only consider a model with fitted rear seat belts.

BED SIZE

21

☐ 21. When you're lying down, you're longer than when you're standing up. This might sound barmy, but it's true! Not only does your body stretch out, but your feet stretch out too, and there's little more irritating than a short bed. On the other hand, if you tend to curl up into the foetal position, many single beds may be too narrow for you, while many double beds may be too narrow for your partner's comfort! Try measuring your own bed at home and comparing it with what's on offer in the manufacturer's brochure.

CONVENIENCE

Can you make an early morning cuppa without having to dismantle the beds? Can you get out of an over-cab or bunk bed to go to the loo in the night without treading on someone's head? In truth, all this and more will only be answered when you try out a vehicle: as good an argument as any for hiring before you buy. See one of the motor caravan magazines or contact the Motor Caravan Information Service or the Caravan Club for addresses of suitable hirers.

WHICH ENGINE?

22

☐ 22. There's no doubt that most motor caravans are slow old things - which is one of the reasons why motor caravan insurance is so inexpensive. But one that is tediously slow will be a pain on a long journey, unless you are an inveterate potterer - and many motor caravanners are! **PETROL ENGINES** are the cheapest to buy, the quietest running, the most powerful (size-for-size) but are a lot less economical to run and consequently depreciate faster. If you do two or three thousand miles a year, that probably won't matter two hoots.

But if you plan to do a large continental mileage, the price difference - petrol can be twice the price of diesel - could make a petrol engine very expensive to run. **DIESEL ENGINES** are usually noisier - the thrum can be tiresome on a long journey - but they often 'lug' well, needing less gearchanging because of their ability to pull away from lower speeds. They hold their value better and are easier to re-sell and they have the economy advantages mentioned above. **TURBO DIESEL ENGINES** give the best of both worlds, albeit at a noticeably higher purchase price. Fuel economy is scarcely any worse than non-turbo diesels but pulling power is far better and turbo-charged diesels often run less noisily than non-turbo diesels.

BASE VEHICLE MANUFACTURER

You pays your money and you takes your pick. Take a look through the correspondence pages of a magazine such as Motorcaravan Motorhome Monthly. Look at it over several months and see which manufacturers are reported most often as experiencing reliability problems. You would expect Mercedes to be best and detail quality is excellent - but you pay more, of course. Volkswagen are regarded by many as among the best in terms of reliability while Ford and Bedford (not many around these days) have always made good, reliable work horses. Peugeot Boxer and Fiat Ducato base vehicles are the most popular and latest versions are probably the easiest vans of their size to drive. Fiats are about the most powerful in their class but tend to be a touch noisier in the engine department. You *must* test drive a good selection and make up your own mind.

WHICH CONVERSION COMPANY?

Quite simply, we recommend that you don't consider buying a motor caravan unless is has the SMMT/NCC Habitation Code of Practice 201 symbol of approval fixed to it.

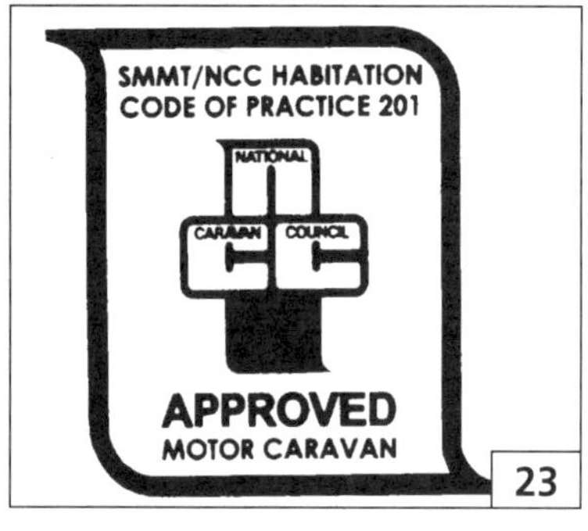

☐ 23. The Society of Motor Manufacturers and Traders and the National Caravan Council have combined to produce Habitation Code 201 which sets standards for Health and Safety requirements in motor caravans to be met by the manufacturers during design and construction.

All members of the SMMT and the NCC must comply with the Code and their entire model ranges must be certificated by NCC engineers. Only then can their vehicles carry the SMMT/NCC code badge.

The demands of the code are quite impressive and include requirements for ventilation, security, emergency escape, water, heating, gas and electricity supplies, fire precautions, insulation and pay loads. There are also detailed requirements for information to be provided to users through the vehicle handbook and for safety notices within vehicles - although it has to be said that some handbooks are still better than others.

☐ 24. Foreign built motor caravans do not appear to be eligible for Code Approval so all you can do if you want to buy foreign, is to ensure that you purchase only a top-name which is handled by a reputable and well established UK importer. Makers such as Eriba-Car, Hymer, Burstner and Pilote are as well known and well established as any.

In the end, only you can tell what you will or will not need in your ideal motor caravan. Get your hands on all the magazines you can, send off for all the brochures, visit as many dealers as you can find in your area and write down on paper the things you couldn't possibly do without, the things you would ideally like to have and the features you don't think you'll need. There's no point paying for more than you have to!

One last tip: make a point of trying out every feature that you possibly can when considering a motor caravan for sale - short of using the loo, the shower and cooking yourself Sunday lunch, of course! Kick your shoes off and try out each of the beds. Go into the w.c./shower compartment and shut the door behind you. Do you feel like a sardine in a tin? Can you and your partner move around and how easy is it to get from one end of the motor caravan to the other (if it's a larger one) with the table in place? Don't be afraid to do all of this, and more - if you're really serious about buying, that is - since you'll be parting with lots and lots of loot and it's all too easy to get carried away in the excitement of the moment, the fun of the search and end up with a Wendy house that you just don't want to play in any more.

PART II: TAKING THE PLUNGE

Where To Buy?

1

1. The Caravan Club reminds members that in general, it's best to buy from a local dealer. This is because motor caravans, like most other consumer goods, can need care and attention, and this is often required during the warranty period. If you were to live in, say, Birmingham but see a motor caravan for sale while you're on holiday in Cornwall, just imagine how many miles you would have to clock-up if you had to return the motor caravan for attention, then go back to collect it only to find that a further trip is necessary because the work is not complete or has not been done to your satisfaction. You could also find that a local dealer may treat you with a little more consideration simply because you live close enough to come back and make a fuss if anything you were promised turns out not to be the case!

Also avoid impulse buying of a foreign motor caravan unless it is imported by a well established UK subsidiary. Foreign makes sometimes come and go and so you may be left with a motor caravan for which it is extremely difficult to obtain spares. Also make absolutely sure that any imported 'van conforms with UK Construction and Use Regulations and to UK Legal Requirements with regard to the electricity supply and the gas supply. You may also find that any mains sockets are not compatible with any of your plugs! A further point worth bearing in mind is that a few continental 'vans are not as well equipped as British ones - usually not being fitted with an oven, for instance - so make sure that an apparent bargain is all that it seems.

Dealing With The Dealers

Most salesmen and women receive a commission for every sale they make, so they will know all the tricks in the book to encourage you to "close" a deal on the spot, whether it's in your best interests or not. Make a BIG POINT whenever going to look at a motor caravan, of never saying you will buy it there and then. Make a pact between yourself and your partner that you will "go away and think about it", no matter what the salesman or woman says. He or she is likely to tell all sorts of porkies, such as that someone else has shown an interest, or that motor caravans of this type/in this condition/at this time of year (delete according to choice) are difficult to come by, but this is virtually never true, so don't be swayed. In fact, if you've never owned a motor caravan before, you should regard the process of deciding which type of motor caravan to buy as part of the fun and spend weeks or months reading the motor caravan magazines and visiting as many sales sites as possible so that you can have an excellent all-round view of the field.

INSIDE INFORMATION: When you think you have identified the right type of motor caravan for you, try hiring one for at least a few days to see if you have made the right decision.

With so many manufacturers to choose from and many more dealerships to visit in the UK, there is a wide variety of motor caravans on offer. And when the used market, including both private and dealer sales, is also taken into consideration, the choice is further increased.

As with the car market, dealers vary from those selling one make of motor caravan to large outlets selling a wide range of manufacturers' motor caravans. Obviously the larger dealers will offer a greater variety of models. However, it is still advisable to shop around, visiting as many different dealerships as possible. Buying a motor caravan is always a major purchase and only by taking your time and by seeing as many different makes and models as possible can you be sure of picking the right one for you.

2

2. As with any purchase, the price of an individual motor caravan is determined by its age, condition, quality and the amount of extras that you get with it - but if you buy an 'oldie', do remember that there will *probably* be extra costs involved in repairs. If you're looking to part exchange your car, motor caravan or present motor caravan for a newer or better equipped alternative, most dealers are only too happy to oblige. However, with part exchanges it is certainly worth shopping around - don't just accept the first offer you are given.

Buying A New Motor Caravan

3

☐ 3. When buying a new motor caravan prices can differ quite substantially from dealer to dealer due to the variety of sales and special offers available across the country. However, it is always particularly worthwhile looking out for special offers around the months of September to December when dealers are particularly keen to clear remaining stock to make room for models for the new year. (Illustration, courtesy Auto-Sleepers)

It's also a good idea to get along to some of the increasing number of major motor caravan shows held each year across the country. The biggest of these are at Earls Court in London, The National Exhibition Centre in Birmingham and G-Mex in Manchester and all - both large and small - are advertised in the motor caravan magazines. These are excellent opportunities to see a wide range of motor caravans under one roof. They are often a great place to get a better than usual deal on a new motor caravan.

All new models should come with at least a year's warranty. Do remember though, that with most motor caravan dealers and manufacturers the warranty only applies to the dealership where you bought the motor caravan. So if you decide to buy a motor caravan from a dealer some miles away, be prepared to have to take it back to that same dealer if any future work is required. This is particularly relevant if you buy a motor caravan at a show where dealers may, for instance, come from the North of England to exhibit in London, or from the West Country to sell in Manchester.

Buying A Used Motor Caravan

When buying a used motor caravan, either privately or through a dealer, it is still advisable to shop around. However, if you are after a specific model you should remember that availability may not be as wide as with a new motor caravan. In such a case you should be prepared to pay slightly above the odds.

When buying a relatively new used motor caravan from a dealer it is worth finding out if a warranty is available, either for free or at extra cost. Spending a few extra pounds on a warranty when you buy the motor caravan might save you a good deal more if a serious problem arises within the following few months.

4

☐ 4. It is extremely doubtful that any sort of warranty will be offered either on very old motor caravans from a dealership or on any motor caravans from a private sale.

Perhaps the most important thing to look out for when buying a used motor caravan is damp, also known as water ingress. Damp can get into a motor caravan through badly sealed seams and damaged bodywork, and may cause extensive damage to the main structure of a motor caravan. See ***Part III, Avoiding a Bad Buy*** for more details.

5

☐ 5. You may be pleasantly surprised to find that the level of equipment on the better equipped older motor caravans is surprisingly high - even if it does *look* reminiscent of days gone by!

Which Layout?

This is almost like asking how long is a piece of string but there are certain points that you should consider in order of priority. The first one is to establish how many berths you will need, remembering that adults as well as children can sleep in the awning. On the other hand, not everyone wants to sleep in the awning if the weather is particularly cold outside!

6

☐ 6. Don't take manufacturers' claims at face value and always use a tape measure to be certain that each berth is long enough. Five or six berth motor caravans may only have two berths long enough for adults! Also bear in mind that the comfort of a bed can make or break your enjoyment of a holiday, especially if you suffer from back problems. Compare cushion depths between motor caravans and also look at the way the small pieces fit together: you'll be surprised how a knee or an elbow can find its way between the cracks in the middle of the night and wake you up with a jolt! All of this is yet another good reason for testing out a motor caravan in real life before committing your hard earned cash. (Illustration, courtesy Auto-Sleepers)

7

☐ 7. A centre kitchen is the ideal layout as far as motor caravan balance on the road is concerned. Most of the weight you carry in your motor caravan will tend to be based over the kitchen - but then this should not be the only consideration because you will also want to enjoy living in the motor caravan when you reach your destination and it is undoubtedly true that, sleeping accommodation permitting, more people seem to prefer the end kitchen shown in this Pilote than a centre one. The way to overcome the problem is simply to pack all of the heavy items in the middle and then repack them into the kitchen area when you arrive on site.

The logistics of living in a motor caravan won't fully occur to you until you actually try one out and after a fortnight away, intelligently planned cupboards, work tops, doors which open without disturbing the cooking area and so on will all be considered more valuable than a pretty fascia!

You should also check out the ease of getting into seats and into the toilet compartment and consider the degree of agility of those who will be using the vehicle.

Equipment

8

☐ 8. Different motor caravans come with different levels of standard equipment, depending on their cost and size. Just about all modern motor caravan have electric lighting, running water and a gas powered hob in the kitchen. And almost all have the facilities to hook up to at least some of the facilities that the most advanced sites have to offer - but do check. The more compact they are, the easier they will be to use on the road - and the more compromises you will have to make inside. (Illustration, courtesy Murvi Motorcaravans)

9

☐ 9. What you will require from a motor caravan will depend on where you want to go, with whom and when. If you intend to visit only well-equipped sites with their own shops, shower and toilet blocks and general amenities, you may not require as much equipment in the motor caravan. More basic vehicles, such as this one, will need the 'outside' w.c. if you want to be on your own in the middle of a field!

If however, you prefer more basic sites with little more than a tap and drain on offer, you will probably require a better equipped vehicle.

10

☐ 10. Similarly, if you are planning to go away in your motor caravan only during the summer months, heating and insulation won't be as much of a concern as if you intend to motor caravan through the winter as well. Then, you'll want an efficient heating system, preferably with blown air to distribute the heat more evenly, and a thermostatic control.

Essential Accessories

Whether you are buying a new or used motor caravan, don't forget the hidden extras that can add quite a few more pounds to the cost. You will certainly require a number of items of equipment that are pretty essential before you can take your motor caravan away. These include gas bottles, a 12-volt leisure battery, and a step to help you get in and out of the motor caravan.

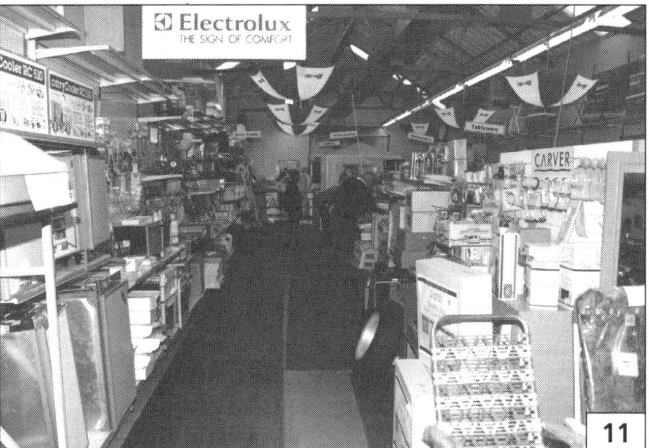

11

☐ 11. Of course the shop at your local motor caravan dealership - this is one of the largest, at Brownhills, near Nottingham - will have displays of numerous other products designed to make motor caravanning a whole lot easier. But to start off with at least, stick to the basics and let time and experience help you decide what else you will need. After all, if you buy everything all at once, not only will you have an overloaded motor caravan but you might not have enough money left to pay for the holiday.

If you are buying your motor caravan from a dealer, you may be able to get some of these essentials thrown in as part of the deal. However, this is certainly a lot less likely with a private sale although second-hand vehicles often come with at least some extras - but do check their condition. Whichever, here's a checklist to help you make sure that you've got all the essentials. It's not a bad idea to make a few copies of this to put up inside your motor caravan so that you can check everything off each time you go away.

Getting What You Pay For

You should always insist on receiving a copy of the users handbook with the motor caravan, whether it is new or used. It is a requirement of the SMMT/NCC Code of Practice that a handbook must be provided covering certain key information. The information you should receive should cover at least: motor caravan type, dimensions, weights, operating instructions and safety precautions. There should also be a separate handbook covering the base vehicle.

i INSIDE INFORMATION: Peugeot UK and Fiat Auto UK tell us that Peugeot in France and Fiat in Italy, respectively, only send one handbook per new vehicle. If you want to buy a second-hand Peugeot or Fiat, make *certain* it's got its original handbook with it or look for a Porter Manuals replacement. i

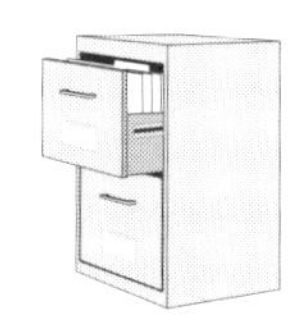

FACT FILE:
ESSENTIAL EQUIPMENT CHECKLIST

- ☐ Waste water container (if necessary)
- ☐ Waste water pipe (if necessary)
- ☐ Gas cylinder/s
- ☐ Gas regulator
- ☐ Mains electricity cable
- ☐ Leisure battery
- ☐ Rear step
- ☐ Toilet chemicals
- ☐ Corner steady winder (if fitted)
- ☐ Wheelclamp
- ☐ Fire extinguisher
- ☐ Set of spare bulbs
- ☐ Spirit level

In addition to the specialist accessories that are necessary for a successful motor caravanning holiday, it's easy to forget a few of those personal and domestic essentials. To help make sure that you don't forget anything, you will find a thorough checklist in *Appendix 2*, towards the back of this book. It's not a bad idea to copy this page and keep it in your motor caravan so that you can check off each item every time you go away.

If a used motor caravan does not have a handbook for the 'living' area, contact the manufacturer and obtain another. If the manufacturer has gone out of existence, contact one of the motor caravan clubs or one of the motor caravanning magazines and see if the manufacturer has been taken over by another who may be able to help out. Much of the information contained in this book should be supplemented by certain pieces of key information from the manufacturer's handbook and your ability to use the motor caravan safely will also be impaired if you can't obtain the right information. Strongly consider not purchasing a motor caravan for which no handbook is available.

Making Comparisons

All of the motor caravan magazines run regular tests on motor caravans and it is possible in most cases to obtain back issues or copies of older tests from the publishers, while the two caravan clubs also offer their members a road-test photocopy service, useful if the particular 'van in which the member is interested has been tested by the club.

Finally some words of advice from The Caravan Club: "You will part with a lot of money when you buy a motor caravan, and to be certain you obtain your money's worth, and exactly what you require, take time in making a decision. Time spent in looking is never wasted." In fact, time spent in looking can be almost as enjoyable as time spent in using your motor caravan, so have fun!

PART III: AVOIDING A BAD BUY

We talked in *Part I: Considering the Options* about how to select a motor caravan whose manufacturer has been approved by the National Caravan Council. We also made some suggestions on how you can go about finding a reliable vehicle. But the majority of people will be buying second-hand and for them, of course, there are the greater risks. There are two 'killers' when it comes to second-hand motor caravans, so let's look at them first.

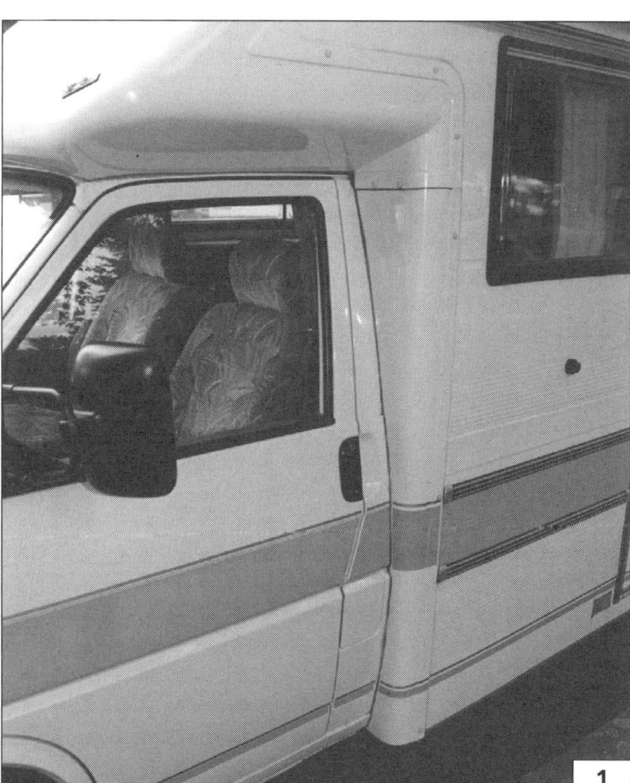

1. All kinds of motor caravan are prone to letting in damp. Coachbuilt and A-Class are most trouble-prone but even van-based vehicles can suffer. Elevating roofs and extra windows can leak in; wheel arches, floors and lower body panels can rust on older vehicles. Check seams carefully for any signs of cracking.

Damp-affected vehicles are well on the slippery slope. Repairs are invariably expensive since body and/or trim panels have to be removed and extensive rot can easily scrap the vehicle. So if you're not careful, you could buy a motor caravan which appears to be OK but which, in reality, has one tyre in the grave.

2. This is one area in which a conversion on a manufacturer's high-top van scores highest - it's the least likely to leak in! And the Fiat Ducato shown here, with front-wheel drive and no rear axle, allows plenty of head-room for a six-footer in a leak-proof shell. But DO check around the windows! (Illustration, courtesy Murvi Motorcaravans)

The first weapon in the fight against damp is your own sense of smell. There's a distinctively sweet, sickly smell about woodwork and upholstery that's going rotten. If such a smell assails you the minute you open the rear door, you'll probably be best giving this one a miss. However, even if it doesn't - maybe the doors and windows have been left open in warm weather - open wardrobe, cupboards and other enclosed spaces (especially low down and near to windows) and sniff again.

INSIDE INFORMATION: If you're not quite sure what the smell of rot is like, try to carry out the sniff test in a really old, clapped-out motor caravan at a dealers (there's usually one tucked away around the back - and never as cheap as it should be!) and work out for yourself the smell you're 'looking' for. Then, you won't confuse the smell of moth balls, herbs and spices, chemical w.c. fluid or any other of the 'OK' smells to be found in a used motor caravan.

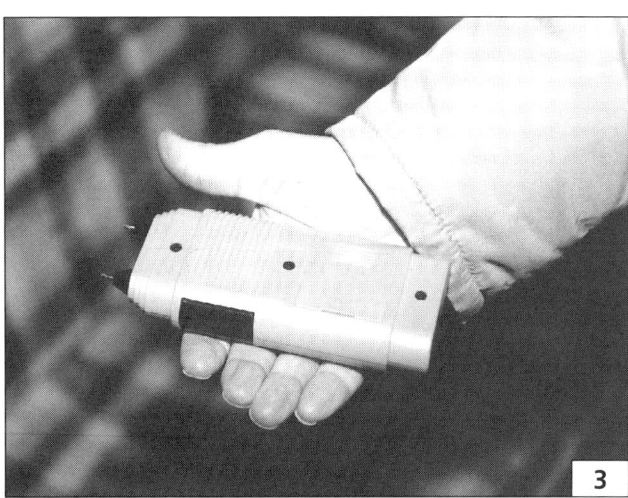
3

4

making it easy! ☐ *3. A damp tester will tell you whether there is any dampness in specific locations which may be covered up by trim or soft furnishings. You press the prongs of the tester into the surface you are testing and you'll soon hear if there is any damp present - try it for yourself on various surfaces in and around the house, and you will see what we mean. Something which is just slightly damp gives a low clicking sound, not unlike a Geiger counter in the movies, while a loud screeching sound is the damp tester emulating the noise **you** will make if you buy a motor caravan with this much damp in it!*

☐ 4. The other big no-no is poorly carried out DIY work - the 'accessory' spotlight just visible in this shot was downright dangerous with loose, partly bare wiring! For some reason, folk will pay many thousands of pounds to purchase a motor caravan and then save a trivial amount by bodging repairs and modifications. Moreover, one man's hook in the wall is another man's eyesore, and 'extras' that may seem indispensable to a former owner could seem monstrous to you.

INSIDE INFORMATION: In general, if it looks as though the manufacturer fitted it, there's no problem. If it doesn't, then the motor caravan has been devalued. If that is so, the extent can only be determined by you, the buyer, but do take the most pessimistic assumption because that's what the salesman will do when you come to trade the vehicle in next time round!

Apart from looking for the obvious checks, don't commit yourself to spending a large sum of money without having an independent authority check the vehicle over for you. The AA or RAC will carry out a check on the base vehicle's mechanical units and if you look in the adverts of the leading motor caravan magazines (or ring the editorial office if you can't see what you need) you should be able to find a qualified engineer who is experienced in checking motor caravans. Alternatively, if you are considering buying privately you may consider asking your nearest dealer if they will carry out a check on your behalf for an agreed fee: they may be only too pleased to add a little work to their workshop and rope you in as a potential future customer at the same time.

CHAPTER 3 USING YOUR MOTOR CARAVAN

There is no more convenient way of going on holiday or taking a short break then by using your motor caravan. However, for the novice or even for those changing their motor caravan for a new one and for those who are planning to take an overseas trip and drive "on the wrong side" for the first time, there's a certain amount of information that will make your trip so much easier and more pleasant.

PART I: ON THE ROAD

We make no apologies for starting off with information on driving your motor caravan since this is something that worries most beginners. If you're an experienced motor caravanner *and* you're used to driving on the continent, you may feel like skipping the first few paragraphs. On the other hand, there might just be something you haven't thought of!

Driving

☐ 1. When you first sit behind the wheel, in the showroom perhaps, the idea of driving something as large as a motor caravan may seem off-putting. But it needn't be! Just think of all those millions of vans, lorries and coaches driven by men and women of all ages, shapes and sizes, and all done in a day's work. If they can do it, so can you! And more to the point, almost all motor caravans, with the exception of the very large American RVs, are far easier to drive than large trucks. In any case, many of those who drive professionally will tell you that they prefer driving their van or truck to their ordinary car. One reason is that they simply *can't* go fast (though they're happy to maintain a steady speed) and there's something calming and enjoyable about sitting up high, being able to see over the roofs of cars in front - and anticipate problems before they reach you - to say nothing of the sheer enjoyment of being able to see over most of the hedges and walls you drive past!

☐ 2. Having said that, there are certain points to bear in mind when driving a motor caravan. They are NOT cars; it's just that after a very short while, they're just as easy if not easier to drive. (Illustration, courtesy Compass)

Even larger petrol engined models and turbo diesels are much slower than most cars. Relax, take it easy, stay in the nearside lane when you're approaching traffic lights on dual carriage-ways or traffic islands, and just go along with the natural speed of the vehicle.

3

3. If you're driving a high-top or coachbuilt, you will feel the effects of crosswinds and buffeting from over taking articulated lorries more than in smaller motor caravans. Don't be frightened by this; just adapt your speed to the prevailing conditions. You haven't got a caravan on the back to worry about and a little 'tug' won't do any harm at all. Do use your common sense in very windy conditions, of course, and adjust your speed accordingly. If this is something that worries you a lot, you may feel comfortable with something like the Auto-Sleepers Trooper, shown here, with a roof that elevates when on-site. (Illustration, courtesy Auto-Sleepers)

4. Vehicle width worries most people. Unnecessarily! Take a look at how much room most cars leave when overtaking stationary vehicles. Most cars are something under six feet (1800 mm) wide. A Volkswagen Transporter panel van is only fractionally wider while a Fiat Ducato/Peugeot Boxer panel van is about 6 feet 8 inches (2030 mm), while coachbuilt vehicles, like the Transit-based Auto-Sleepers shown, are frequently around the 7 feet wide mark (2130 mm) so at worst, you've got between 12 and 18 inches (300-450 mm) extra to worry about. Now, think back to how much room cars give when they overtake: No problem, is there!

4

THINK LENGTH!

Although the width is important, the extra wheelbase is even more important when going around corners, especially in town.

making it easy! *• You should always set your nearside mirror so that you can see down the side of the van as well as any traffic you may have overtaken.*
• As you go round a corner, glance in the mirror to give yourself an idea how close you are getting.
• Prompt your partner, positioned in the passenger seat of course, to calmly give you an indication of how much leeway you have.

The trick is to take corners a little more slowly than you would in your car, to turn in a little later and to give a slightly wider berth. The rear end of your motor caravan will 'cut-in' because of its extra length - but it won't take you any time at all to get used to it.

5

5. Judging the width is still something that some drivers find a little tricky especially with the largest A-class and coachbuilt vehicles. When driving on the continent for the first time, you may think things will be even more daunting. In practice, because you are now sitting on the kerb-side of the vehicle, you shouldn't have too much difficulty in placing it correctly. Once again, get your partner to help guide you into the correct position relative to the centre line of the road. (In fact, since he/she is the one who will be sitting facing the on-rushing MANs and Saviems, you can take it for granted that you will be the first to know!)

making it easy! *•One tip which some drivers find helps them to position the vehicle accurately is to stick a piece of masking tape or a label onto the windscreen in the driver's eye-line to the kerb. In other words, with the driver sitting relaxed in his/her natural driving position, when glancing down at the kerb, the marker strip should just line up.*
•This can be extra-useful when driving on the continent for the first time if you are not sure of your bearings with regard to the right-hand kerb.
•Before you go, find a completely clear stretch of road, park on the 'wrong' side with the vehicle about the right distance from the kerb for driving along and place your marker. That way, when you get off the ferry or Shuttle, you'll be prepared.

REVERSING AND PARKING

6

☐ 6. For most people, reversing a motor caravan is a new skill. Even on the smaller conversions, you may not be able to see out of the side windows or even the rear window so you'll have to learn the truck drivers' trick of reversing with your mirrors. You will be amazed at how easy it becomes after a little practice. Find yourself a deserted area, such as a car park (with no height barriers!) after closing time or some other suitable area and try it out for yourself.

SAFETY FIRST!

It is absolutely essential that you have an assistant see you back while you are reversing. You almost certainly don't have the experience of a professional driver; the damage you could cause to your or other vehicles could run into hundreds or thousands of pounds; the risk of running over an animal or - stuff or nightmares! - a small child means that you would be reckless not to take advantage of any help that may be available.

BRAKING

7

☐ 7. Do remember that your motor caravan will be on or near the weight limit for the van on which it is based. Allow plenty of braking distance, especially in wet or slippery conditions and be sure to use your gearbox when going down very long very steep hills, such as in the Alps, so that your brakes don't fade - a terrifying experience!

DRIVER TRAINING

At the time of writing, the Caravan Club in Great Britain is planning a series of "Motor Caravan Familiarisation Courses" for those who have just take up motor caravanning or are considering doing so. These will be a mixture of lecture, discussion and use of supplied vehicles, including five hours of practical work. There could be no finer way of learning the techniques for manoeuvring a large vehicle and we strongly recommend that anyone who has never driven a vehicle as large as a motor caravan joins the Caravan Club and takes part on one of these training days.

PART II: GETTING READY TO GO

Weight Watching

There are two things that you must bear in mind when loading up: weight and weight. The first is the weight of the 'extras' you will be carrying and the second is the positioning of those weights.

WEIGHT (ONE)

Before going any further, you should look up three crucial figures in your handbook. One is the Maximum Allowable Mass (MAM) - formerly known as the Gross Vehicle Weight. Another is the Unladen Mass/Weight. The third is the Maximum Payload. The difference between numbers one and two should be the third figure, that of your Maximum Payload. If is isn't, check again - check with your dealer and/or, check with the manufacturer!

FACT FILE: CALCULATING PAYLOADS

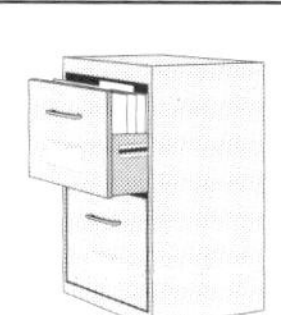

- Different manufacturers may use different methods of calculating both the unladen weight and the Maximum Authorised Mass (MAM) sometimes called Maximum Authorised Weight (MAW) and previously called Maximum Laden Weight (MLW) - of their vehicles.
- Volkswagen, for instance, include in the unladen weight an allowance for ten litres of fuel but the driver and passenger and optional equipment are excluded.
- The Gross Vehicle Weight, however, must include the weight of the driver and passenger or passengers, so these figures will have to be borne in mind.
- The unladen weight of motor caravans traditionally includes a 75 kg allowance for the driver and an allowance for 90% of the fuel weight. Auto-Sleepers, for instance, also include the weight of the spare wheel, the crockery and the fire extinguisher.
- The only way you can be sure is to check with your handbook, your dealer or with the manufacturer.

INSIDE INFORMATION: If you don't have a handbook with your motor caravan, check with the original manufacturer. If the information isn't available for any reason, find out the MAM from the base vehicle manufacturer (visit your local dealership or ring the manufacturers themselves and ask for Customer Services) or take your motor caravan to a weigh bridge (see Yellow Pages) and have it weighed with about half a tank of fuel but before it is packed for a journey. The difference between the two figures will be the maximum amount you can pack in. MAKE A NOTE OF THESE FIGURES IN *AUTO-BIOGRAPHY* AT THE FRONT OF THIS BOOK!

Do note, however, that if you pack your vehicle up to its MAM, there won't be any available capacity for those bottles of wine or other goodies you might come across. And if you do go over the weight limit, you could fall foul of a police spot check and be prosecuted.

FACT FILE: WEIGHTS OF 'EXTRAS'

The following list provides you with a rough guide to how a few items of equipment typically weigh.

Equipment	kg	lb
Awning (drive away)	20	44
Battery (12v) and carrier box	20	44
Portable TV	15	33
Fire Extinguisher	2	4
Step	2	4
Lifting Jack	2-4	4-8
Additional LPG above 15 kg allowance i.e. total 2 full 7 kg cylinders	15	33
WC fluid (2.5 litres)	2.5	5
Wheel levellers (typical)	4	9

In addition, water weighs exactly 1 kg per litre, or around 10 lbs per gallon. And the waste and w.c. water weighs the same!

WEIGHT (TWO)

1. If your motor caravan has an end kitchen, there's a great temptation to put all the tins of food, crockery, etc. in their normal positions. Do remember, however, that you should try to avoid putting too much weight behind the rear axle line of the vehicle or in the top lockers. As a general rule, save the top lockers for lighter items, such as bedding, clothes and toiletries and place all the heavier stuff (which includes books and magazines if, like many of us, you cart loads of them around with you) in the lower lockers. (Illustration, courtesy Murvi Motorcaravans)

1

Heaviest items of all should go towards the middle of the vehicle. This will help to make the vehicle more stable when cornering, less prone to being pulled off line by crosswinds and it will help to some extent to avoid over-loading the rear axle - the more weight you have in the overhang, the more downwards leverage will be applied.

It is also important to note that each vehicle has its own front-and-rear axle maximum weights which again, must not be exceeded. In practice, it is extremely difficult to judge how much weight has been placed over each axle, but it does emphasise the point that you should try to spread the weight as evenly as possible - and it re-emphasises the point that any weight placed in the overhang has an even larger effect on the weight to be supported by the rear suspension.

Setting Out

Before moving off, check the following:

A. Make sure that the seat is positioned to give the best driving position and maximum visibility. Also, adjust and clean the mirrors to give the best rear view, especially for overtaking and pulling on to motorways.

A

B. Check that gas cylinders and all gas operated equipment have been turned off including fridge, cooker, heater and water heater.

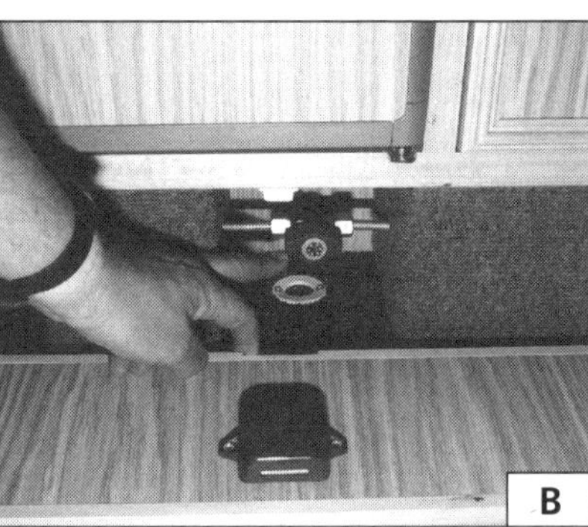
B

C. Check that the gas cylinders are securely mounted. (Illustration, courtesy Auto-Trail)

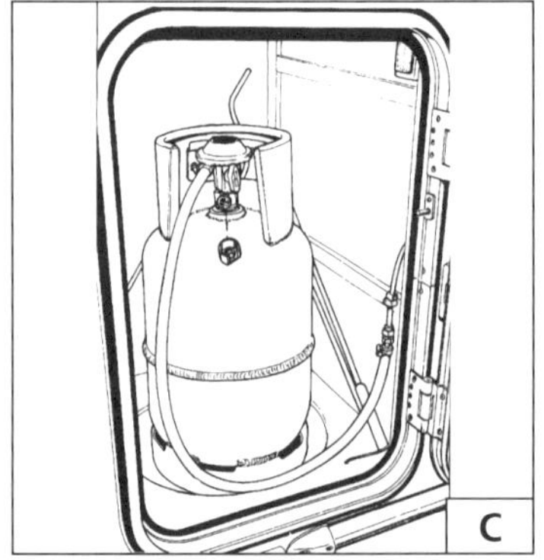
C

☐ D. Switch fridge to 12 volt and ensure that the door lock is set.

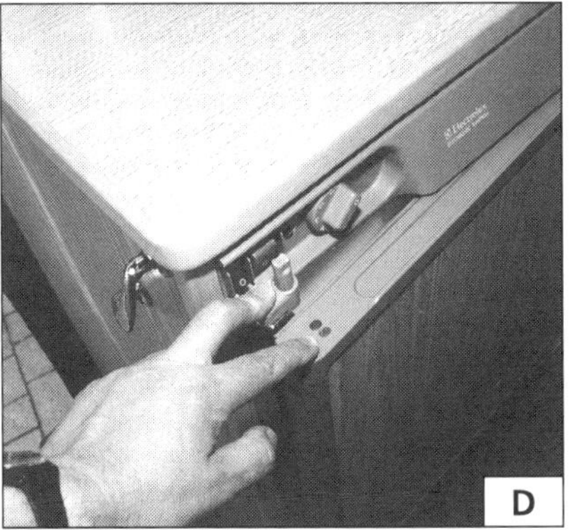

D

☐ E. Ensure that the battery selection switch is in the OFF position. (Illustration, courtesy Swift)

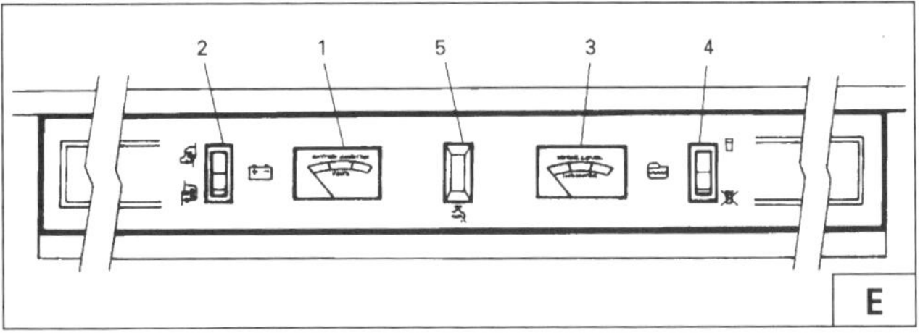

E

☐ F. Make certain that the 240 volt mains input flap is properly closed.

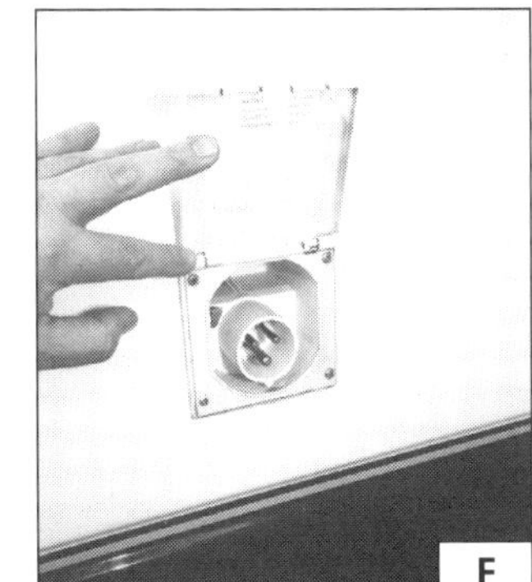

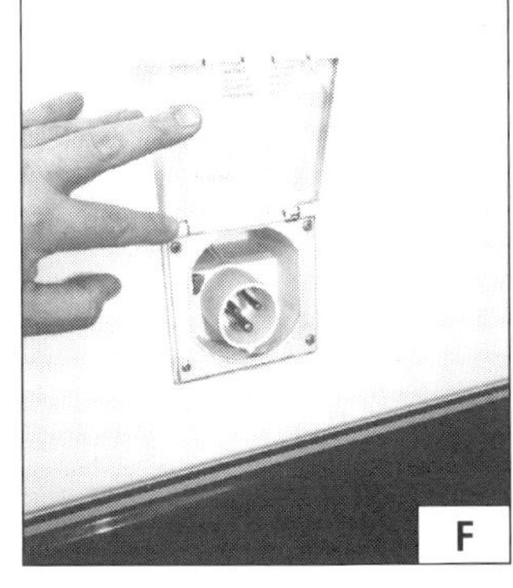

F

☐ G. Make sure that all roof lights are closed and secured, including that in the w.c.

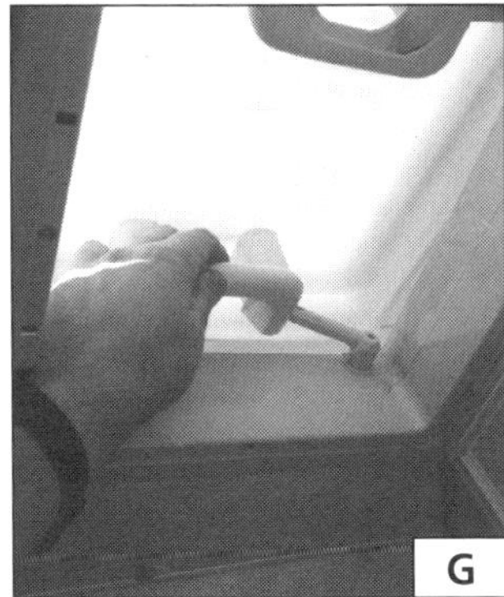

G

☐ H. Check that all top-hinged windows, as well as any in the luton are tight closed, to prevent damage.

H

☐ I. Ensure that the caravan exterior door and all locker and cupboard doors are closed and locked or secured shut.

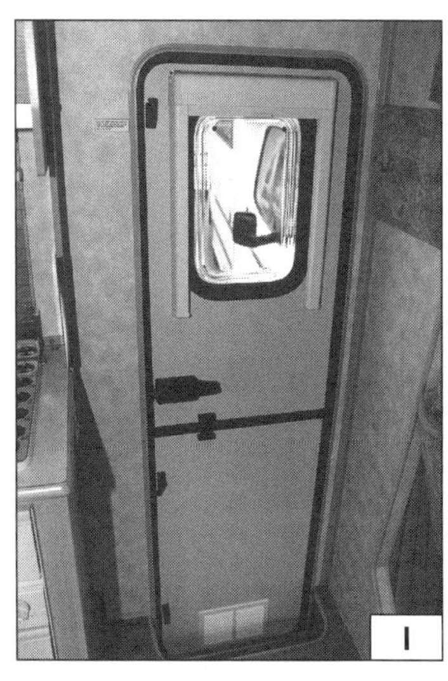

I

☐ J. Be sure that all loose articles are securely stowed, and that bunks and ladders are strapped or clipped into the manufacturer's recommended positions.

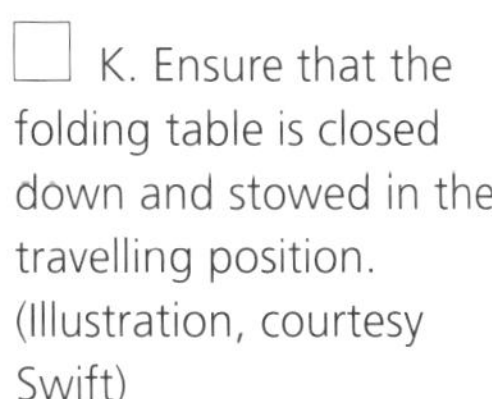

J

☐ K. Ensure that the folding table is closed down and stowed in the travelling position. (Illustration, courtesy Swift)

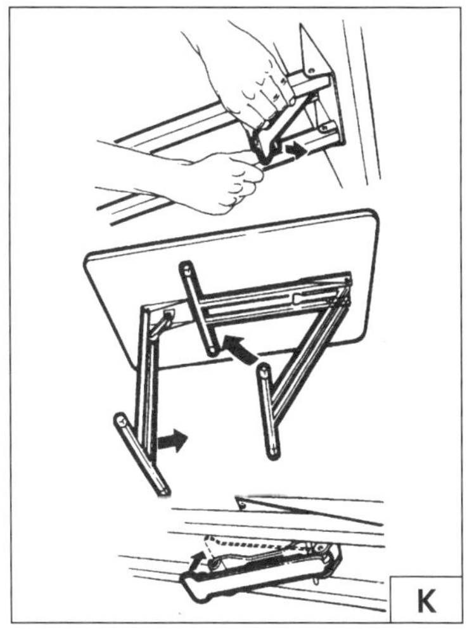

K

☐ L. Outside the vehicle, check that all drain taps are closed. (Illustration, courtesy Auto-Trail)

L

☐ M. Check that the rear corner steadies (if fitted) are raised.

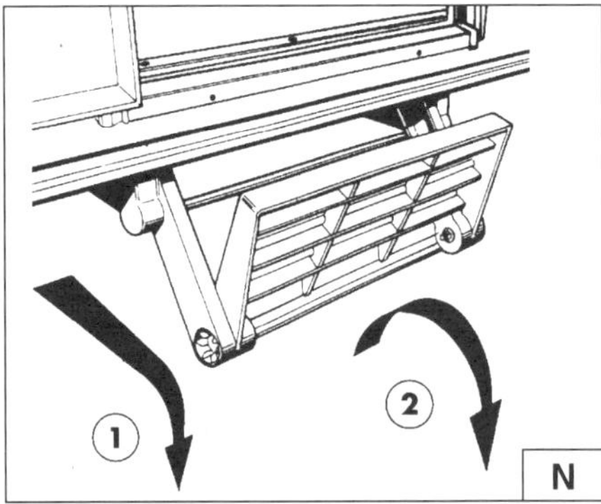

☐ N. Check that the folding step (if fitted) is retracted. (Illustration, courtesy Auto-Trail)

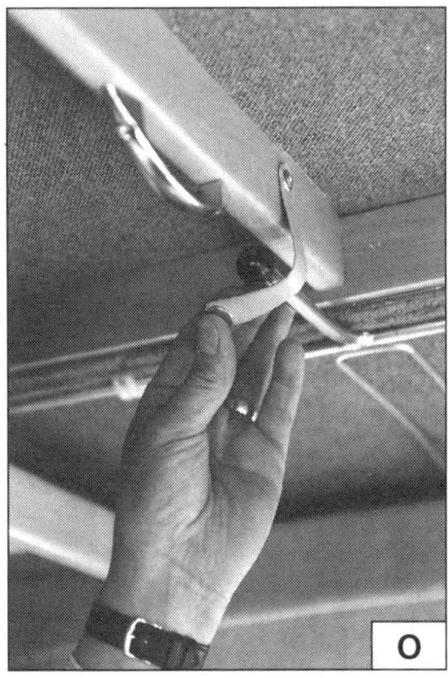

☐ O. Check that the elevating roof (if fitted) is closed and correctly secured.

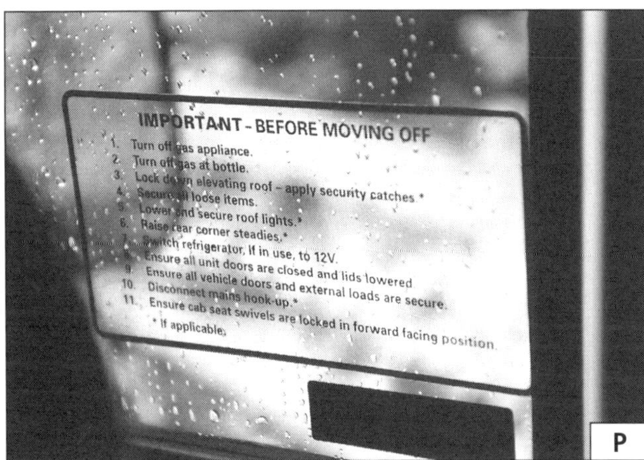

☐ P. Your motor caravan should be fitted with a reminder label, so that you don't drive off without checking the main points, shown above.

If yours isn't, photocopy this label and secure it somewhere suitable so that your checklist is always to hand. (Illustration, courtesy Auto-Sleepers)

IMPORTANT - BEFORE MOVING OFF

1. **Turn off gas appliance.**
2. **Turn off gas at bottle.**
3. **Lock down elevating roof – apply security catches.***
4. **Secure all loose items.**
5. **Lower and secure roof lights.***
6. **Raise rear corner steadies.***
7. **Switch refrigerator, if in use, to 12V.**
8. **Ensure all unit doors are closed and lids lowered.**
9. **Ensure all vehicle doors and external loads are secure.**
10. **Disconnect mains hook-up.***
11. **Ensure cab seat swivels are locked in forward facing position.**

*** If applicable.**

IMPORTANT NOTE: There are also several vitally important service jobs that you should carry out before starting out on any extended trip. See *Chapters 5 and 6.*

FACT FILE: USING YOUR MOTOR CARAVAN

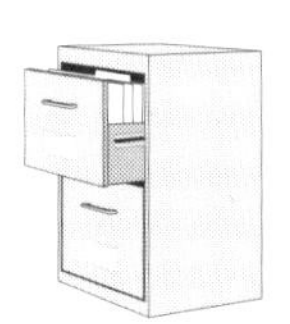

The following Motor Caravan Code of Conduct has been produced by the National Caravan Council.

PARKING

- Motor caravans should only be parked in approved places.
- When using the facilities of a motor caravan at such times care and consideration should be given to those around them.

DRIVING

- When using a motor caravan on either the public highway or private roads, the Highway Code should be complied with and full consideration given to other road users.
- In the event of a motor caravan travelling slowly and there being a queue of traffic behind, the driver of the motor caravan should, where possible, pull over in order to let the other traffic pass.
- When the vehicle is in motion it is compulsory that all passengers are seated and seat restraint straps worn.
- Before moving off, elevating roofs should be lowered and correctly secured, and top hinged windows closed. Likewise all doors and access lockers for gas containers and chemical toilets must be properly closed.
- Exterior steps should be properly retracted and secured.
- When the vehicle is being refuelled, or on a ferry, all gas systems must be turned off.
- Gas appliances should only be used when the vehicle is in motion when such use is permitted by the manufacturer of the appliance.

PART III: ON SITE

Arrival on Site

Unless you're particularly adventurous, it's a good idea to ring your chosen site prior to arrival. In-season, the site may be fully booked and out of season, it might be closed. You will also want to know if the site is locked at night and what time the site office closes, if you intend making a late arrival.

Your first port of call should, of course, be the site office where - open or closed - you should be able to obtain an idea of the site regulations.

If the site is closed, there will often be a temporary pitch near the entrance, specially for latecomers and to avoid disturbing others' beauty sleep.

DRIVING ON SITE

Drive only on the constructed road-ways unless the site warden directs you otherwise. Always adhere strictly to speed limits and note that these are generally around 10 mph.

> **SAFETY FIRST!**
>
> ***Remember that the stopping distance on grass particularly when it is wet, is not so very different from driving on snow or ice and will be far greater than when driving on tarmac.***

FINDING A PITCH

Motor caravans are, by their nature, more difficult to level than towed caravans so it goes without saying that you should try to find yourself as level a pitch as possible. The ideal area will be dry, fairly level and with a hard base.

> *making it easy!* *• If you have to pitch on an area with a slope, make sure that you will be able to drive off down the slope. Otherwise, especially if the weather turns wet, you may not be able to get back off again!*

LEVELLING UP AND STABILISING

> **FACT FILE: LEVELLING UP**
>
> 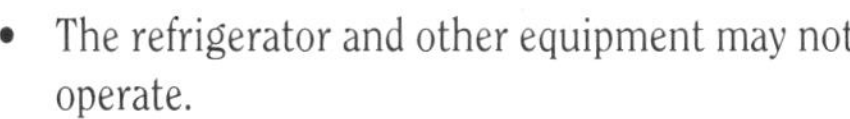
>
> If the motor caravan is not correctly levelled, you can encounter a number of problems:
>
> - The refrigerator and other equipment may not operate.
> - The 'caravan' door, especially on coachbuilt models, may not close properly.

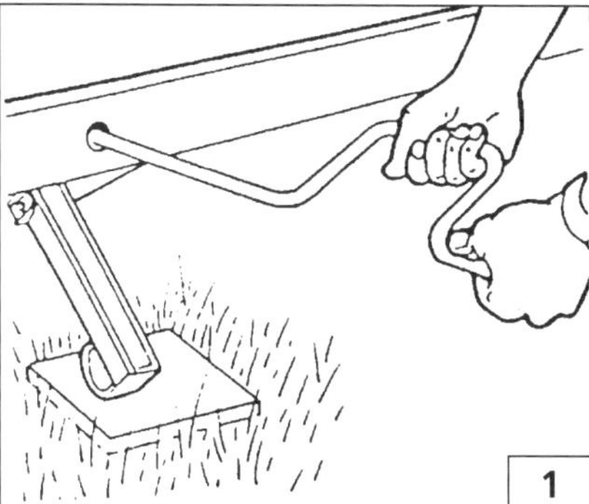

1. Apply the handbrake and put the motor caravan in gear or select PARK in the case of automatics. If you are on a level pitch and your motor caravan is fitted with rear corner steadies, place a pad between the corner steady and the ground to stop it sinking in and wind the corner steadies until they are in firm contact with the ground. (Illustration, courtesy Swift)

IMPORTANT NOTE: Do not use the steadies as a jack since they are not built to take the weight of the motor caravan.

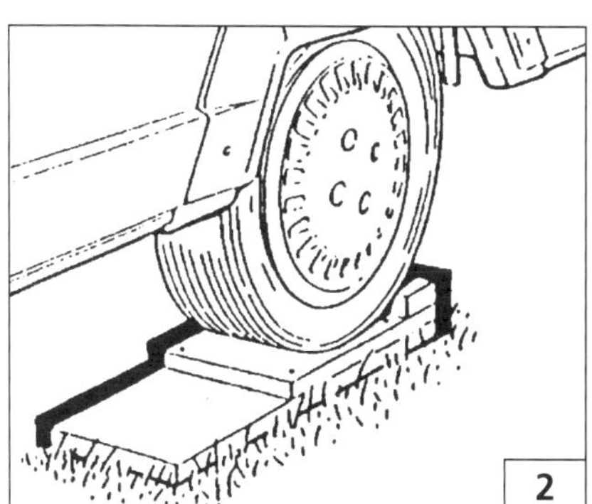

2. A pair of DIY levelling boards are usually sufficient to level the motor caravan on all but the most severe slopes. Purpose-made varieties, which may be lighter and more versatile, can be purchased from your motor caravan accessory shop. (Illustration, courtesy Swift)

Awnings

> **ENVIRONMENT FIRST!**
>
> ***When a canvass awning is left in place for more than a few days on grass, the ground sheet and/or sideflaps should be raised or removed for a day at a time to avoid damage to the ground.***

1. Whether yours is a pull-out awning or a tent-type construction, you should obtain permission from the site office and note that there may be an additional charge. (Illustration, courtesy CGI Camping/Apache Awnings)

CONNECTING UP TO POWER, ON SITE

SAFETY FIRST!

- ***You are recommended to use up to, but no more than, 25 metres of 3-core flexible cable, each core of 2.5 mm.***
- ***The cable should be orange, so that it can easily be seen in grass, and both end connectors (one male; one female) should be blue.***
- ***If you buy ready made-up cable, ensure that it and the connectors are marked as being to BS 4343 (CEE17) standards.***

INSIDE INFORMATION: Most mains supplies are designed to operate on a voltage of between 220 and 240 volts AC. Some continental sites may produce a lower voltage but most equipment will continue to work, albeit less efficiently. But see *FACT FILE: SITE SUPPLIES* on page *29*.

☐ 3. Open the cover to the mains inlet provided at the motor caravan and insert the blue (female) connector of the supply flexible cable. (Illustration, courtesy Auto-Trail)

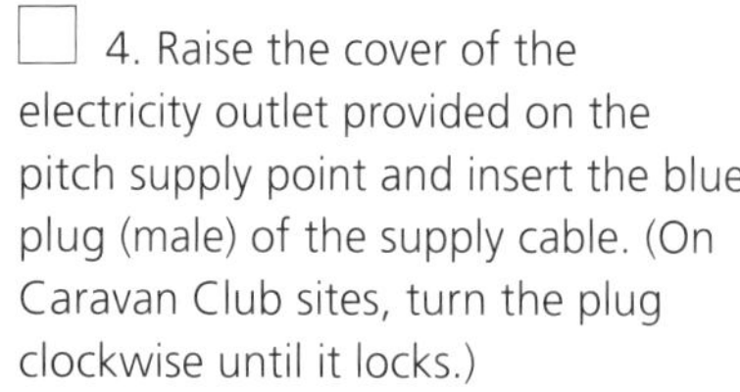

☐ 4. Raise the cover of the electricity outlet provided on the pitch supply point and insert the blue plug (male) of the supply cable. (On Caravan Club sites, turn the plug clockwise until it locks.)

INSIDE INFORMATION: On some sites, you will have to ask the warden to turn on the power supply at a central point, especially at quiet times.

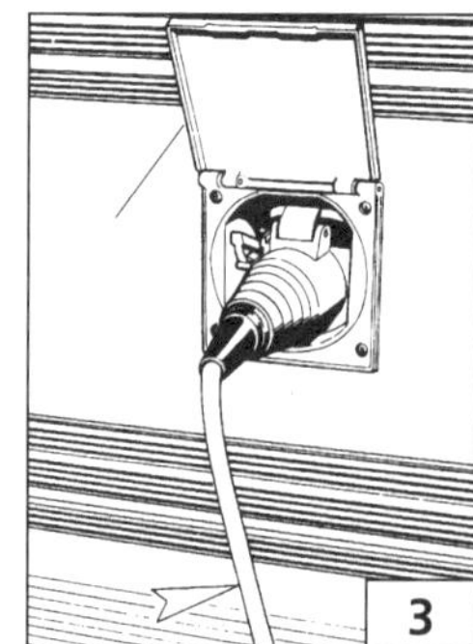

3

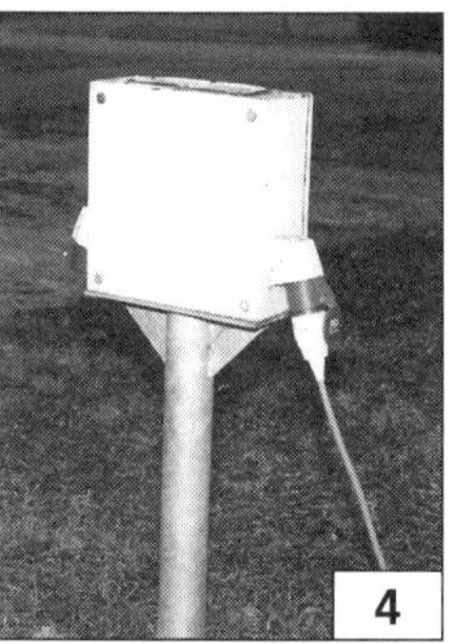

4

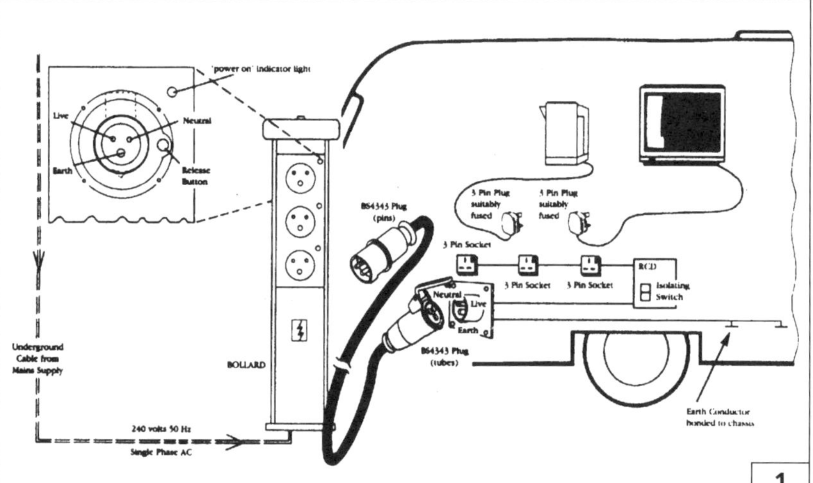

1

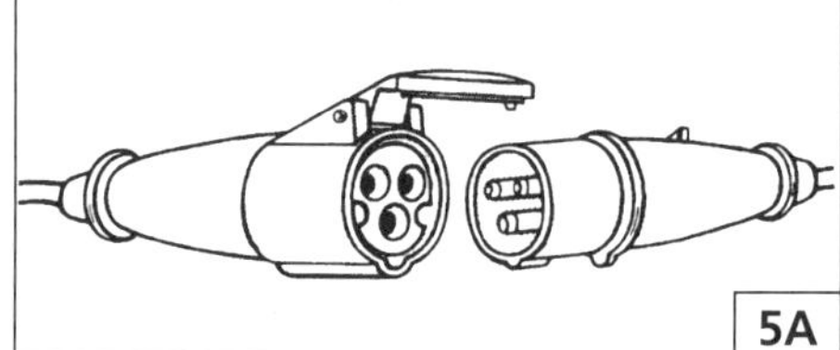

5A

☐ 5A. These are the two 'ends' (female, left; male, right) of the motor caravan-to-site connectors.

☐ 1. The following information is supplied by the Caravan Club to its members. The Club emphasises to its members that motor caravanners are personally responsible for the safety of all of the electrical appliances and equipment inside the caravan. Before connecting the motor caravan installation to the mains supply, check that the supply available at the caravan pitch supply point is suitable for the motor caravan electrical installation and appliances. (Illustration, courtesy The Caravan Club)

☐ 2. Check that the motor caravan mains isolating switch is in the OFF position.

2

☐ 5B. The female socket must be connected up as shown here...

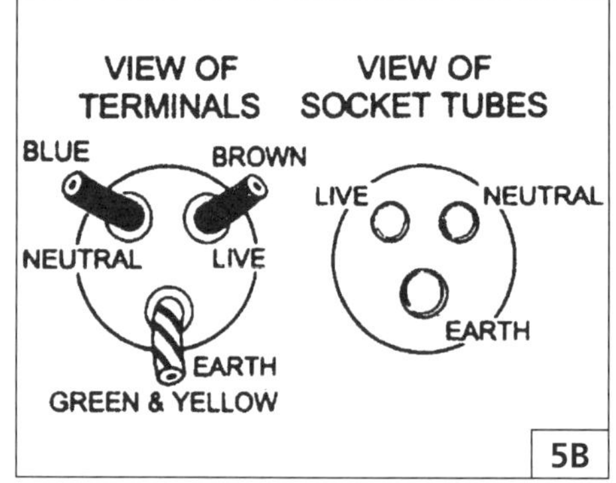

5B

☐ 5C. ...while the male plug must be connected up like this. (Illustrations, courtesy The Caravan Club)

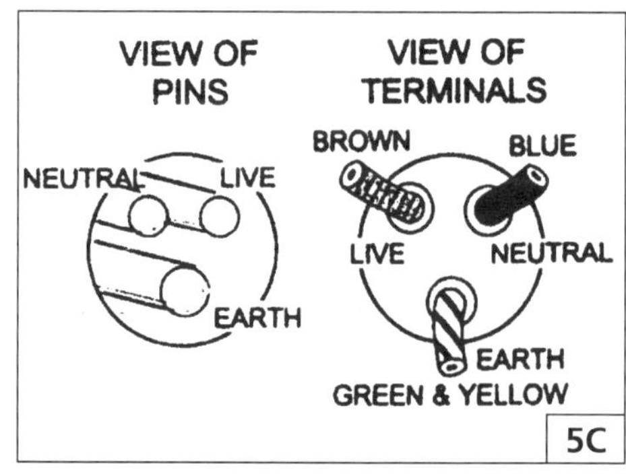

5C

SAFETY FIRST!

- ***The motor caravan flexible cable must be fully uncoiled to avoid damage by overheating. In case of doubt or the supply does not become available, or if the supply fails, consult the caravan park operator or his agent or a qualified electrician.***
- ***Check that the polarity is correct, either by checking the polarity indicator light (if fitted) or using a polarity check meter. If it is not correct, reverse the input polarity on your extension cable or use a polarity reverser - see below.***
- ***Switch on at the motor caravan mains isolating switch.***
- ***Check the operation of the RCDs (residual current devices) if any, fitted in the motor caravan by depressing the test button.***

6

☐ 6. With the supply turned on, check that the supply polarity is correct. You can buy a polarity tester from an accessory shop. DO NOT use the mains if the polarity is incorrect!

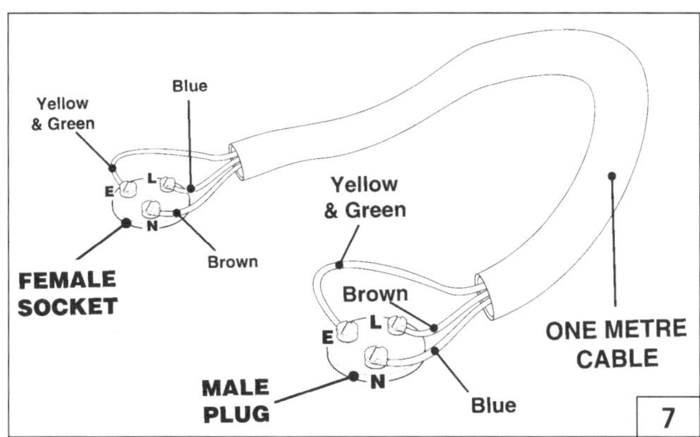

7

☐ 7. You can make your own polarity converter - or have a competent electrician make one up for you - using a male plug, a female socket, one metre of cable and a CLEAR LABEL THAT CAN'T COME OFF indicating what the adaptor is for. Use the wiring plan shown here.

CONTINENTAL EUROPEAN CONNECTIONS

All British electrical connections comply with the European Standard, called CEE17 but not all continental sites comply, as yet. As time goes by, the situation changes but you will probably find that in Denmark, Germany and the Benelux countries that all sites are fitted with CEE17 hook-ups. As you would possibly expect, Spain, France and Italy are slower to change and you are more likely to encounter older style hook-ups.

FRANCE: The traditional French electrical fitting is a two-pin (female) plus earth (male) socket and a corresponding plug, not unlike their domestic connectors.

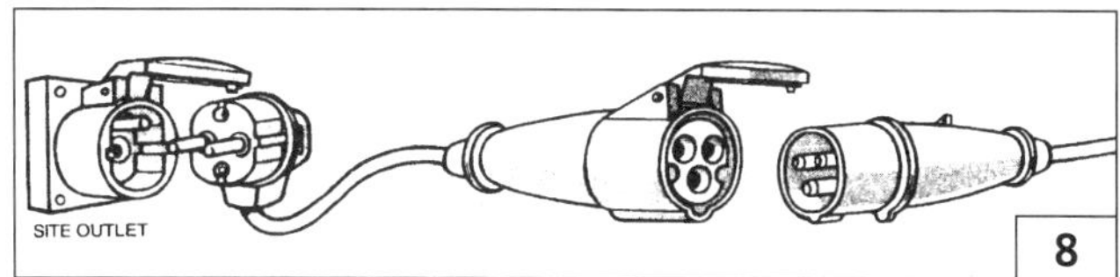

8

☐ 8. This type of adaptor for traditional French sites is commonly available from UK caravan accessory shops. (Illustration, courtesy The Caravan Club)

GERMANY: The two-pin, plus two earth strip type of connector can still be found in Holland, Norway and Sweden and may conceivably still be found in Germany. Adaptors - see below.

DENMARK: A smaller type of three-pin plug is still sometimes in use in Denmark.

ADAPTORS: Those for the older German and Danish type of fittings can often be borrowed from the campsite office when you arrive.

SAFETY: Do be aware that if a site does not have a modern CEE17 supply, you can not be certain that the supply is properly protected or properly earthed.

INSIDE INFORMATION: Hardy types who take their motor caravans on skiing trips must remember to move their mains cable every day if they don't want to have to abandon it, after it has been swallowed by the frozen snow. The slight amount of heat generated within the cable causes it to sink ever deeper into the snow until it is frozen deep and irretrievable.

FACT FILE: SITE SUPPLIES

The following is an extract from a Caravan Club information leaflet:

•Although the [motor] caravan installation is designed for a maximum current of 16 Amp, some sites may, for technical or economic reasons, limit the maximum current loading per [motor] caravan to a lower figure, usually 10 Amp in the UK and sometimes 5 Amp or less abroad (refer to Site warden for the relevant amperage on a Club Site).

•On arrival at a site, check the maximum permitted current, and make sure that this figure is never exceeded. Failure to do so will result in tripped circuit breakers - at the site rather then in the [motor] caravan - and this will not endear the culprit to the site warden!

•It is now more common for appliance power to be quoted in watts and kilowatts (1 kilowatt (kW) = 1,000 watts (w)). In general it may be assumed that a total electrical load of 1 kW will require a 5 Amp supply at 240V. Hence the normal supply of 16 Amp in the UK would be suitable for a total load of approximately 3 kW (although this may exceed the circuit limitations of the [motor] caravan).

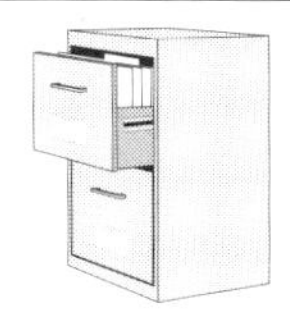

•Note therefore, that the average domestic kettle/jug having a power consumption in excess of 2000 watts may not be usable with outlets at present limited to 10 Amp. Lower consumption kettles/ jugs should be readily available at any well stocked accessory shop.

•Remember that, although an individual [motor] caravan can be supplied with 16 amps on a suitable site, there is a demand limitation when the site is busy and if everyone switches everything on at once the circuit protectors might trip. So be economical with your use of electrical power, for everyone's benefit.

•In the UK a Club Site Warden may refuse to offer a supply if it is believed that the installation may be unsafe.

TO DISCONNECT

Switch off at the caravan mains isolating switch, switch off at the pitch supply point and unplug both ends of the cable, site supply end first. (On Caravan Club sites, press the plug release button.)

FACT FILE: POWER CONSUMPTION OF APPLIANCES

In order to help with your calculations, this chart, reproduced here courtesy of The Caravan Club, gives some typical power consumption ratings of a number of appliances used in motor caravans. Be sure to check the specific ratings of the appliances you actually use.

Mains and 12V - Appliance Power Consumption in Amperes

Typical Appliance	Mains 240V AC	12V DC
Refrigerator	0.5	9.6
Black &White Television	0.1	1.25
Colour Television	0.2	4.2
Video Cassette Player	0.1	1.25 to 2.0
Microwave Cooker	5.0	N/A
2 KW Kettle	8.3	N/A
750 Watt Kettle	3.1	N/A
1 KW Fan Heater	4.2	N/A
Low Wattage Panel Heater	from 0.4	N/A
Carver Water Heater	2.75	N/A
Battery Charger	0.03	1.5
Carver Fanmaster	4.2 (slow) to 8.3	1.5 (max speed)
Water Pump	N/A	2 to 3
Fluorescent Lighting	N/A	0.5 to 1.5
Spot Lighting	N/A	0.8 to 1.75
TV Antenna	negligible	negligible
Powered Jockey Wheel	N/A	25 (running)
Cassette Toilet Flush	N/A	2.3 max
Car Type Vacuum Cleaner	N/A	6 (typically)

INSIDE INFORMATION: You can calculate the capacity of equipment by using the formula: Amps equals Watts divided by Volts. Therefore, if you have a 2 kilowatt (2,000 watt) kettle, and a 240 volt supply, when you divide 2,000 by 240, you can see that you will be using up 8.4 of your 'allocation' of amps to boil up for a cup of tea - but you really should use a non-domestic low-wattage kettle.

SAFETY FIRST!

To summarise, these are the Caravan Club's main recommendations:
•HAVE THE MOTOR CARAVAN MAIN ELECTRICAL SYSTEM CHECKED BY A QUALIFIED ELECTRICIAN AT REGULAR INTERVALS - ANNUALLY IF YOU COVER HIGH MILEAGES.*
•Maintain equipment in good order, and have appliances serviced as recommended by the manufacturer.
•Have damaged or worn cables replaced immediately.
•Do not abuse appliances by forcing them to perform in excess of their capability.
•Switch off ALL caravan internal appliances before connecting to or disconnecting from site supply.
•Check operation of RCD by means of test button every time caravan is connected to a site supply (NOTE: Supply must be switched on at site socket outlet.)
•In the event of a blown fuse or appliance malfunction, switch off the supply at the main switch before replacing a fuse or removing an appliance for inspection.
**A member of the ECA (the Electrical Contractors Association or the Electrical Contractors Association of Scotland) or of the NICEIC (the National Inspection Council for Electrical Installation Contracting) or the equivalent in other countries outside the UK.*

The Superpitch

1. An improved alternative to the usual pitching procedure for a motor caravan on site has become available over recent years. Superpitch is a system fitted to a number of new motor caravans that allows them to have all their services, gas, electricity, water and the cassette toilet, plus the option of satellite television and even a telephone line, connected up to their caravan through a single service point.

In order to work, the Superpitch requires the motor caravan to be placed on a specially developed pitch, and at present these are in relatively short supply. However, they are slowly increasing in popularity. For us on standard pitches, adaptors are available so that motor caravans with Superpitch facilities can be used as usual.

Towing

The 'Car-A-Tow' system allows you to tow a small car behind your motor caravan. It comes complete with a braked over-run system and lighting connections which appear to turn your car into a 'braked 4-wheel trailer' under the meaning of current towing legislation. This does imply that those who first pass their test after 1 January 1997 won't be able to 'Car-A-Tow", unless they have passed the separate trailer test. See *Chapter 4, Job 38* for connecting up with a 'Car-A-Tow'.

CHAPTER 4
OPERATING INSTRUCTIONS

This chapter consists of a kind of 'Owner's Handbook' for features common to all motor caravans and all the most popular appliances.

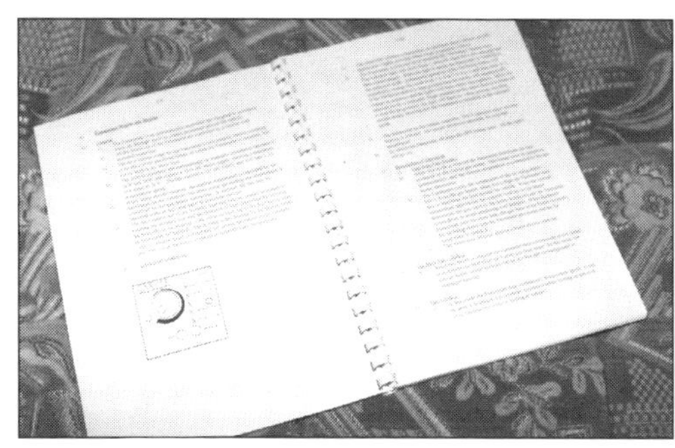

Please read this chapter in conjunction with the vehicle's handbook and the component manufacturer's manuals, where available.

PART I: THE BASE VEHICLE

Changing a Wheel

☐ I. First, remove the spare wheel. On this VW Transporter van conversion, you use the wheel bolt brace to remove the under-body wheel pan bolt. (Illustration, courtesy Volkswagen)

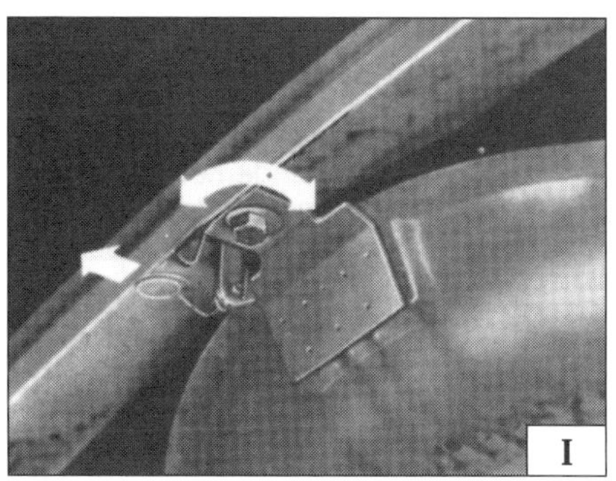

I

SAFETY FIRST!

The wheel is heavy - keep clear as - on some vehicles - the pan or retainer falls down.

☐ II. On some coachbuilt models, such as this Transit-based Auto-Sleepers, you remove a blanking plug by unscrewing it with the 'wrong' end of the wheel brace...

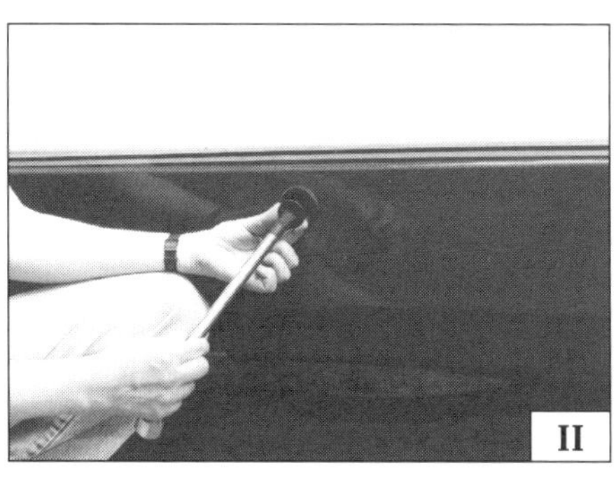

II

☐ III. ...then insert the spare wheel 'winder' so that the squared end locates in the mechanism beneath the vehicle (tricky!)...

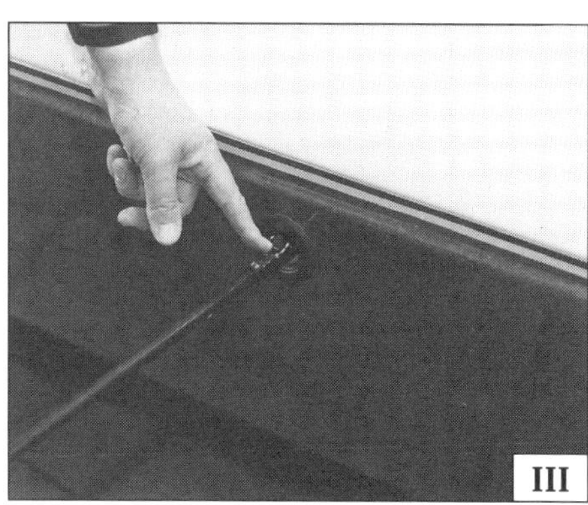

III

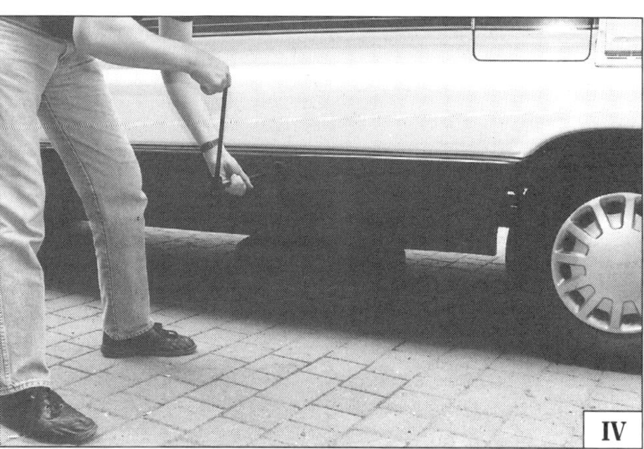

IV

☐ IV. ...and wind the wheel to the ground where it is unscrewed from its lowering chain and pulled free.

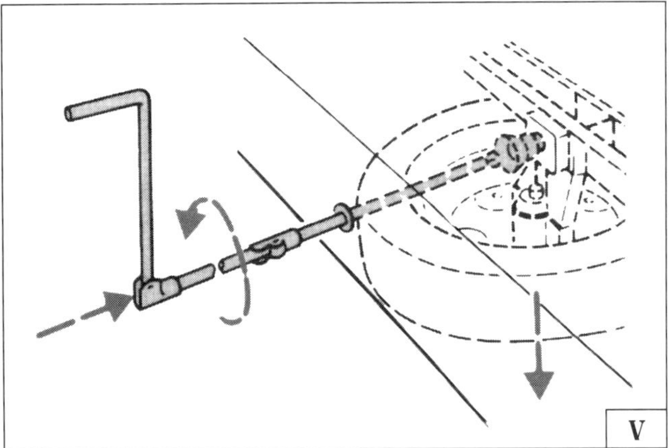

☐ V. On some Transits - mainly van conversions - spare wheel access is from the rear, but is the same in principle. (Illustration, courtesy Ford)

☐ VI. Apply the handbrake and chock front-and-back the wheel diagonally opposite the one to be changed.

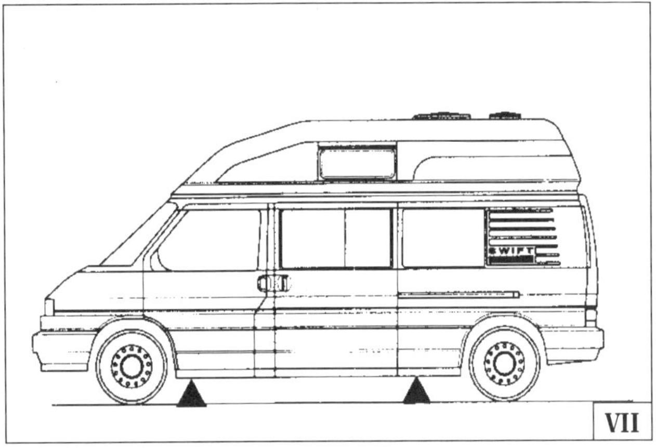

☐ VII. Position the jack under the appropriate jacking point - see your handbook. These are the jacking point locations on the Swift Carrera and Scorpio models. (Illustration, courtesy Swift)

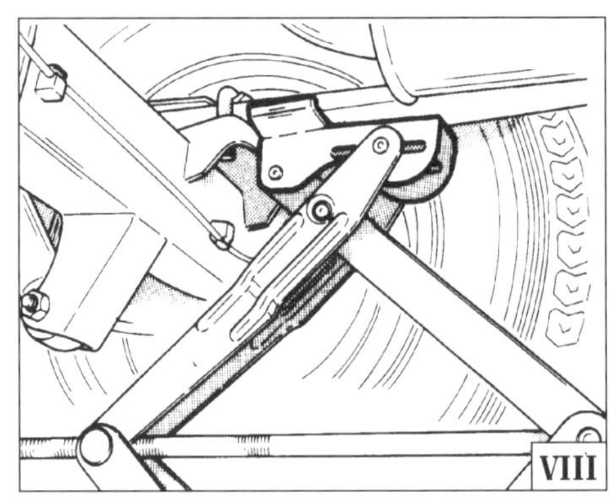

☐ VIII. If you don't have the original jack, ensure that you *only* use a scissors jack or bottle jack that is man enough for the job. A typical car-sized jack won't do. You could jack under the rear road spring, as near to the axle as possible...

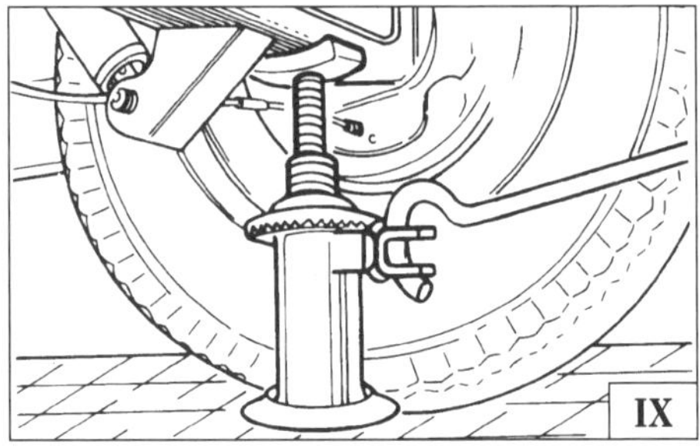

☐ IX. ...or better still, if the area is flat and stable, under the axle itself. In the case of Transporters, Ducatos and Boxers and others with independent rear suspension, you *must* use the manufacturer's jacking points.

☐ X. At the front, use the outer end of the crossmember or some other suitable NON-MOVING load-bearing component adjacent to the front suspension - or best of all, the manufacturer's recommended jacking points, once again. (Illustration, courtesy Ford)

☐ XI. Remove the wheel trim, when fitted, levering carefully until free.

☐ XII. Use the wheel brace to slacken off the wheel bolts or nuts on the wheel to be changed while it is still on the ground. If you jack up first, the wheel will turn instead of the bolts! (Illustration, courtesy Fiat)

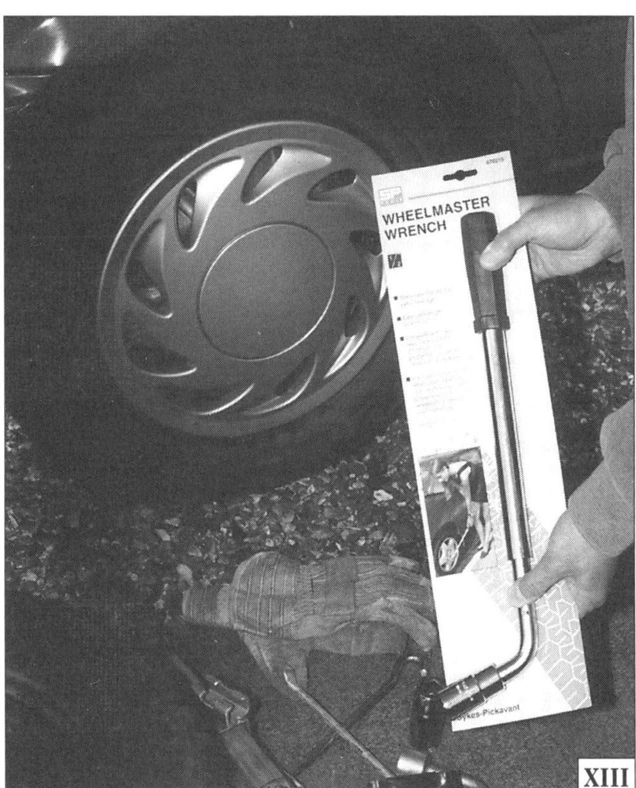

making it easy! *• XIII. Wheel bolts should be done up to a specified degree of tightness, but all too often they're done up by a chap behaving like a gorilla with a toothache!*

• Give yourself a better chance by buying one of these extendible wrenches, complete with the right-sized socket to fit your wheel bolts.

• Its superior strength and leverage will shift wheel bolts that the car-kit brace wouldn't even look at - it's an absolute 'must', not just for those who haven't got the strength of a raging gorilla, but also to replace that feeble wheel brace in the boot.

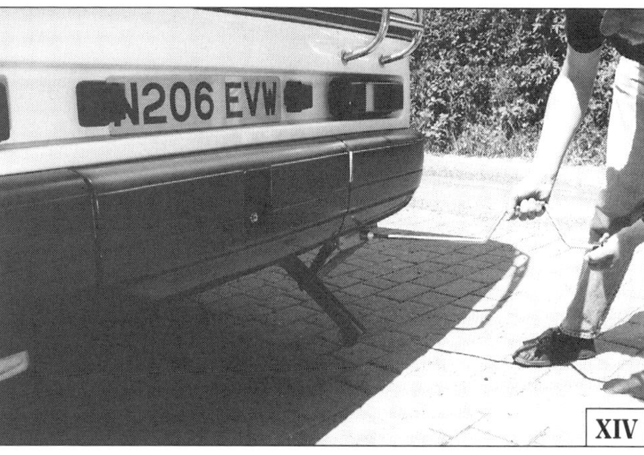

☐ XIV. As an additional safety measure, lower the corner steady (if fitted), on the relevant side if a rear wheel is being removed - DO NOT use it to take the weight of the vehicle!

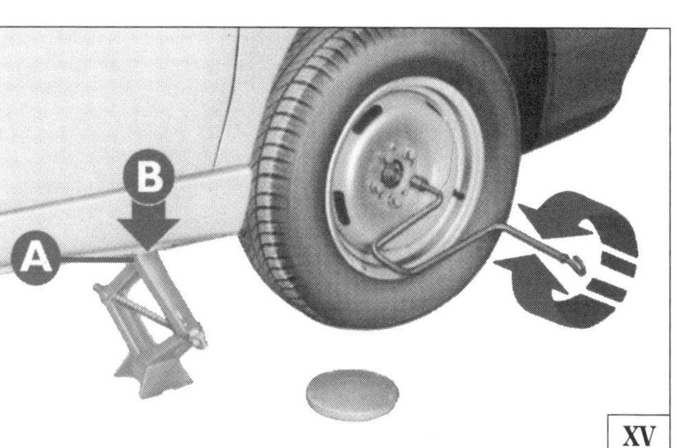

☐ XV. Jack up the motor caravan until the wheel for removal is just off the ground, unless the tyre is punctured in which case you will have to raise it high enough to get on a fully inflated tyre. You can now remove the wheel bolts or nuts and remove the wheel. Remember that the wheel will be heavier than one fitted to your car so be prepared for the extra weight. (Illustration, courtesy Fiat)

☐ XVI. Fit the spare wheel ensuring that any locating pegs in the hub are fitted into the wheel, and tighten the wheel nuts. Lower the vehicle to the ground and tighten the wheel nuts fully in the order shown. (Illustration, courtesy Swift)

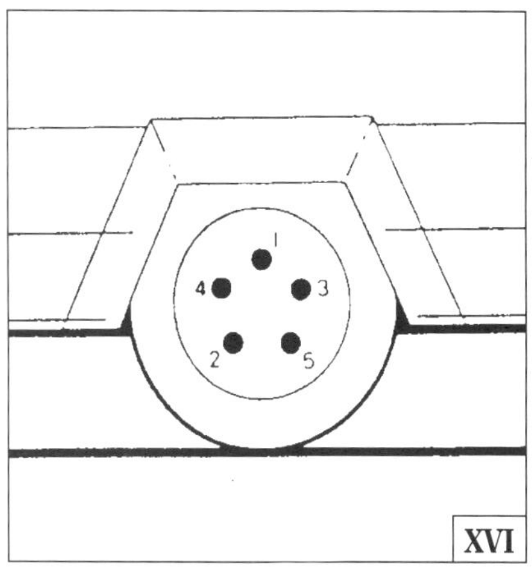

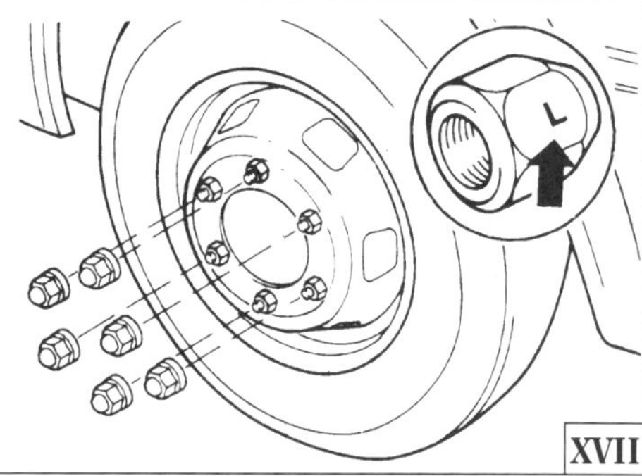

XVII. A few motor caravans, such as Transits with 6-nut fittings, have wheel nuts which are 'handed' for the left or right-hand side of the vehicle. Those on the left have a left-hand thread and are marked 'L', as shown. (Illustration, courtesy Ford)

Make sure you know the recommended bolt or nut torque for your vehicle and torque all the bolts up to the correct figure. For instance, Swift recommend 118 lbs/ft (16 Nm) for all of their vehicles.

making it easy!

- *You will probably find great difficulty in lifting the replacement wheel on to the wheel hub, especially if the vehicle is fitted with bolts, in which case there will be no studs on which to hang the wheel.*
- *Use a shovel, a plank of wood or any other lever that you may have to hand to help in lifting the wheel to the required height.*

Changing Bulbs and Lenses

All motor caravans have extra lights fitted to them and the larger coachbuilt and A-class models even have exterior lights which are not always those used by the manufacturer of the base vehicle.

EXTERIOR LIGHTS

1. The taller coachbuilt and A-class vehicles often have auxiliary side lights at the top of the bodywork. These lenses are a little more prone to being cracked than most because of their vulnerable position...

2. ...and in this case, the lens is simply held in place with two cross-head screws.

INSIDE INFORMATION: When refitting, always ensure that the rubber seal is in good condition and if necessary, replace. If the seal isn't a hundred percent efficient, water will get in and the bulb holder assembly will invariably corrode.

3. At the rear, many coachbuilt motor caravans use caravan or trailer-type light units. The lens for this one is held in place with a plastic clip...

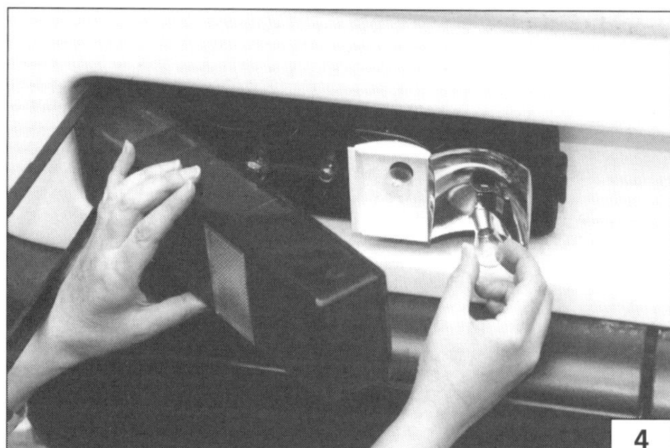

4. ...and when it's removed, the lens surround hinges back and the lens itself can be pealed out of its rubber seating. All of the bulbs are replaced by pressing in slightly, turning part of a turn anti-clockwise and pulling out.

PART II: THE LIVING ACCOMMODATION

Interior Lights

SAFETY FIRST!

Always disconnect the leisure battery, or turn off the power to the living accommodation before dismantling any of the light units.

1

☐ 1. Some lights, such as this one near the footwell, are simply removed by carefully levering the unit out of its retaining aperture.

2

☐ 2. **INSIDE INFORMATION: The festoon-type bulb is simple enough to remove from its holder, but you might find that the reflector-come-heat shield flops about loosely. Bend it so that it springs back into place and is held tight.**

SAFETY FIRST!

If you touch a halogen bulb while it is hot, or fit a new one with the power turned on to the light unit, your fingers can be badly burnt.

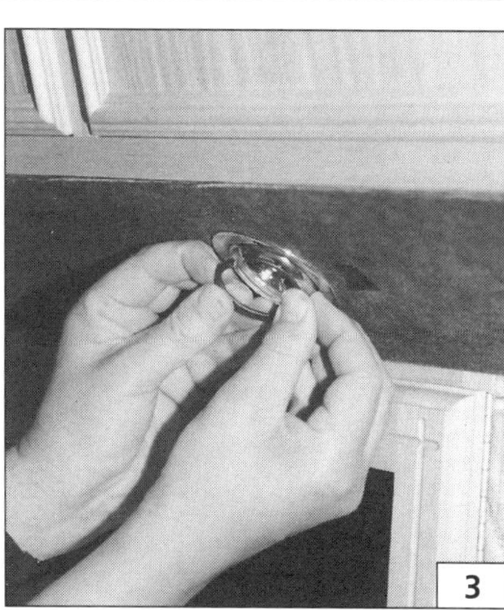
3

☐ 3. These mini-spot lights have clear lenses which are held in place with a spring clip which you have to carefully prise away.

4

☐ 4. IMPORTANT NOTE: You must never touch the small halogen bulbs with your fingers, otherwise they will burn out shortly after reconnecting them. Always hold the bulbs with a clean cloth or tissue.

INSIDE INFORMATION: If you should accidentally touch the bulb, wipe the glass clean with methylated spirits before refitting it.

Gas System

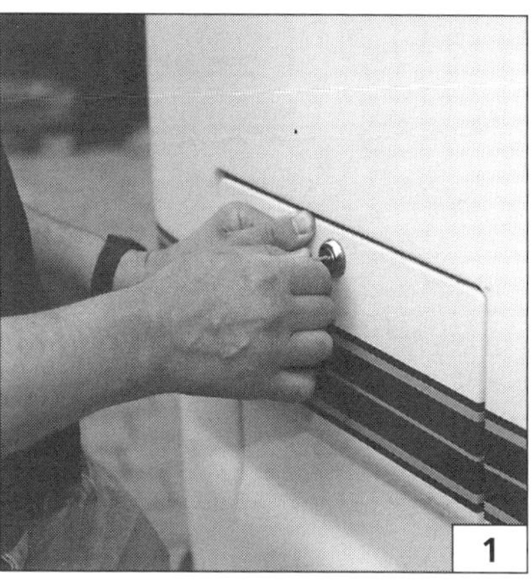
1

☐ 1. On most coachbuilt caravans, there will be a gas locker reached from outside the vehicle. On smaller motor caravans the locker is sometimes reached from inside the vehicle or when one of the rear doors is open on a panel van. (In all cases, the locker should be sealed from the living accommodation and vented in the floor of the locker.)

The gas system can be used for the hob, grill, oven (if fitted), room heater and water heater, so make sure that you are carrying enough with you.

SAFETY FIRST!

When either in use or in storage, a gas bottle should always stand on its base and never be allowed to rest on its side.

☐ 2.Two types of gas are commonly used for motor caravanning - butane and propane. Butane is available in blue bottles and propane in red.

For identification Butane is supplied in BLUE cylinders and Propane in RED cylinders.

2

3

☐ 3. Each requires its own type of regulator, which is a device that adapts the bottle pressure to one that suits the equipment in the motor caravan. These regulators are designed so that it is impossible to fit one to the wrong type of gas bottle. Propane regulators (centre) have a male thread; screw-on Butane regulators (right) have a female thread. See (5) below for the left-hand regulator. (Illustration, courtesy Calor Gas Ltd.)

While butane is more readily available and burns hotter than propane, it will freeze when temperatures drop below 2 degrees Celcius. Propane, however, will not burn quite as hot but will remain usable at temperatures down to minus 40 degrees C. It is therefore common for motor caravanners to use butane during the Summer and Spring and Propane in the Winter and Autumn.

4

☐ 4. As different types of regulators are used on different types and sizes of gas bottles, knowing how to use each one is essential. Before fitting either regulator, the safety cap will have to be removed from the top of the cylinder. This is done by pulling the wire cage holding the cap in place to the side and taking the cap off the top of the cylinder. (Illustration, courtesy Calor Gas Ltd.)

BUTANE CYLINDERS

4.5kg size (handwheel valve)

This cylinder takes a regulator or flow controller which screws on to the valve outlet. Both have a connecting nut which incorporates a black sealing washer.

CONNECTING A CYLINDER

1 Check that the valve handwheel is OFF by turning clockwise.

2 Remove protective black cap and keep to replace later.

3 Inspect the black sealing washer for damage before connecting. Replace the washer if faulty.

4 Fit the connecting nut (left hand thread), to the cylinder using a Calor Gas spanner. Tighten firmly, but do not overtighten as this can damage the washer.

5 When gas is required, turn the valve handwheel anti-clockwise.

5

☐ 5. To fit the regulators fitted to all propane and the small 4.5 kg butane cylinders you will need to screw the regulator into place, remembering that it is a LEFT-HAND thread. After checking that the sealing washer is in place, hand-turn the nut ANTI-CLOCKWISE, then tighten firmly (but not over-tight) in the direction shown. A suitable spanner is used to secure the lock nut into position. Turn the gas tap fully anti-clockwise to start the gas flow and fully clockwise to stop the gas flow. (Illustration, courtesy Calor Gas Ltd.)

☐ 6. With the 7 kg and 15 kg bottles, the procedure is slightly more complex, though no spanner is required. To attach the regulator to the bottle, check that the black sealing washer is fitted inside the cylinder valve, depress the spring catch in the middle of the regulator switch and turn the switch so that it's pointing downwards.

6

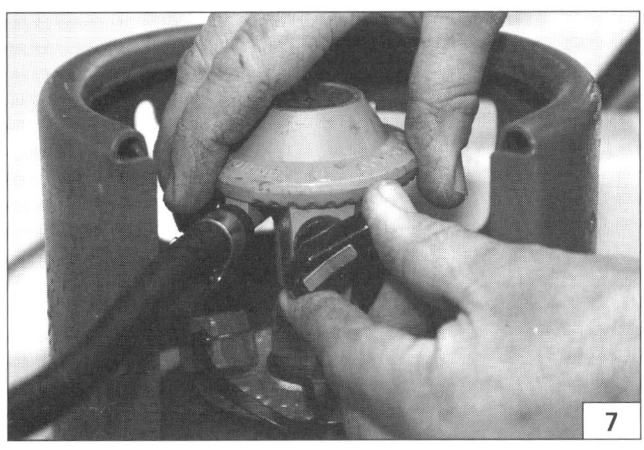
7

☐ 7. Then put the regulator into position on top of the gas cylinder and turn the switch back 90 degrees anti-clockwise. This will attach the regulator to the cylinder without actually turning the gas on. To turn the gas on, turn the regulator switch a further 90 degrees anti-clockwise.

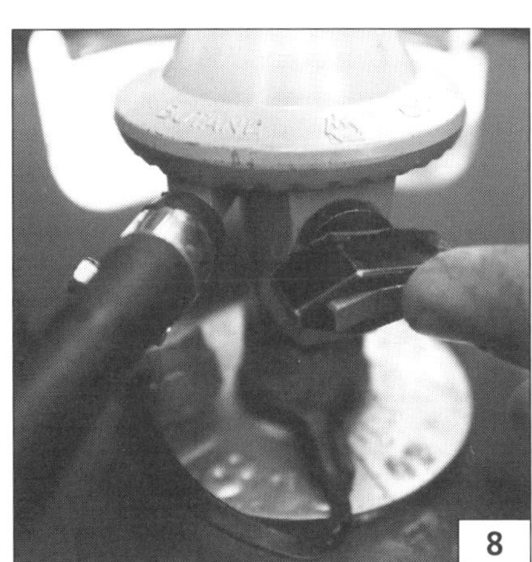
8

☐ 8. To release the regulator, depress the spring catch and turn the switch 180 degrees clockwise.

INSIDE INFORMATION: Most motor caravan sites and dealerships will carry replacement gas cylinders for when the cylinders in your motor caravan run out. However, if your cylinder is running low, telephone ahead to the site you are travelling towards, to check that they stock the size, type and brand that you use, otherwise you may not be able to make the necessary switch.

SAFETY FIRST!

Only a fully qualified engineer should attempt to carry out any repairs or alterations to the gas system. If your motor caravan develops any sort of problem with the gas system, turn the supply off immediately at the bottle, make sure all pilot lights are extinguished and seek expert help.

FACT FILE: CAMPING GAZ CYLINDERS

☐ 9. • When travelling on the continent it pays to carry a Camping Gaz Solo Regulator as an emergency standby.

• You may not be able to get refills for the cylinders you are carrying (Calor refills are certainly not available outside this country) but you would be able to switch to a Camping Gaz CV470 valved gas cartridge as an emergency measure.

• Alternatively, if you know that you are going to need more than an emergency top-up, you could invest in a larger Camping Gaz cylinder (the 901, 904 and 907 range) for which you will need a different type of regulator known as the Camping Gaz Regulator Tap. (Illustration, courtesy Camping Gaz (GB) Ltd.)

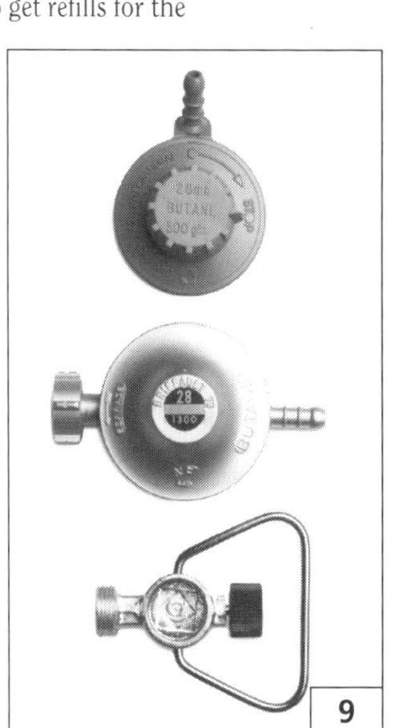
9

Electrical System

12 VOLT SUPPLY

In all but the oldest motor caravans, there will be some form of electrical distribution panel which acts as a central control point for the 12 volt system. While the number of controls and meters will vary from vehicle to vehicle, operating this panel is very straightforward.

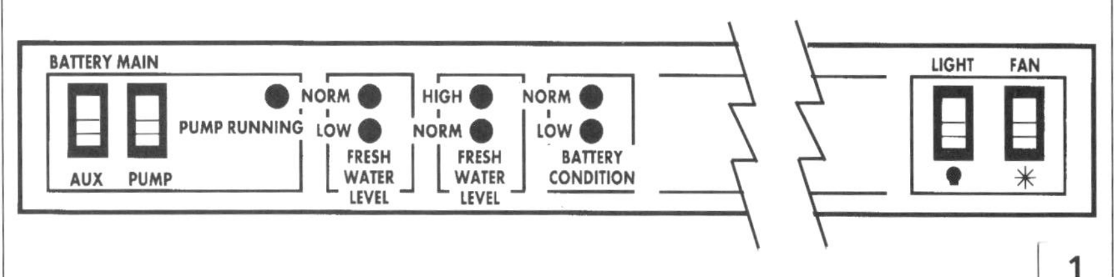

1

☐ 1. Almost all distribution panels use a rocker switch to select the 12-volt power source when required. This is usually simply labelled ON and OFF. When the vehicle is in use, the 12 volt control panel should be set to the OFF position and only turned ON when the vehicle's ignition is turned off and the 12 volt system is needed. Nearby will often be a water pump switch and, although this is dealt with more fully under a different section of this manual, it is worth noting that it should be turned off to avoid the pump ticking away when you don't need it. There may also be a battery power level indicator which may only be operated by pressing a button. (Illustration, courtesy Auto-Trail)

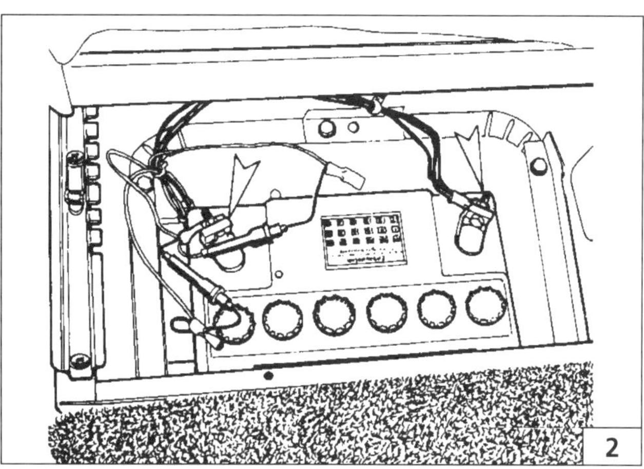

2

☐ 2. Every motor caravan should have an auxiliary battery so that you don't have to run the 12-volt system off the vehicle battery. This is so that, if the 12-volt battery is drained, there will still be ample power to start the engine. (Illustration, courtesy Auto-Trail)

i INSIDE INFORMATION: A second reason is that the auxiliary battery is designed to operate on different load cycles to that of the vehicle battery and, theoretically at least, it should be of a type this is specially built for the job. However, some motor caravanners swear that a (much cheaper!) regular car battery does the job just as well! i

In almost all motor caravans, the auxiliary battery will be charged either by the vehicle's alternator as it is being driven along or by the 240 volt system when plugged in. On some vehicles, the change over is automatic but on others, there is a switch on the control panel.

3

☐ 3. On most models, the 12-volt fuse box is in or adjacent to the control panel. On this Zig unit, the fuse box cover is levered away...

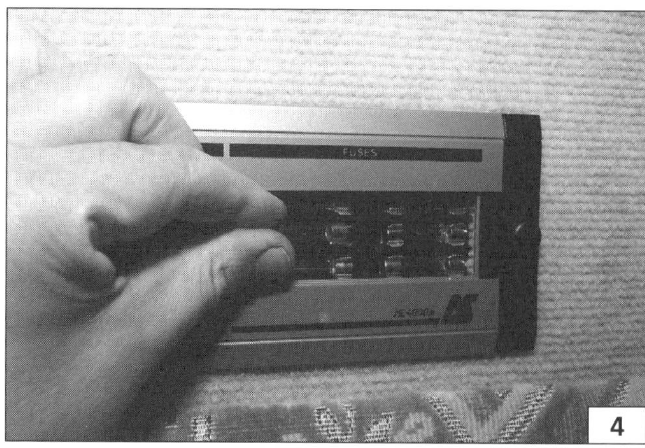

4

☐ 4. ...exposing the fuses beneath which can be replaced by being carefully levered out of their clips. DISCONNECT THE BATTERY FIRST! The glass tubes on this type contain the fuse wires and it is obvious when they are broken.

i INSIDE INFORMATION: Always carry a set of 12-volt fuses suitable for your control box and matching the values of the original fuses. Then, if you accidentally short out a connection, a fuse will be to hand. i

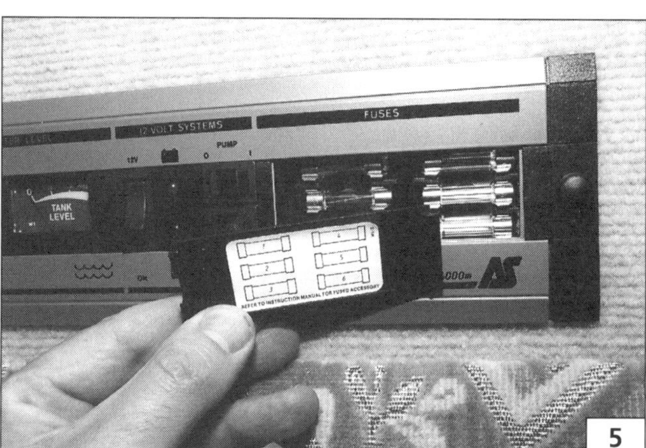

5

making it easy! ☐ *5. Write the fuse values and what they control on a label on the inside of the fuse box cover. That way, you'll be able to track down faults or use the correct replacement without unnecessary detective work.*

IMPORTANT NOTE: If a fuse continues to blow, there is a fault in the circuit of the component and you should not attempt to use it. You should NEVER bridge a fuse or use one with a higher value than the original.

MAINS SUPPLY

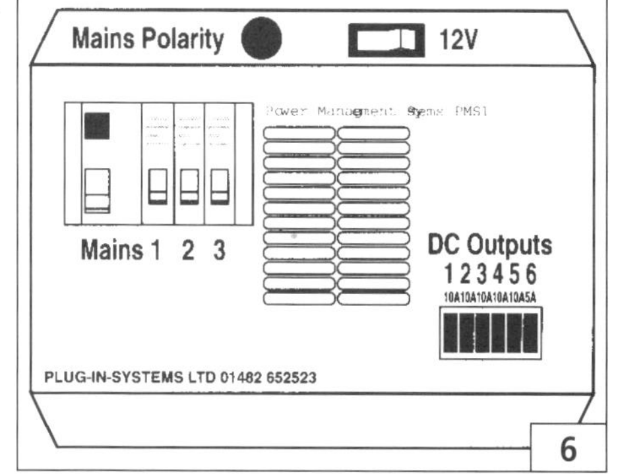

6

☐ 6. This is the Plug-In Systems Limited control panel with main switches, DC fuses, the 12 volt charging switch and a mains polarity light. When this pilot light illuminates, it tells you that the polarity of the mains input is reversed (all too often, this is still the case on some continental sites) and needs to be corrected. You can purchase a polarity reversing plug to enable you to switch the feed over without rewiring. Also, see page 29 for a DIY version. (Illustration, courtesy Auto-Trail)

• The MCB, is better described as a mechanical fuse which 'blows' to the OFF position in the event of an overload. In normal use, it should be left in the ON position, of course.

• The RCD on the other hand is fitted to provide protection against earth faults and possible electric shock. In the event of an earth fault which would cause a current leakage to earth, either directly or through the human body, the unit should immediately trip and switch to the OFF position.

7

☐ 7. You must test the operation of the RCD by pressing the TEST or 'T' button at which, the unit should immediately switch to the OFF position. If it does so, all is correct and the switch should be returned to the ON position.

SAFETY FIRST!

When the battery charger is operating, the power management system and the battery charger itself may become warm to the touch and it is therefore important that sufficient ventilation is maintained in the surrounding area.

Heating Systems

There are two main types of heaters in a motor caravan, the majority incorporating a flue, while there are also those of the catalytic variety.

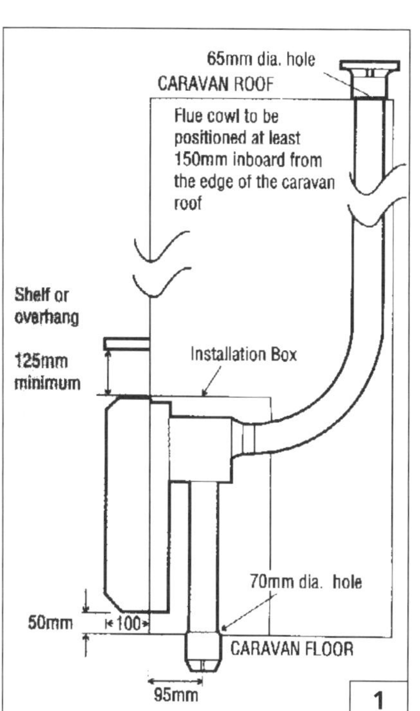

1

☐ 1. Flued heaters are completely room-sealed units with sealed air intake and gas output pipework and all are based on the principle of a well proven and extremely efficient heat exchanger. (Illustration, courtesy Belling)

2

☐ 2. A cheaper, although much less efficient, alternative to the flued heaters fitted to most motor caravans is the catalytic variety. These differ from the flued type of heater in that they don't require a vent for exhaust gases. Instead catalytic heaters are designed to burn off their own exhaust gases. However, if your motor caravan has one of these catalytic type of heaters fitted it is still ***strongly*** advised that the motor caravan is well ventilated whenever the heater is in use.

☐ 3. With the far more efficient flued type of heater, the gas burner is situated at the bottom of a vertical passage which permits complete combustion of the gas before meeting the heat exchanger surfaces above. The combustion gases travel along the top horizontal section and then downwards through further galleries while transferring their heat to the motor caravan. They are kept moving by the thermal drive of the rising column of hot gases from the flame.

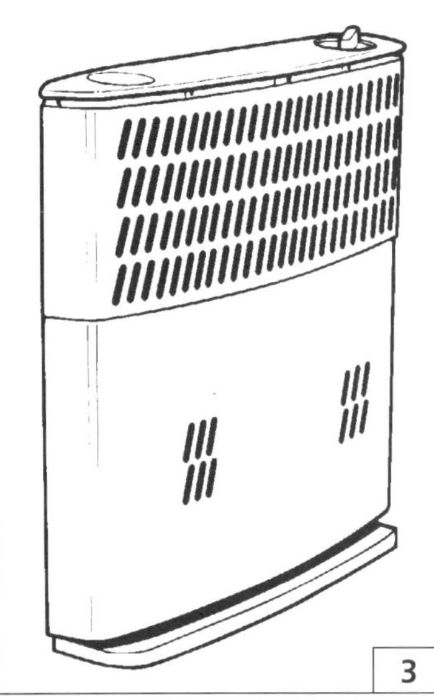

3

The flue outlet of the heater is at the bottom of the heat exchanger ensuring that the majority of the heat is extracted from the combustion products before they leave the heat exchanger. The combustion path is completely sealed from the living space, all the air for combustion being discharged through the adjacent flue.

Control and adjustment of the heater is by the gas control knob mounted on the top of the heater. Incorporated in the gas control is a flame failure device. If, for any reason, the burner flame is extinguished, the flame failure device goes 'cold' and the heater will automatically go to fail-safe, shutting off the gas. Ignition is by piezo spark, operated by pressing the ignition button mounted adjacent to the gas control knob. (Illustration, courtesy Carver)

All models have underfloor vents and, as a result, require unrestricted ventilation beneath the caravan. To allow the heater to work efficiently and safely it is essential that at least three sides of the vehicle must be open at one time. If the sides get blocked up by, for example, the build-up of snow, the heater shouldn't be used until the obstruction is cleared.

USING A FLUED HEATER

☐ 4. To switch on a motor caravan's standard gas heater, first make sure that the gas supply is turned on. Then turn the heater's thermostat control fully anti-clockwise and push the knob right in. While doing this, press the igniter switch several times.

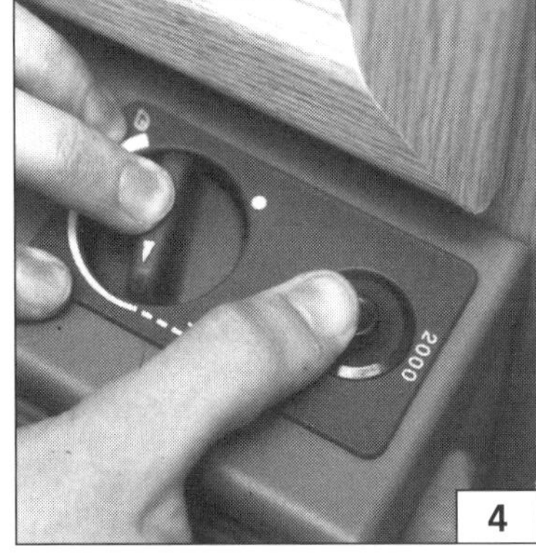

4

☐ 5. Where there is no separate igniter switch, turn the knob to the 'Ignition' position and press down firmly. You'll hear a click - or repeated clicking, in the case of electrical auto-ignition - as the igniter tries to light the burner. If the gas pipes leading to the burner are empty, you'll have to repeat this again and again until gas comes through and the burner lights. (Illustration, courtesy Carver)

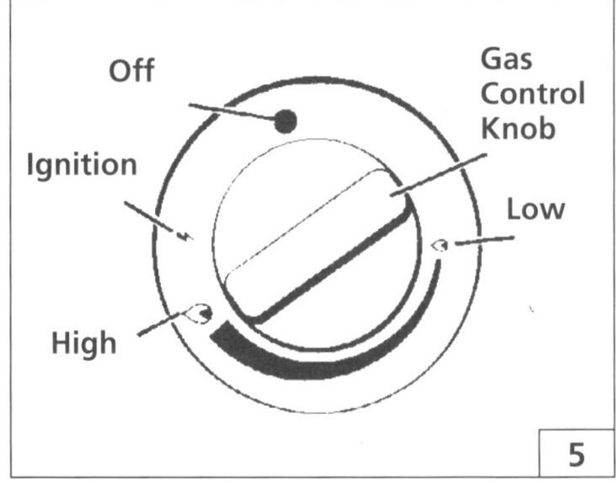

5

☐ 6. Keeping the control knob depressed, look for the pilot light through the viewing hole near the heater's base, or through the vents, according to model. When the pilot light is visible, keep the knob held down for about 30 seconds and then release. The burner should now stay alight and can be adjusted to the desired heat setting.

6

IMPORTANT NOTE: If the pilot light flame lights and then goes out again for any reason, WAIT 3 MINUTES before attempting to relight the heater.

AUTOMATIC MODELS: When you hold the knob down in the 'Ignition' position, the igniter clicks continuously until the flame is alight. Once the flame can be seen (see above) hold the knob down for a further 20 seconds. IMPORTANT NOTE: If the flame goes out, the auto-igniter will click continuously until the flame re-ignites or the knob is turned off. After turning off, WAIT 3 MINUTES before attempting to relight the heater.

ROOM TEMPERATURE on all models will be maintained automatically, depending on the setting on the control knob. The main burner will turn itself on and off, as required by the thermostat, while the pilot light stays alight.

To turn the heater off simply turn the thermostat to the 'OFF' or 'O' position.

BLOWN AIR CENTRAL HEATING

This is a very popular feature on modern motor caravans and is a 'must' for larger ones, where a static system simply can't circulate the heat widely enough. It is available either as standard equipment on newer and better equipped motor caravans or as kits to be fitted to older or more basic motor caravans.

☐ 7. Blown air central heating refers to an 12-volt electric fan system that can be fitted to the back of some motor caravan heaters and blows the heat through ducting out of vents situated throughout the motor caravan. (Illustration, courtesy Carver)

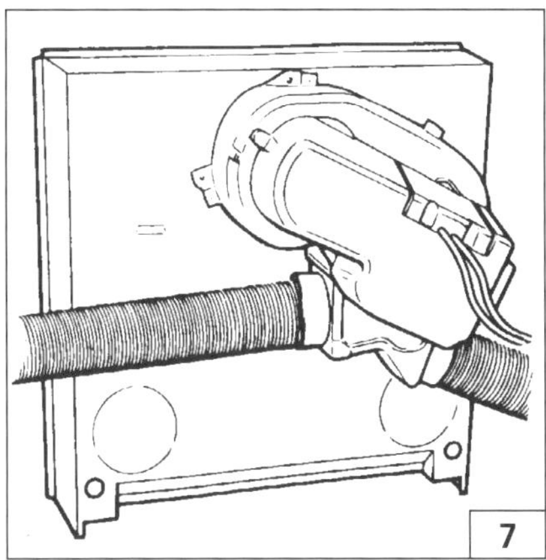

7

There are two types of Carver blown air central heating (the most popular type), known as the Senior and Junior systems. The Junior fan is designed for use in smaller motor caravans. When combined with an 1800, 2000 or 3000 heater it provides an effective way of introducing blown air heating. A 12-volt distribution fan operates at two selectable speed settings. The Junior Fan can be operated while the heater is in operation or, on hot summer days, the fan can circulate air around the motor caravan. The Junior Fan is also very quiet on slow speed.

The Senior Fan incorporates a more powerful fan and is suited to larger motor caravans fitted with 3000 or 5000 heaters. The Senior Fan has two control options: 'Auto Fan' and 'Manual Fan'. Auto Fan monitors the temperature output of the gas heater and adjusts its speed accordingly, so that constant warm air is distributed around your motor caravan. Manual control allows you to set the speed of the fan, making it ideal for night-time use or in the summer for cool air distribution.

☐ 8. To operate this model of blown air heating, locate the 'Trumavent' control switch, consisting off a circular thermostat control and a three-position switch. Leaving the switch in the central position will turn the fan off. Putting the switch in the top position allows the fan to circulate cold air. The 'A' position, meanwhile, is automatic speed control which increases the speed of the fan as the thermostat control is turned to higher settings and decreases the speed of the fan as the thermostat control is turned to lower settings.

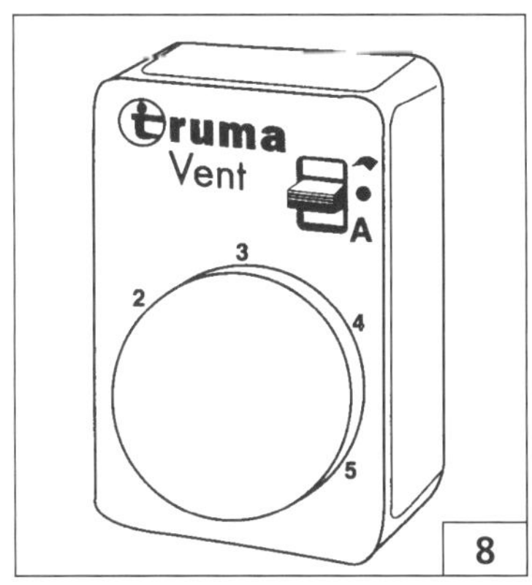

8

THE FANMASTER SYSTEM

☐ 9. At the top end of blown air heating range is the Fanmaster. Suitable for all motor caravans, it is compatible with Carver 1800, 2000 and 3000 heaters. It has a 230-volt AC heating element and a 12-volt DC distribution fan, giving blown air heating from the electric heating element or the on-board heater. Alternatively, in the summer the fan may be operated without any heat input to distribute cool air around the motor caravan.

9

The Fanmaster is operated by a remote, wall-mounted control panel. When using electric heating the motor caravan temperature is regulated by the thermostat on the control panel but when using gas heating the temperature is regulated by the gas heater thermostat.

☐ 10. The control panel contains a thermostat, an 'On/Select' button, an 'Off' button and five lights to show which mode is selected.

10

To turn the Fanmaster on, press the 'On/Select' button once and the mode indicator light will show 'mode 1' selected, flash for a few seconds and then remain steady.

Pressing the 'On/Select' button further will select modes from 1, to 2, to 3, to 4, to 5 and then back to 1 again.

The thermostat on the control panel only operates when electric heating is selected. Movement clockwise increases the selected temperature. To switch the Fanmaster off, simply press the OFF button once.

As for the mode settings, different modes have different effects on the output of the heater. 'Gas Auto Fan Mode 1' distributes the heat produced by the gas heater and is controlled by the heater's thermostat. The Fanmaster speed tracks the temperature of the air being drawn into it from the heater. When the temperature is high the Fanmaster runs faster to distribute the heat around the motor caravan.

When the motor caravan temperature approaches the comfort level set on the heater thermostat, the gas input to the heater is reduced and the Fanmaster slows down to avoid producing cool draughts. When the heater thermostat then calls for more heat, the gas input to the heater increases, the air being drawn into the Fanmaster gets hotter and the fan speed rises to match it.

This mode may be used without a mains electric hook-up.

When 'Gas Slow Fan Mode 2' is selected the Fanmaster runs continuously at a low speed to distribute the heat from the heater.

In 'Fan Mode 3' the Fanmaster runs continuously at maximum speed. This can be used to maintain maximum air circulation while heating on gas only, or to circulate air without heating in the summer. When set at 'Electric Auto Fan Mode 4', the Fanmaster runs at maximum speed with the integral 2kW electric element operating. When the comfort level set on the Fanmaster control is achieved the electrical input is reduced to 1kW and the fan speed is reduced. If the temperature continues to rise the element is switched off but the fan continues to run at a slow speed. A drop in temperature will reverse the sequence.

A mains hook-up is needed for this mode and the maximum current will be approximately 8 Amps.

Finally, 'Electric Slow Fan Mode 5' means the Fanmaster runs continuously at low speed and the 1kW element is in operation. When the comfort level set on the Fanmaster control is achieved the element is switched off but the fan continues to run.

It is not recommended that electric and gas heating is used simultaneously with the Fanmaster system.

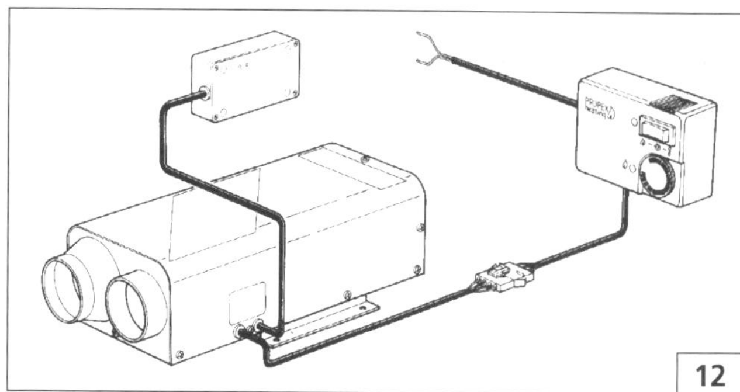

12. Another popular system is the Carver Propex system. This is commonly fitted to van conversions and where space is at a premium - there is only a blown air system and no separate heater unit in the room. (Illustration, courtesy Carver)

13. Outlet vents distribute the warm (or cold, if you prefer) air around the interior...

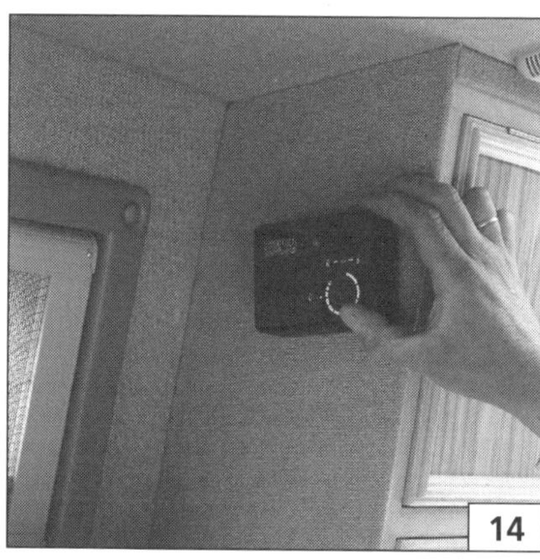

14. ...while a wall-mounted thermostat is all that's on display. As with other non-catalytic heaters, fresh air is drawn from outside while the exhaust passes out through a separate flue.

FACT FILE: FANMASTER OPERATING INSTRUCTIONS

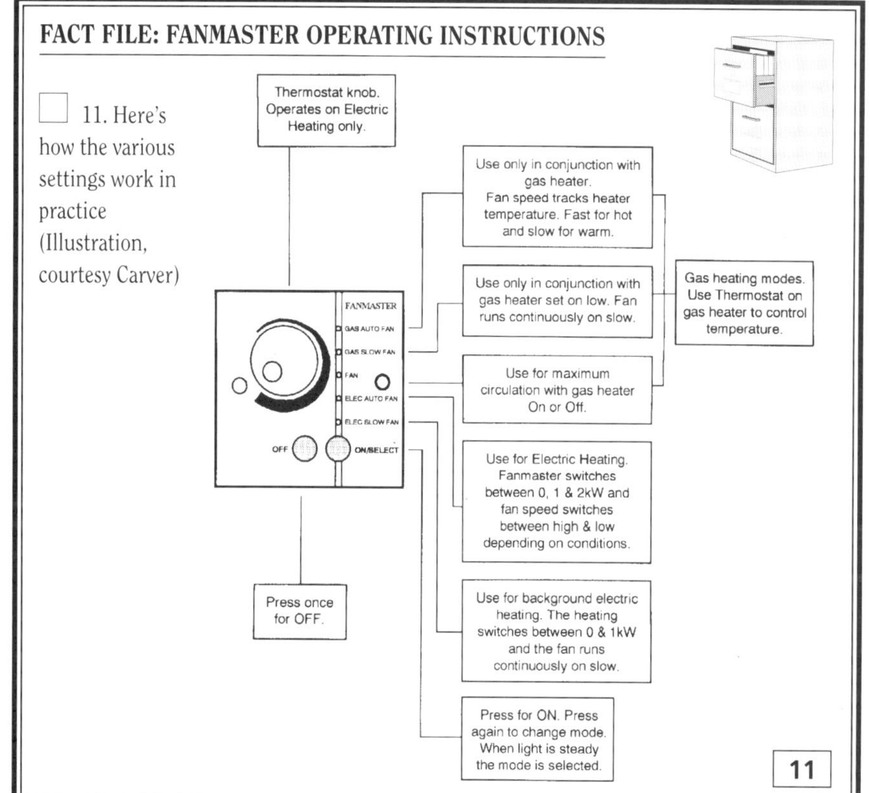

11. Here's how the various settings work in practice (Illustration, courtesy Carver)

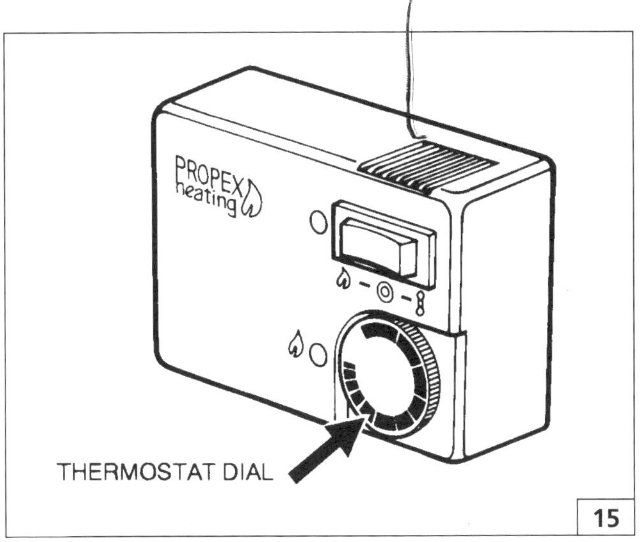

15

15. To light and control the heater:

i) Ensure that the gas is turned on at the cylinder and isolating valve and that the 12v or 24v electrical supply is switched on.

ii) Rotate the thermostat dial fully anti-clockwise and press the left-hand side of the 3 position switch. The red 'power-on' LED will light.

iii) Rotate the thermostat dial clockwise until the green LED (next to the thermostat marks) lights. The heater will now go through its ignition sequence, the fan will start and run for about 6 seconds to pre-purge the heat exchanger then the internal gas valve will open with a click and the igniter will operate to light the burner. A regular ticking may be heard as this happens.

iv) The heater will run until the thermostat is satisfied when the green light will go out and the burner will shut down. The fan may run on to cool the heat exchanger down.

As the temperature of the living space drops the thermostat will switch the heater on again and paragraphs iii) and iv), above, will be repeated.

v) The temperature of the living space is controlled by rotating the thermostat knob. Once a satisfactory comfort setting has been established the knob may be left in that position and the heater lit by operating the switch alone.

To switch the heater off: Centralise the 3 position switch. The red and green LEDs will go out and the burner will shut down. The fan may run on to cool the heat exchanger.

To circulate cool air: Press the right hand side of the 3 position switch. The fan will start but the burner will not. The 'power on' LED next to the switch will light up green. The thermostat is inoperative in this mode.

FACT FILE:
PROPEX HEATER TROUBLE-SHOOTING

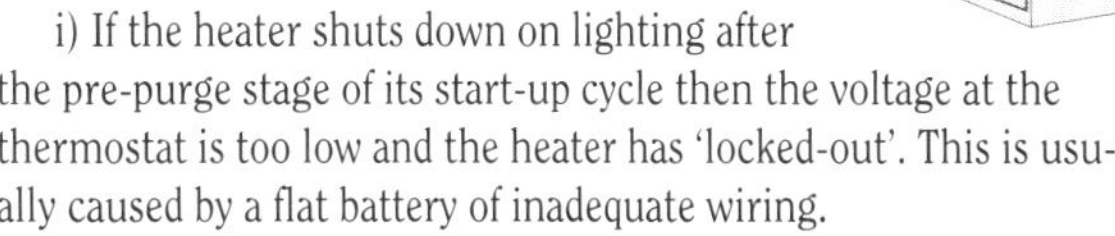

Low Battery Symptoms:

i) If the heater shuts down on lighting after the pre-purge stage of its start-up cycle then the voltage at the thermostat is too low and the heater has 'locked-out'. This is usually caused by a flat battery of inadequate wiring.

ii) After curing the fault, re-set the controls by switching off and on again at the thermostat.

iii) Another indication of low voltage is the illumination of the red LED on the control unit near the heater.

Gas Supply Failure Symptoms:

iv) If the heater shuts down on lighting after the ignition stage of its start-up cycle it is usually due to a failure of the gas supply and the heater has 'locked-out'. Lock-out can be confirmed by the green LED on the control box near the heater being out, while the green LED on the thermostat is lit.

This can be caused by the gas not being turned on, cylinder empty, cylinder temperature below 0 degrees C on butane, or air in the gas line. The latter often occurs in new installations or after long periods of non-use.

v) Check the state of the cylinder and ensure the gas is turned on.

vi) The control is re-set by switching off and on again at the thermostat.

vii) If there is air in the gas line, iv) and vi) may have to be repeated several times.

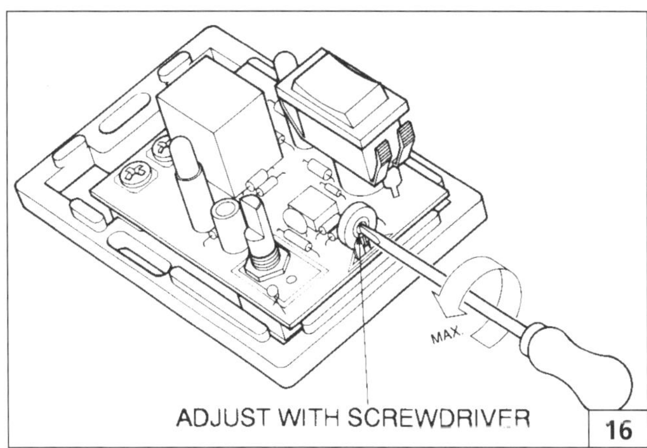

16

16. The sensitivity of the thermostat is adjustable.

If the vehicle is getting too hot before the thermostat turns the heater off and too cold before it turns it on again the sensitivity is low. If the heater is cycling on and off too often the sensitivity is too high.

To adjust the sensitivity gently pull the knob off the thermostat, undo the screw beneath it and remove the cover.

The adjustment may be made as shown by very gently using a small screwdriver or a cocktail stick sharpened to a screwdriver point. (Illustration, courtesy Carver)

SAFETY FIRST!

• The gas supply to the heater must be from a regulator of adequate capacity providing a working pressure of 28mbar on butane or 37mbar on propane. Under NO circumstances should an industrial or adjustable regulator be used.

• The electrical supply to the heater must be 12v or 24v negative earth, fused at the manufacturer's recommended rating.

• The heater must NOT be operated: a) While refuelling. b) When the vehicle is in a confined space such as a garage. c) When the motor caravan is on the move.

• Ensure that the path between the recirculation intake on the heater and the recirculation grill into the heater enclosure is not obstructed.

• Regularly check the exhaust and combustion air intake ducts beneath the vehicle for crushing, splits, obstructions and droops that could lead to water pockets.

• If exhaust fumes from the heater are detected inside the vehicle turn the heater off immediately. Do not use until the cause has been found and cured.

• It is recommended that the heater isolating valve, if fitted, is kept closed if the heater is not in use.

• Never block or cover the vents and grills at the top of the heater or outside the motor caravan.

• When children are in the motor caravan, position a safety guard around the heater at all times.

Water and Waste Systems

Modern motor caravan water and waste systems are remarkably sophisticated affairs and contribute greatly towards that home-from-home feeling.

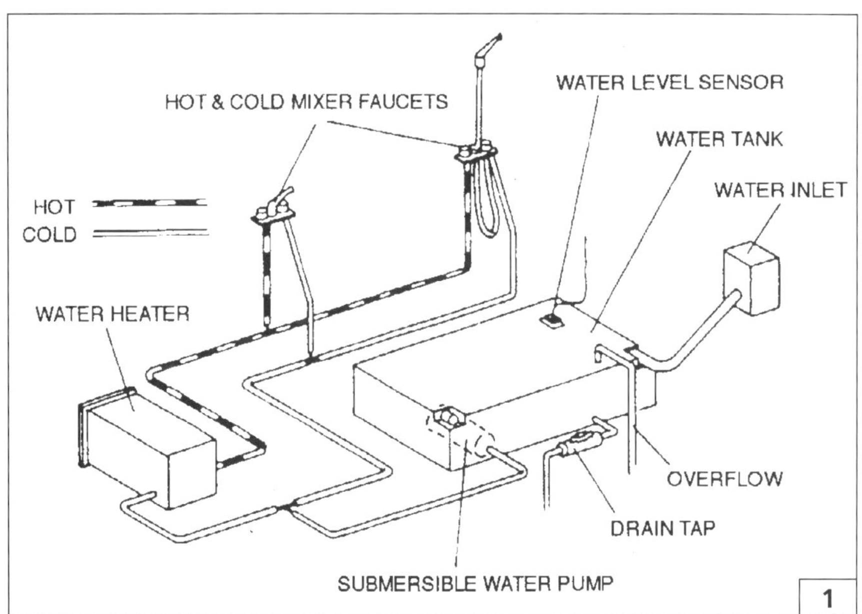

1

☐ 1. Most now contain an on-board water tank and all have a pumped system of some sort. If you are thinking of topping-up your motor caravan's water tank before setting out on a journey, think again! One litre of water weighs 1 kg. (In other words, a gallon weighs around 10 lbs.) So even if your waste water tank is empty (of which, more anon) you could easily be carrying 90 litres, or 90 kg of water as you drive along. This could be enough to tip you over the weight limit and will certainly waste fuel. (Illustration, courtesy Swift)

2

☐ 2. You'll quite often find the water tank level gauge built in to a larger control panel, such as this one...

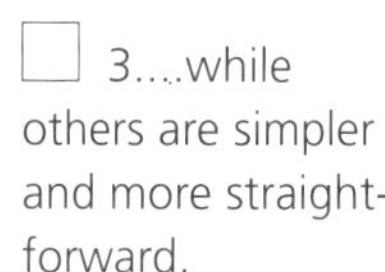

☐ 3....while others are simpler and more straight-forward.

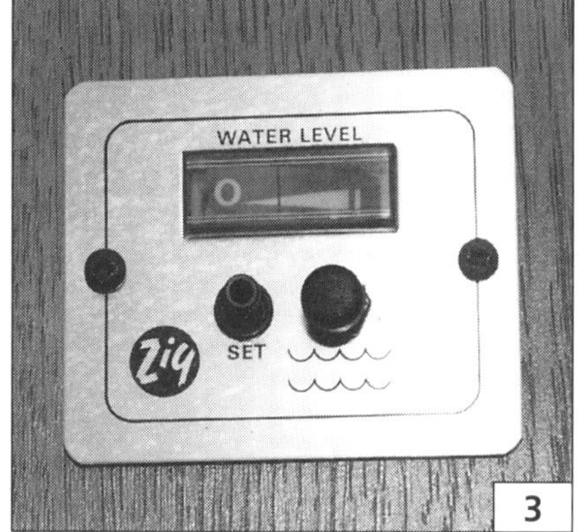

3

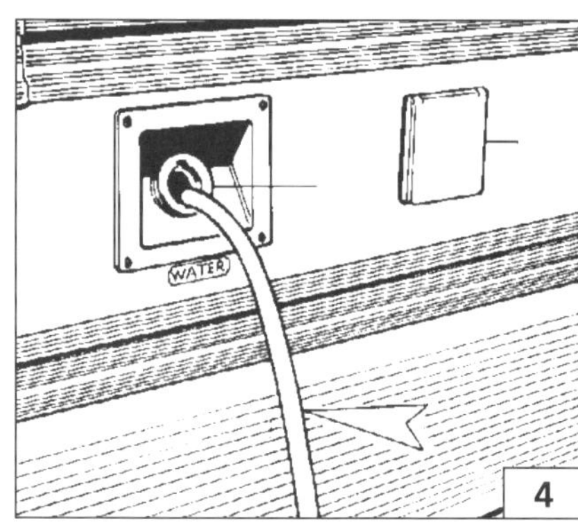

4

☐ 4. When topping-up the water tank from a mains supply, all you have to do is insert one end of a suitable length of pipe into the filler aperture after having removed the lockable filler cap. (Illustration, courtesy Auto-Trail)

You must make sure that the hose pipe is made from a non-toxic food-quality material. Suitable hoses are available from your motor caravan and caravan accessory shop.

IMPORTANT NOTE: The fresh water filler cap must be lockable and must be fitted with a label clearly identifying it as 'WATER'. You don't want anyone accidentally topping up with petrol or diesel!

5

☐ 5. Where you can't get at a mains supply, fill your fresh water container and place it near to the motor caravan's water inlet point. Place a submersible pump, as shown here, into the water container and top-up your water supply. You could, of course, pour but that would be slow and laborious.

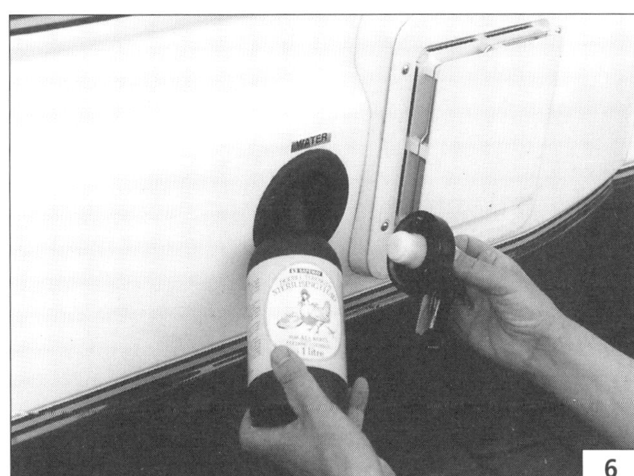

6

☐ 6. If a motor caravan's water system is left unused for a period of time, it will go brackish and the water coming out of the system will be polluted with bacteria. Use diluted Milton's Fluid (or a cheaper supermarket's own brand alternative) to flush through the system but beware: if you use it too often, it will add its own taste to your water system. The best solution (no pun intended) is to flush through the system as often as possible.

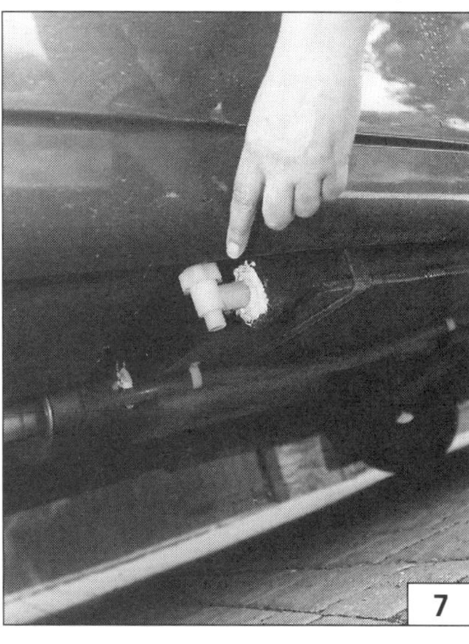
7

☐ 7. Most motor caravans of any size, have a holding tank for the waste system. This can be drained from beneath the vehicle and in fact, should be drained before every journey. Residual waste in the tank can cause smells in the motor caravan and it can once again be flushed through with Miltons.

The drain tap is made to have a flexible pipe pushed on to the end of it so that you can drive the motor caravan near to the waste water disposal point and drain the waste water away. For the sake of hygiene, always use the appropriate waste water disposal point and never the drain adjacent to the fresh water tap.

8

☐ 8. Older and smaller motor caravans may not have an integral waste tank, in which case the waste water container should be connected up to the waste outlet when you arrive on site. Make sure that the top of the container is lower than the waste outlet point. Otherwise, a situation occurs where old water sits in the waste pipe which, in time, can create an unpleasant smell.

9

☐ 9. For those without an on-board waste water tank and also those who wish to leave their motor caravan connected up to an awning and to remain in place on-site for an extended period, a rollaway waste water tank will be an invaluable accessory.

WATER HEATERS

For motor caravans with a water heater fitted as standard equipment, there are several different types such as the Carver Cascade 2 and 2 PLUS, the Carver Cascade 2 GE and 2GE PLUS, the Maxol Malaga and the Trumastore, all of which run on gas alone or gas and electricity. For instance, the Cascade 2 PLUS uses just gas to heat the water while the Cascade 2 GE PLUS uses either gas or mains electricity, or a combination of the two.

SAFETY FIRST!

• Never attempt to operate a water heater unless it is filled with water. Run the hot water tap - water will only come out if the heater tank is full.

• The exhaust and intake cowls must not be obstructed in any way. During winter use, ensure that the cowl is not blocked by driven snow.

• After switching off or the heater going to safety shutdown, wait for three minutes (or longer if the manufacturer recommends it) before relighting.

• Do not operate the water heater while the motor caravan is in motion.

• Drain the system in frosty weather, as shown below, so that no frost damage can occur.

• Do not attempt to service a water heater yourself: in common with all gas appliances, an annual service by an approved dealer is strongly recommended.

☐ 1. The most popular heater in the UK, the Carver Cascade, is installed through the wall of the motor caravan with only the flue cowl visible on the outside. The whole unit is a self-contained module. The control panel is sited somewhere suitable inside the motor caravan. With earlier models of Cascade (those without a 'PLUS' suffix) there is also a separate control with an ON-OFF switch - see below.

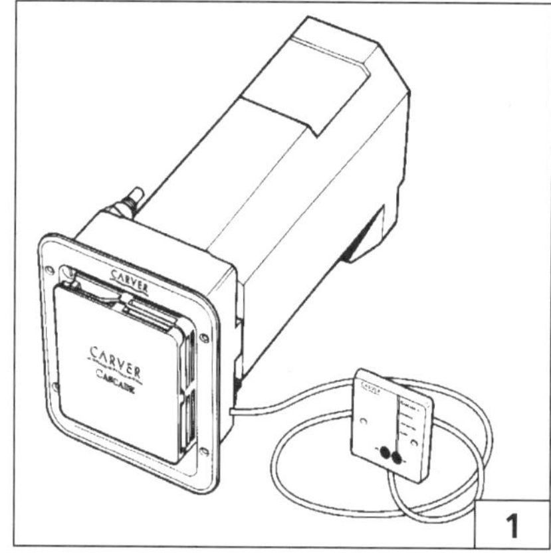

1

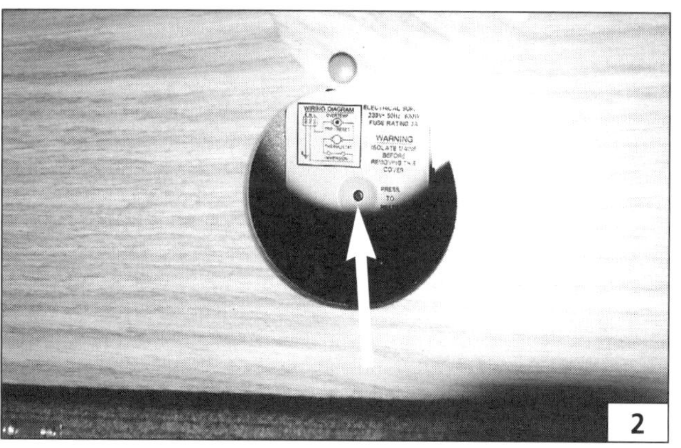

2

☐ 2. Cascade heaters include the following safety features.

i) On the inner end of the heater is an over-temperature cut-out with a reset button (arrowed). If your heater doesn't work, work out where the button is located inside your motor caravan and try resetting it. The cut-out switch shown here only applies to the GE models with an electrical immersion heater.

ii) There is also a pressure release valve which automatically opens if the internal pressure exceeds three bar (44 psi), ejecting water through the cowl, then closes when the pressure drops.

In case of direst emergency, there is a fusable plug situated above the burner. If the internal temperature of the unit goes above 96 degrees C, the plug melts and sprays water onto the burner, causing the heater to go to safety shutdown. (Illustration, courtesy Auto-Trail)

☐ 3. Earlier models of Cascade are also fitted with a separate control switch as shown here. The slide switch is up for ON and down for OFF. The green indicator shows that the heater is working satisfactorily; green and yellow on together shows that the DC voltage is below the 10.5 volts required and the battery needs to be recharged; green and red on together shows that the heater has failed to ignite or has gone to safety shutdown. This is usually caused by failure by the gas supply or air in the gas system after fitting a new cylinder. If air in the system is the problem, you will need several attempts to relight the heater before all the air has been purged from the system. (Illustration, courtesy Auto-Trail)

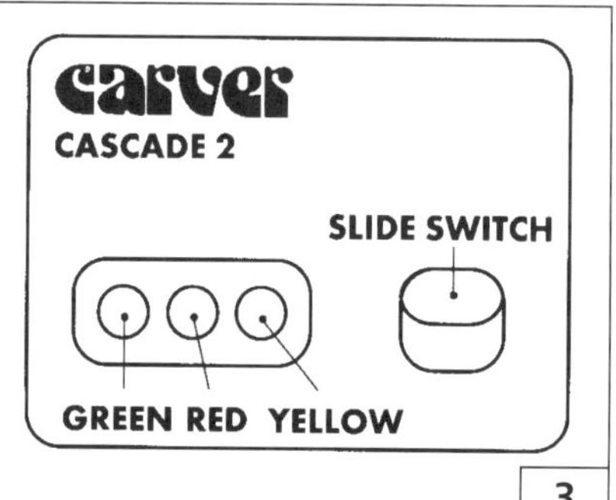

3

IMPORTANT NOTE: Wait three minutes after switching off the heater before attempting to relight it.

GAS OPERATION: Ensure that the gas is turned on and that the system is full of water (check that water flows from the hot taps). Ensure that the 12 volt supply is connected. Do not use a battery charger as the only source of power.

In the case of earlier (pre-PLUS models), slide the switch to the ON position. See **3** above.

☐ 4. In the case of all Cascade models, press the ON button on the power controller. And that's all there is to it!

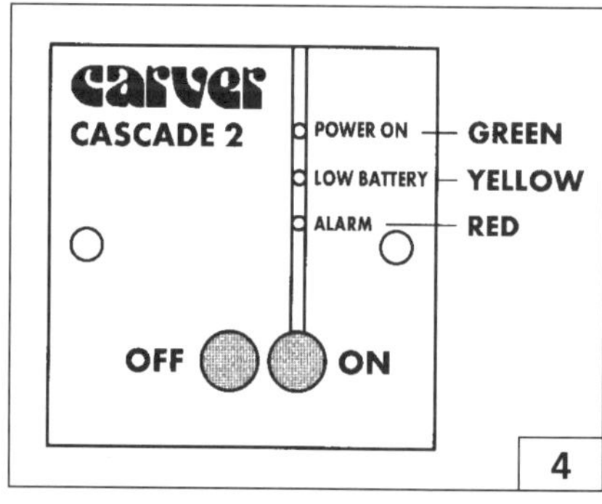

4

FACT FILE: CARVER CASCADE

- The thermostat is pre-set to approximately 70 degrees C and cannot be reset.
- When a GE system is fitted, the electric immersion heater uses approximately 2.75 amps.
- Carver claim that some water will be available at 55 degrees C to 60 degrees C after 30 minutes of switching on when used on gas and after 55 minutes of switching on when used on electricity.
- Both gas and electricity can be used together for warming up but should not be used together after the initial warm-up period.
- Carver estimate that approximately 140 grams of gas will supply 23 litres (5 gallons) of hot water per day.
- Cascade heaters have either a 6 litre (1.3 gallons) or 9 litre (2 gallons) capacity, according to model.

ELECTRICAL OPERATION: Ensure that the heater is full of water (check that water flows from the hot tap when it is turned on) and make sure that the site mains supply is adequate. See FACT FILE above.

Carver do not supply an electrical isolation ON-OFF switch but one must have been fitted by the installer when the unit was installed. Make sure it is turned on. It is strongly recommended that the separate switch is fitted with a light so that you can tell when the immersion heater is on.

If the trip switch referred to in **2** above, continues to trip out, do not use the immersion heater until a Carver dealer or qualified electrician has checked the system.

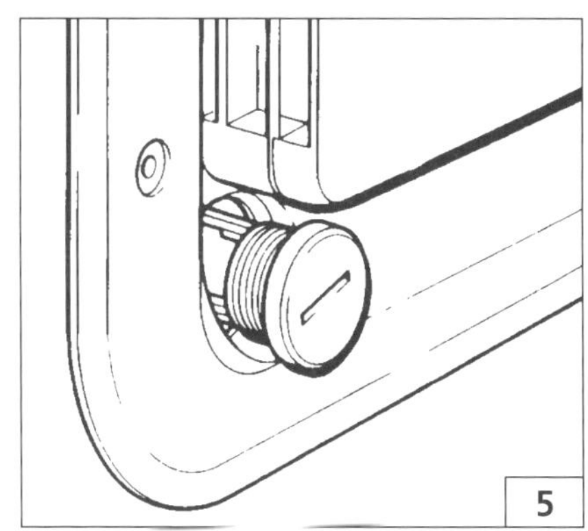

5

☐ 5. **DRAINING THE SYSTEM:** This should be done at the end of the season or in frosty weather. See *Chapter 5, Job 77* for details. (Illustration, courtesy Auto-Trail)

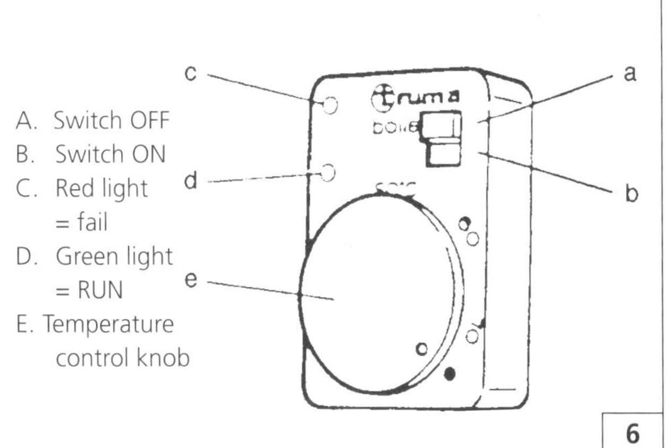

A. Switch OFF
B. Switch ON
C. Red light = fail
D. Green light = RUN
E. Temperature control knob

6

☐ 6. The TRUMASTORE water heater, as with other water heaters, has to be filled before turning on. To fill the heater for the first time or after draining:

- Check that the safety valve is closed.
- Make sure the water pump is switched on and open the hot tap.
- Air will escape from the tap as the heater is filling with water and when water flows with no more air, the heater is full.

TRUMASTORE GAS OPERATION: Ensure that the gas and the 12 volt supply are fully charged, connected up and turned on. Set the control knob to the temperature required and move the switch to the position A. The green RUN light (D) should come on. If the gas pipe is full of air, it may take up to a minute for the air to be purged. If the red FAIL light (C) comes on during this time, repeat the process by switching the heater off (to position A) to reset it and then ON again.

RED FAIL LIGHT: This light comes on if there is any failure of the gas supply or a defective safety device. Reset by switching off and then on again. If the fail light comes on after trying to ignite unsuccessfully for the second time, wait 10 minutes before trying again.

DRAINING THE SYSTEM: Switch the pump off and open a hot tap. Lift the drain handle on the drain valves to the vertical position and close the valves again when the water has completely drained out.

7

☐ 7. On some models, an electric heater is also fitted. As with the Carver system, this can be used in conjunction with the gas system for a quick warm-up. It consists of no more than the ON-OFF switch, arrowed. The water temperature is not adjustable and is set for approximately 70 degrees C.

A number of less common 240-volt water heaters are available to be fitted to motor caravans. These are generally operated through a simple on/off switch and adjustable thermostat. However, this type of water heater obviously requires a site with a sufficient mains electrical power supply.

INSIDE INFORMATION: Using a motor caravan's Fanmaster system and mains electric water heater at the same time will sometimes be too much for many site electricity supplies and may cause the supply to cut-out. Check with the staff on site, when you arrive, and where necessary, try not to use both appliances at the same time.

SAFETY FIRST!

All gas water heaters must be switched off when the motor caravan is in motion.

Portable Toilet

Many older motor caravans, smaller vehicles and van conversions are fitted with portable-type toilets with the flush-water tank mounted above the waste tank. In many cases, these are built in to cupboard units so that they slide away and out of sight when not in use.

All of the line drawings in this section have been used courtesy, Thetford.

☐ 1. The Thetford Porta Potti range is the most popular of this type of toilet.

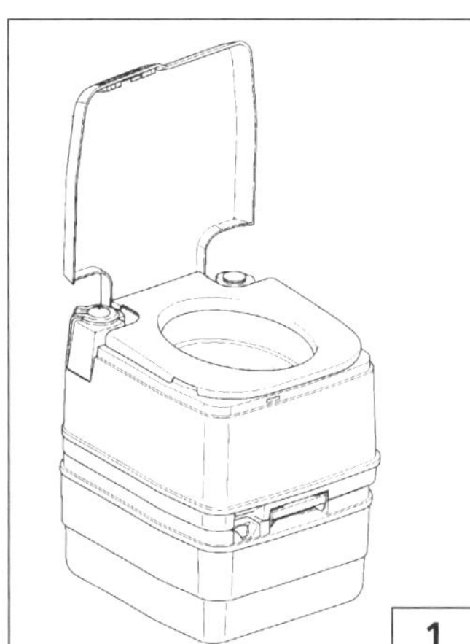

☐ 2. To empty a Porta Potti, you slide the latch to one side while simultaneously removing the water tank from the waste tank. Note that when the flush water tank is removed from the waste tank, the valve handle locks.

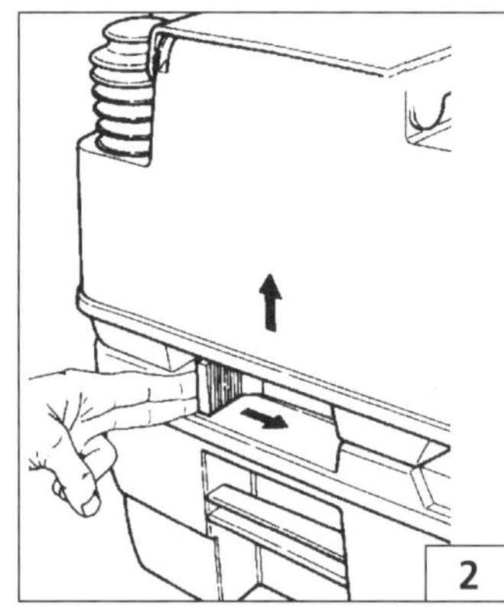

☐ 3. The waste tank can be carried to the disposal point using the integral carrying handle.

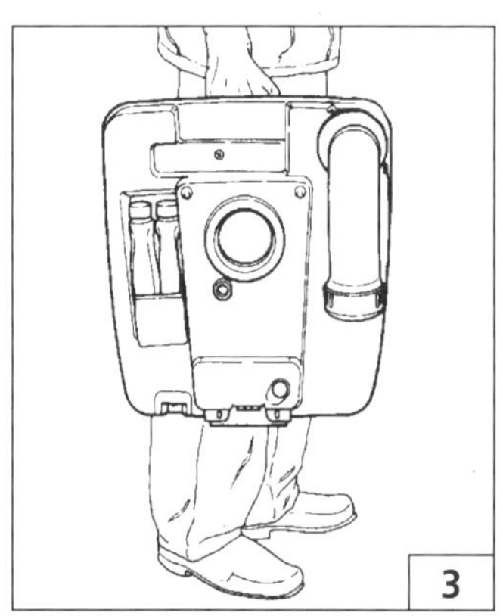

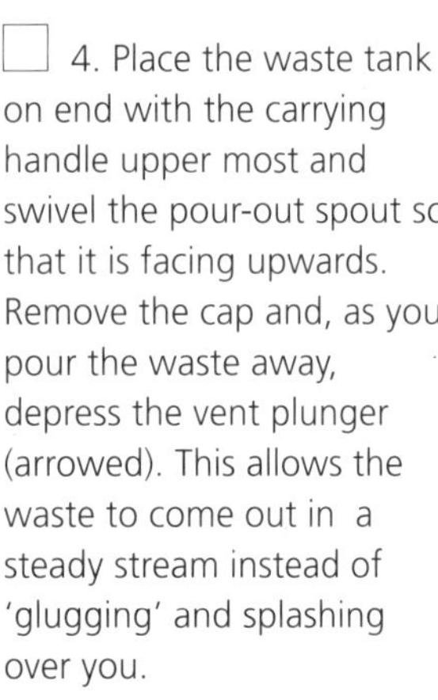

☐ 4. Place the waste tank on end with the carrying handle upper most and swivel the pour-out spout so that it is facing upwards. Remove the cap and, as you pour the waste away, depress the vent plunger (arrowed). This allows the waste to come out in a steady stream instead of 'glugging' and splashing over you.

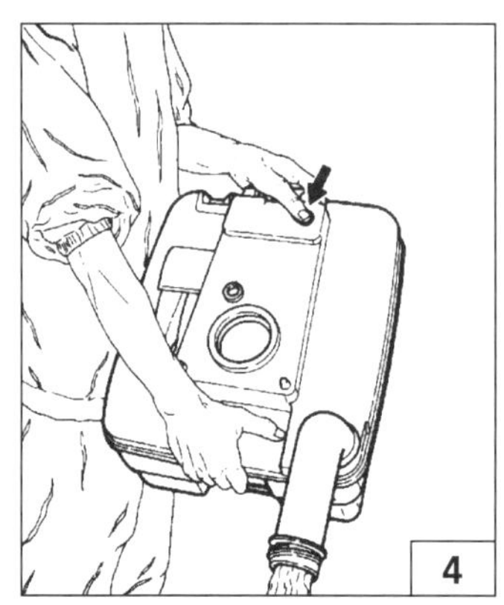

☐ 5. Pour approximately two litres of water into the waste holding tank and add an appropriate amount of toilet fluid. On some models, the cap doubles as a measuring cup; on others, use the measures shown on the bottle of fluid.

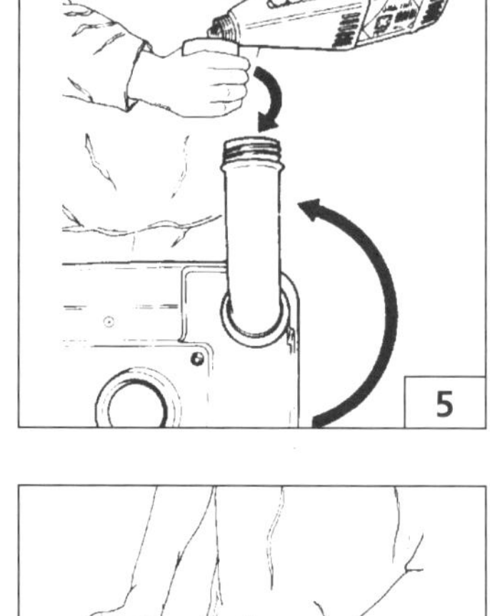

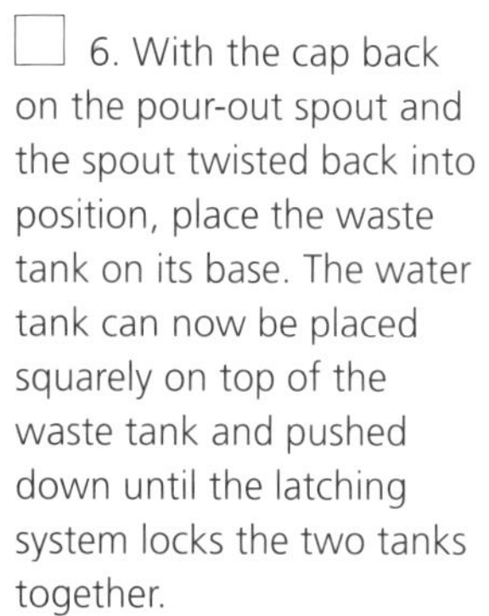

☐ 6. With the cap back on the pour-out spout and the spout twisted back into position, place the waste tank on its base. The water tank can now be placed squarely on top of the waste tank and pushed down until the latching system locks the two tanks together.

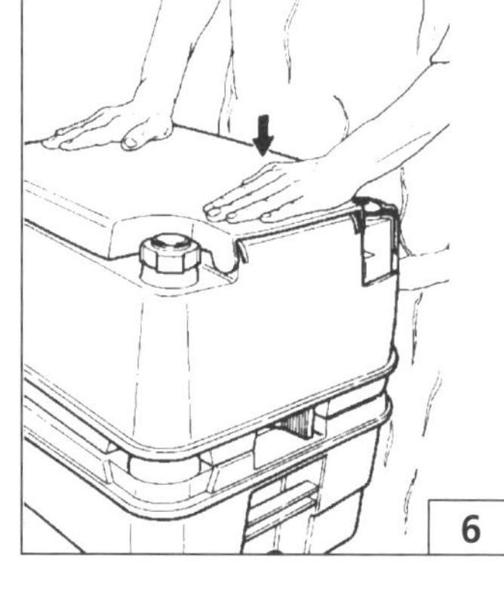

SAFETY FIRST!

Keep all toilet chemicals out of the reach of small children. It's advisable to wear protective gloves when using the fluid and if any gets into contact with your eyes, wash them immediately with cold water and seek medical advice.

☐ 7. Remove the cap of the flush-water tank and fill the tank with clean water. Add the appropriate amount of toilet rinse and replace the cap.

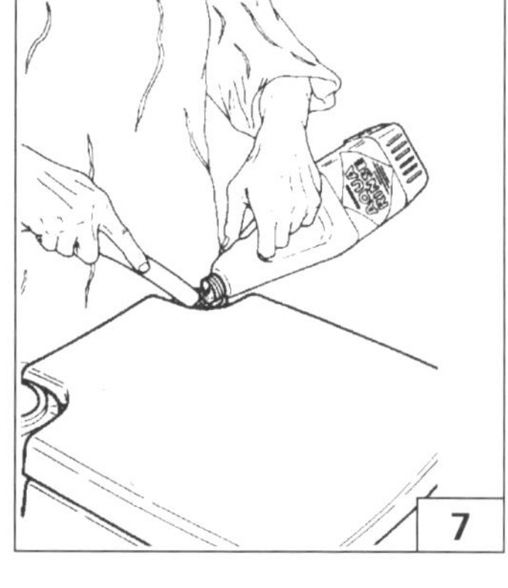

☐ 8. In order to prevent any pressure build up, hold the lid closed and open and close the waste tank valve blade once.

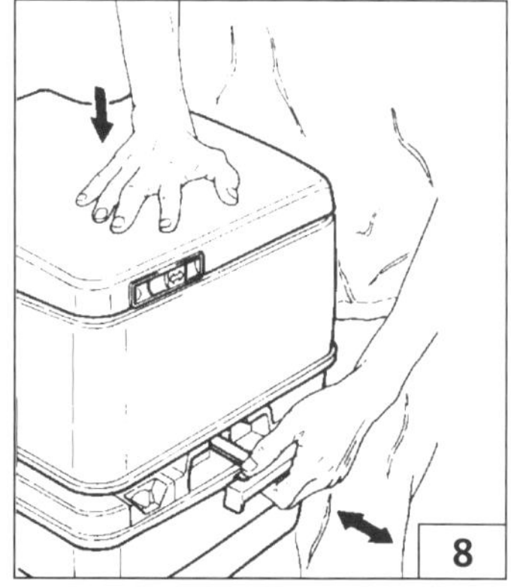

☐ 9. Before using the toilet, press the pump (or the pump button on electric models) so that there is a little flushing water in the bowl.

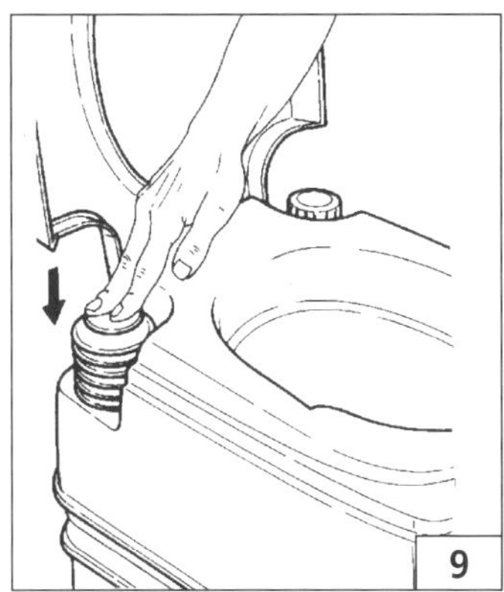

9

☐ 10. After using the toilet, open the valve blade by pulling out the valve handle. Now flush the toilet by pressing the pump or the pump button (three to four short, sharp flushes are recommended with electric models) then close the valve.

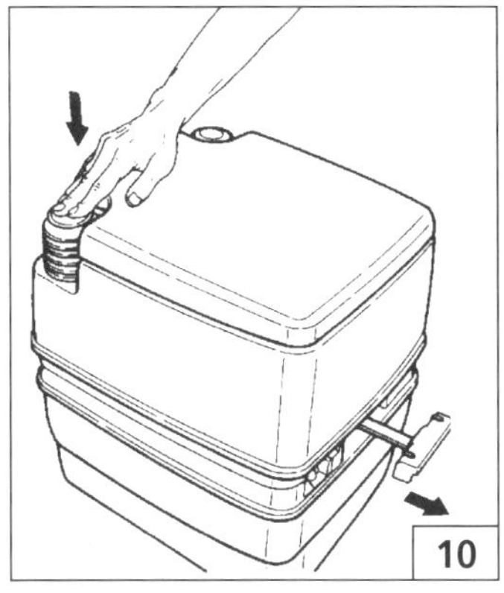

10

☐ 11. On electric models, alkaline batteries are usually good for 500 to 600 flushes. When there is not enough power to pump through enough water to cover the toilet bowl completely, the batteries should be replaced. Depress the latch of the battery housing and pull the housing upwards and out of the pump.

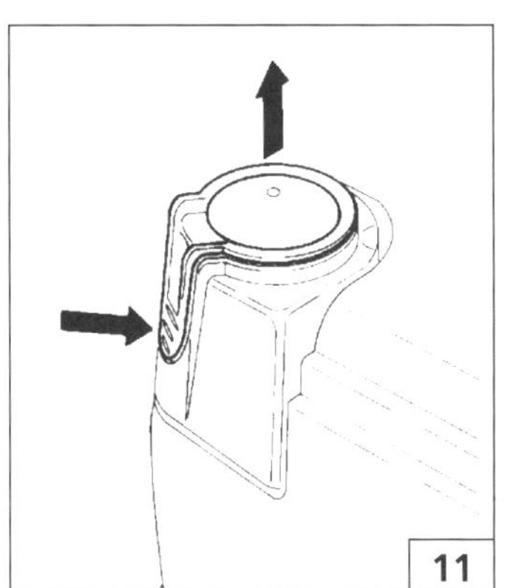

11

☐ 12. The battery housing takes six Penlight/AA 1.4/1.5 alkaline batteries, as indicated.

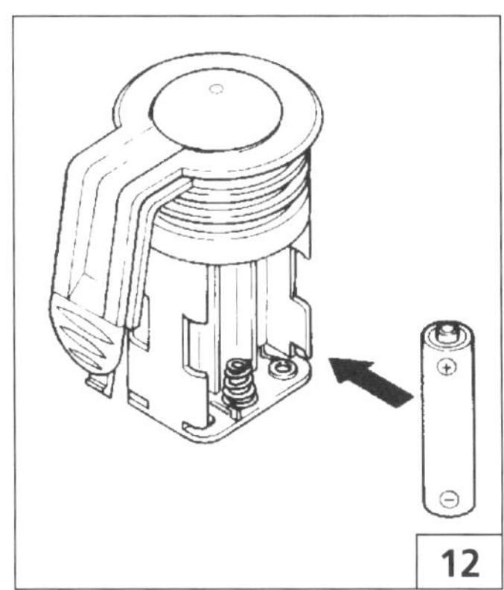

12

Cassette Toilet

Many motor caravans are now fitted with cassette toilets, so that you don't need to rely on site facilities, and the most common models are those produced by Thetford. The cassette toilet is a permanently fitted design which operates much like a domestic toilet, although generally with a turning flush knob rather than a push down lever.

☐ 1. To empty or prepare the toilet for use, you have to go outside the motor caravan and open up the access hatch, generally found to the rear of the offside wall.

1

Fill the toilet's water tank through a filler that folds out from the toilet compartment. This usually holds ten litres of water and should always be virtually empty when the motor caravan is on the move - with just enough for emergency purposes!

A 'rinse' chemical should also be added at this stage. On some models fitted with an electric flush facility, a level indicator shows when enough water has been added.

☐ 2. You can now remove the cassette, by releasing the large retaining clip at its base.

2

3

☐ 3. Pull the cassette out of its compartment taking hold of the other handle as it appears in view. The cassette will be heavy when full!

☐ 4. The cassette can be carried with the pouring spout at the upper end.

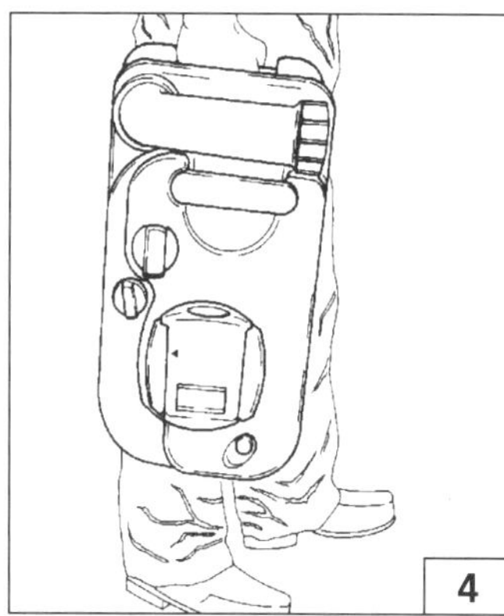

4

5

making it easy! ☐ *5. As a cassette can be quite heavy when full, there are a number of trolleys on the market to help you transport the cassette from the motor caravan to the waste disposal point.*

☐ 6. Place the cassette on the ground with the pouring tube uppermost. Swivel the tube into the vertical position and unscrew the cap. Grip the cassette as shown and when pouring, be sure to depress the air release button (arrowed) so that the fluid pours out smoothly without 'glugging' back and over your feet!

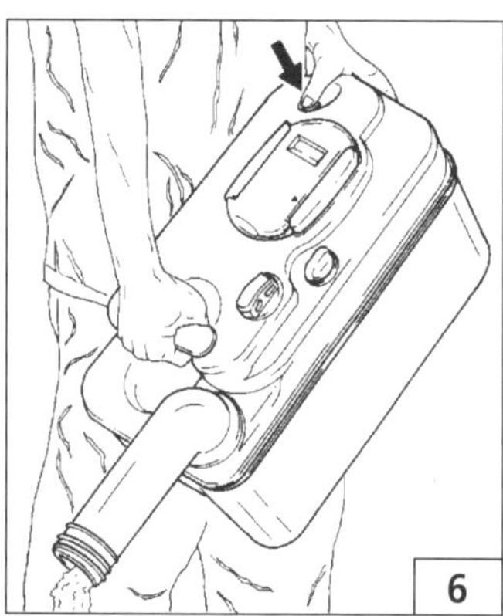

6

☐ 7. On some models, there is space to store flushing fluid and waste tank fluid underneath the cassette. Approximately two litres of water should be poured into the holding tank followed by the appropriate quantity of toilet fluid. On some models, the cap may act as a measure; in all other cases, follow the measurements on the fluid container.

7

After replacing the cap, the emptying spout can be swivelled back to its original position.

IMPORTANT NOTE: Ensure that when the holding tank is pushed back into place, it is held securely by the retaining clip. Note that the holding tank does not have to be 'opened' in any way; the mechanism inside the toilet opens and closes the flap as required.

making it easy! ☐ *8. You won't feel comfortable taking the cassette waste container to the fresh water point to put your two litres of fluid in - and, in any case, how will you know when you've got two litres? A plastic two litre water bottle weighs next to nothing to carry around with you and makes a much more hygienic way of taking two litres of water to the holding tank.*

8

SAFETY FIRST!

Keep all toilet chemicals out of the reach of small children. It's advisable to wear protective gloves when using the fluid and if any gets into contact with your eyes, wash them immediately with cold water and seek medical advice.

☐ 9. You should now add water and rinse fluid to the holding tank. On some models, such as the C200CW, water is added through a filler point on the motor caravan itself.

☐ 10. On most, however, the filler neck swings out from inside the cassette door.

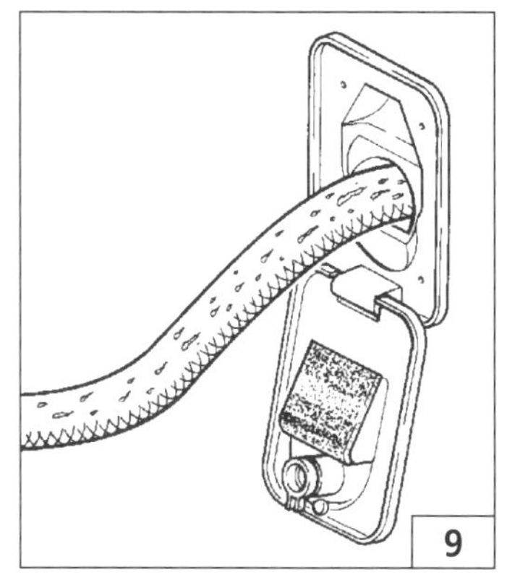

9

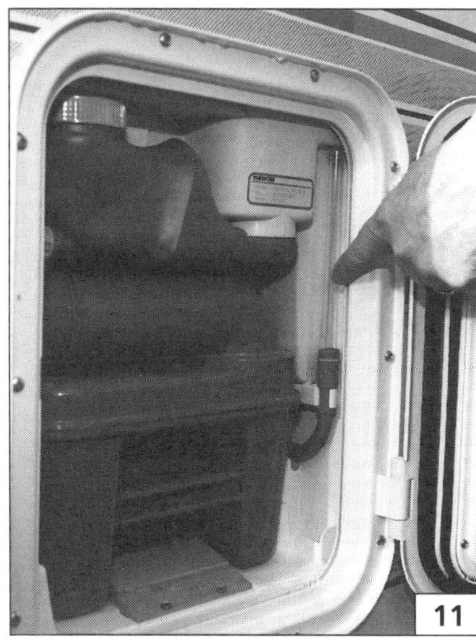

10

☐ 11. On some models, a sight glass lets you see how much fluid is left in the tank.

11

☐ 12. Before using the toilet press down the flush knob. On this model, you press the flush knob down and turn it in an anti-clockwise direction.

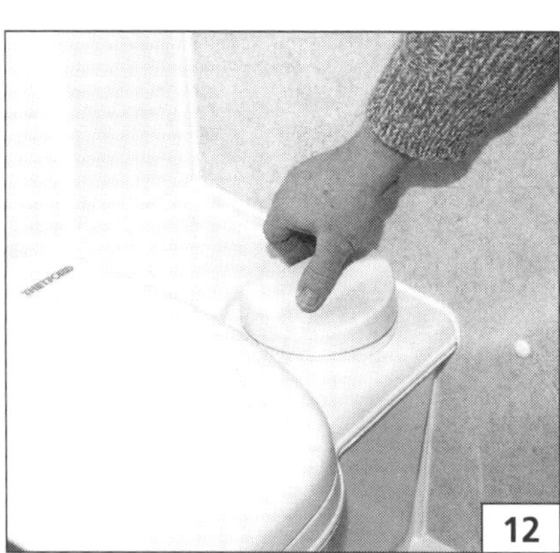

12

☐ 13. With this one you raise and lower the plunger...

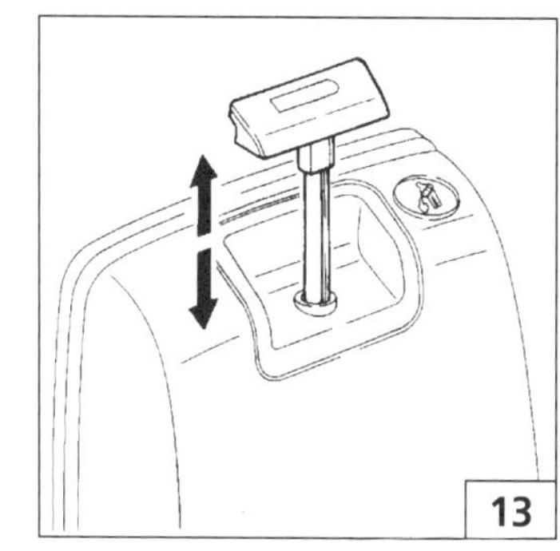

13

☐ 14. ...while with this one, you press the relevant button.

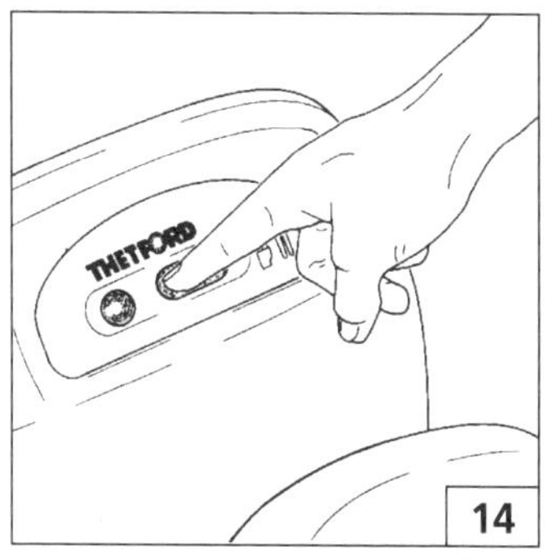

14

☐ 15. After using the toilet, you open the base of the bowl to the cassette tank beneath.

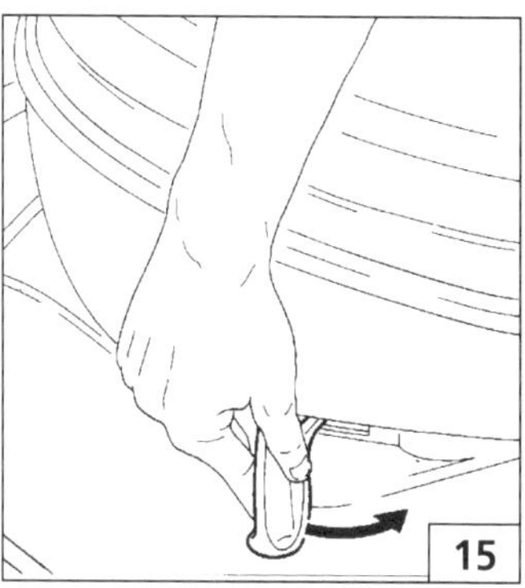

15

☐ 16. On this model, you press the left-hand button to open the blade and the right-hand button to close it again.

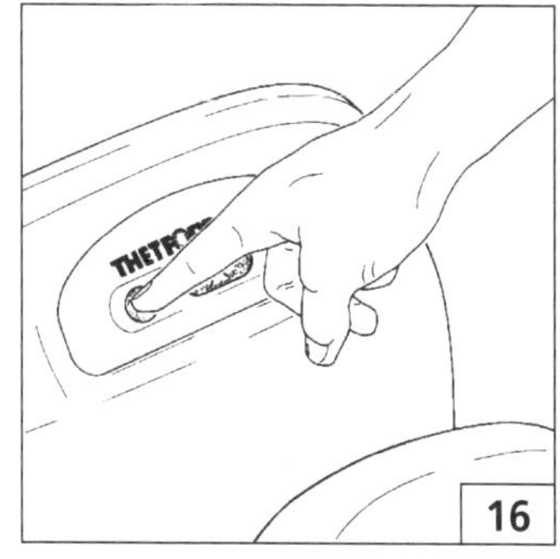

16

☐ 17. All models have a level indicator to tell you when the tank is full, or almost full and requires emptying. On no account should the cassette be allowed to become overfilled.

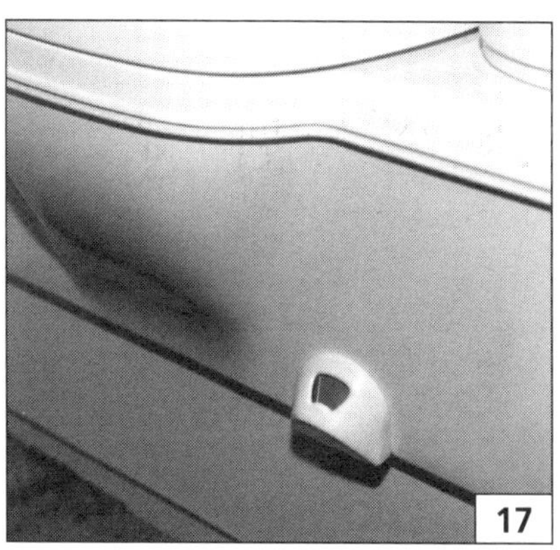

17

☐ 18. Some models have an integral toilet roll holder which is invaluable for keeping the loo paper dry when the toilet area doubles as a shower compartment.

18

☐ 19. These are the component parts of one of the most common of the Thetford cassette toilets.

☐ 20. If the cassette toilet flush motor doesn't work, check the fuse. Either the glass tube-type or spade-type may be used. It's fitted (rather inconveniently!) inside the waste tank housing, in the 'roof' beneath the mechanism accessed through the external door.

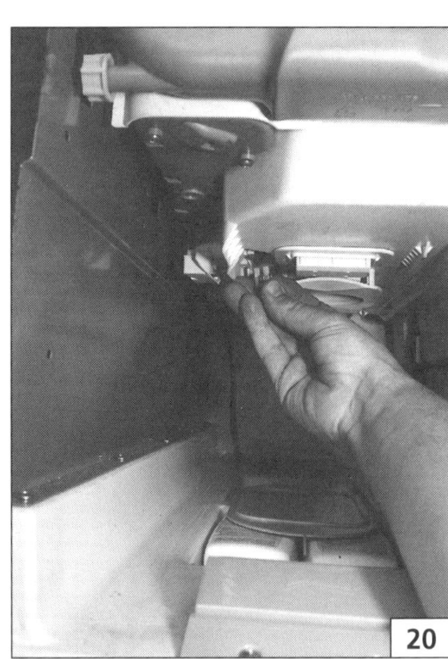

20

1. Flush and valve blade opener knob - opens and closes valve blade. Also adds water to bowl by means of an electric pump.
2. Removable seat and cover.
3. Toilet tissue storage compartment - keeps tissue clean and dry.
4. Toilet tissue wall mount bracket.
5. Waster level indicator - indicates when Cassette is full.
6. Toilet fluid storage compartments. (only with high models).
7. Drip tray - collects drops from bowl, when holding tank is out.
8. Cassette retainer clip - holds holding tank in locked position.
10. Automatic holding tank vent.
11. Valve blade opener.
12. Cassette valve blade.
13. Sliding cover, provides optimal hygiene, opens and closes when tank is taken out.
14. Upper carrying handles - makes carrying and emptying easy.
15. Air release valve - ensures smooth emptying without splashing.
16. Lower carrying handles.
17. Hand grip.
18. Rotating pour out spout - makes emptying Cassette easy and convenient.
19. Cassette access door - locks from outside Caravan.

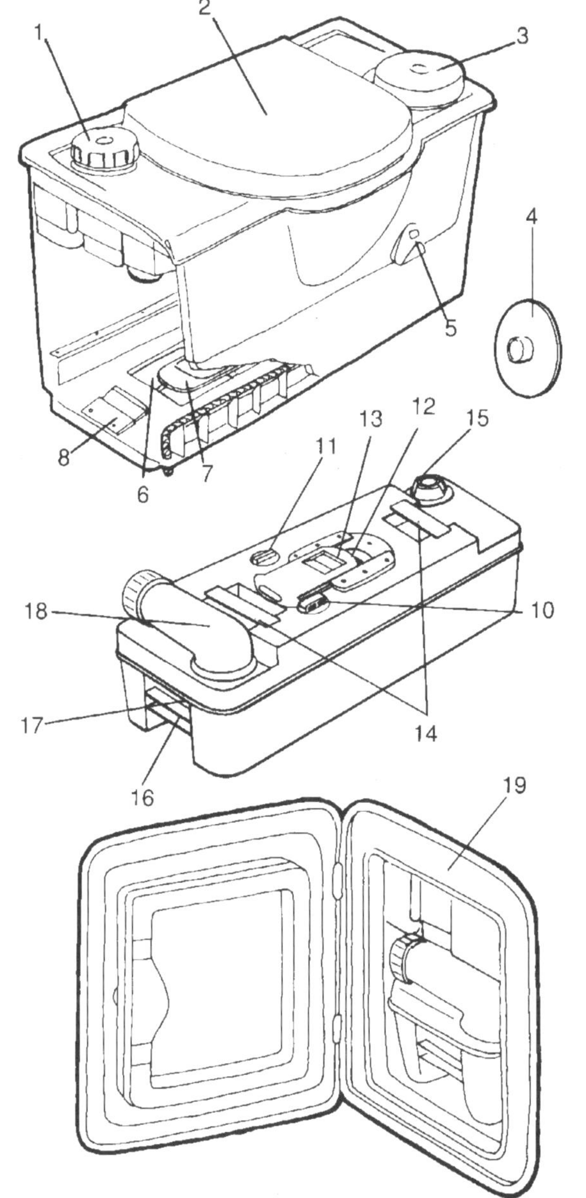

19

Cooking Equipment

The gas cooking equipment in a motor caravan's kitchen works in very much the same way as that in most homes. But if you are not familiar with the set-up because your house is "all electric", here goes...

1

☐ 1. When using a lighted match (or an igniter, as shown) to ignite a burner, put the match in position next to the burner before turning on the gas.

Then, depress the gas control before turning it anti-clockwise to the 'full' position. Hold down for five seconds, **with the gas alight** to allow the flame failure device to warm up. See illustration 2.

To turn the burner off, simply turn the tap clockwise until it won't go any further.

For motor caravans fitted with automatic ignition, hold the ignition button down and then turn and hold down the gas control into the fully 'on' position as before. After the burner has lit, continue to hold the gas control down for 20 seconds. If there's no spark, check to see if the battery needs replacing.

SAFETY FIRST!

• The hob, grill and oven must be turned off when the caravan is in motion.
• Under no circumstances should the cooker be used as a heater.
• Always ventilate the motor caravan when the cooker is in use, whatever the weather.
• Ensure that your motor caravan is equipped with a suitable fire extinguisher and a fire blanket.

FLAME FAILURE DEVICE

2

☐ 2. All motor caravans built since 1994, and most high-spec models since 1992 will have flame failure devices fitted to all gas appliances. This will automatically turn off the gas supply should any of the cooking flames or pilot lights go out.

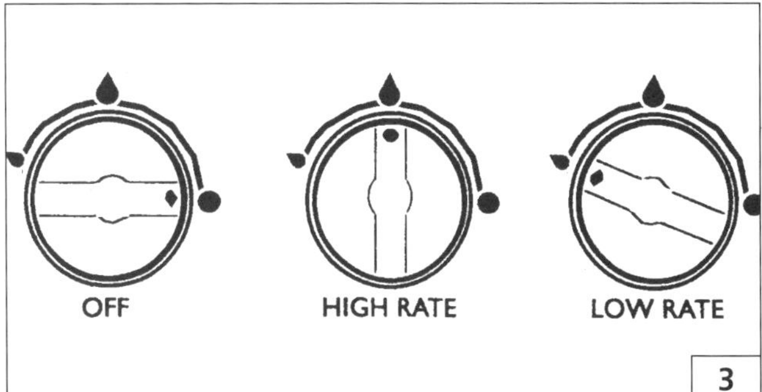

3

☐ 3. These are the usual knob settings. Note that the LOW setting is beyond the HIGH setting. (Illustration, courtesy Spinflo Ltd)

4

SAFETY FIRST!

☐ 4. Make sure that pan handles are turned inwards (especially if there are small children about) but make sure they're NOT over an adjacent burner ring.
• ALWAYS open extra ventilation to the living area, whenever using the cooker.

The Refrigerator

Modern motor caravan fridges can be powered by any one of three supplies - 12-volt electricity, 240-volt electricity or gas. The 12-volt supply should only be used when the outfit is on the move. Otherwise the fridge will run the auxiliary battery down in less than an hour. 240-volt is generally used whenever there is a power supply on site.

Before setting out on a journey, it is best to start on gas to get the fridge down to an operating temperature before turning to electricity, because keeping the temperature low takes less energy than getting it there in the first place.

Turn the power supply switch to gas and make sure that, if there's a voltage selector switch, it is set to '0'.

1

☐ 1. Then turn the gas supply knob to its highest setting and push it inwards towards the fridge. While it's being held in, press in the ignition button four or five times in quick succession.

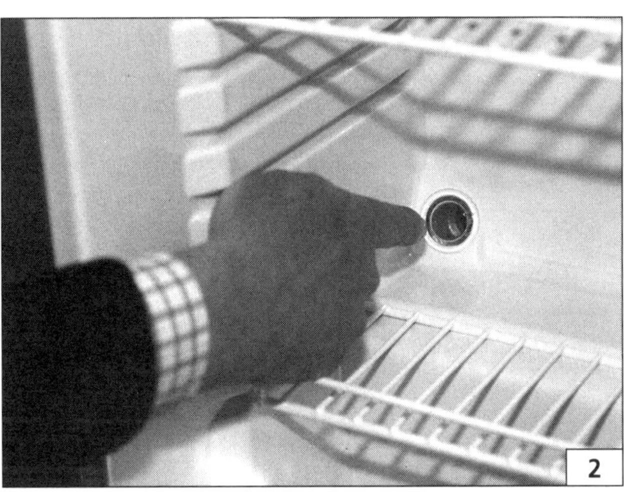

2

☐ 2. As you're doing this, look for the pilot light through a viewing glass usually in the bottom corner of the fridge. When this is alight, continue to hold the gas control knob down for a further 10 to 15 seconds and then release.

3

☐ 3. To change the fridge over to mains 240-volt operation, turn the gas supply knob to '0' and select the mains voltage switch. In this case it's next to the transformer, beneath one of the beds. It's often part of a main control panel on the wall or in a wardrobe. Check your handbook. Then turn the thermostat knob to the desired setting.

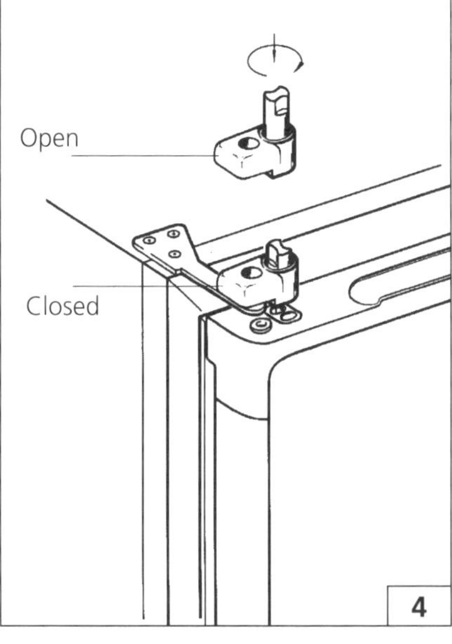

4

☐ **4. i INSIDE INFORMATION: When a refrigerator is not in use, it tends to go mouldy inside. If your motor caravan refrigerator has a storage position latch fitted to it, clip the door into this position when the motor caravan is not in use. Otherwise, tape a piece of card or something similar onto the floor of the refrigerator so that the door cannot fully close. Also, note that on modern Electrolux fridges, doors are now 'locked' shut. (Illustration, courtesy Electrolux) i**

making it easy! *You may find the tiny knob difficult to turn. Try pressing lightly on the door as you turn, so that the pressure is taken off it.*

5

☐ 5. On Auto-Sleeper's motor caravans, there is an extension to the latch designed to hold the door open. It is there because the door would otherwise be held back against the refrigerator outlet vent and this could obstruct the flow. The extension only needs to be used when the refrigerator is used on gas, not on electricity.

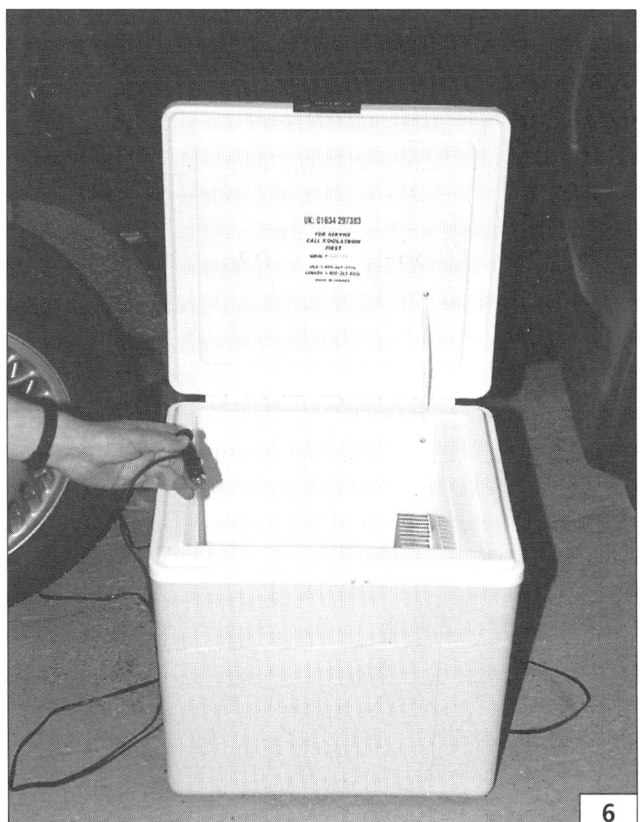

6

☐ 6. A coolbox 'fridge', such as this Koolatron unit, which plugs into the cigarette lighter, gives extra cooling capacity and doubles up as a portable coolbox while you're away.

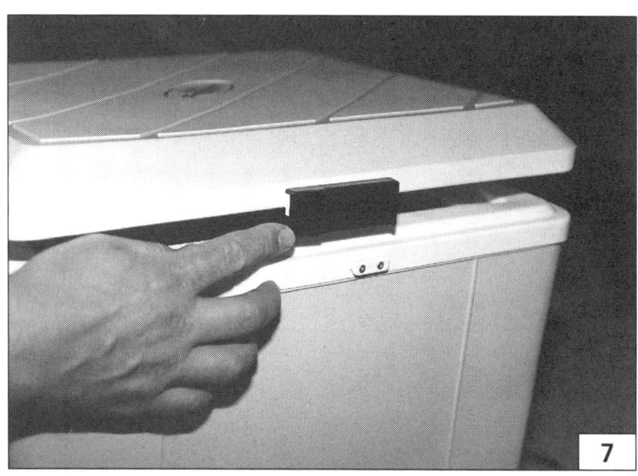

7

☐ 7. When stored, the Koolatron latch should be placed in the 'closed' position before the lid is shut, leaving a small gap for air flow to prevent smells forming.

Sleeping Arrangements

While not considered as 'technical' equipment, constructing the motor caravan's bedding in the correct manner is essential for a good night's sleep. Making the main front seating area up into a double bed will either mean using the table top as a bed base to make up the gap between the two seating areas, or utilising a slatted bed base, according to model.

When the table top is used it sits along narrow ledges situated on the edge of the bed bases. Unfortunately, when using the table top as a bed base the problem of a build-up of condensation often occurs. This can be dealt with in one of two ways: Either, put a thick towel between the table top and the cushioning above to soak up any condensation. Or the second way is to make yourself a slatted bed base.

1

☐ 1. Some motor caravans are fitted with slatted bed bases as standard. They are generally stored at the front of the motor caravan either beneath the seating or within the base of a chest of drawers.

2

☐ 2. To use a slatted bed base, simply grasp the front rail and pull the assembly out along the holding rails until it is fully extended.

Slatted bed bases not only cure the problem of condensation but also generally offer better support for your back when in bed.

INSIDE INFORMATION: When using the motor caravan's seating cushions as mattresses, it is generally recommended that you turn them upside down. This helps create a more even sleeping surface and saves wear on the upper fabric.

3

☐ 3. When a motor caravan is fitted with bunks, care should always be taken to follow the manufacturer's instructions to the letter of the law when constructing them. Also be careful to check the bunk's weight limit to make sure that it is capable of taking the weight of its occupant.

4

☐ 4. The overcab bed should have some form of safety device to prevent the occupant rolling out of bed. This Auto-Sleeper uses boards...

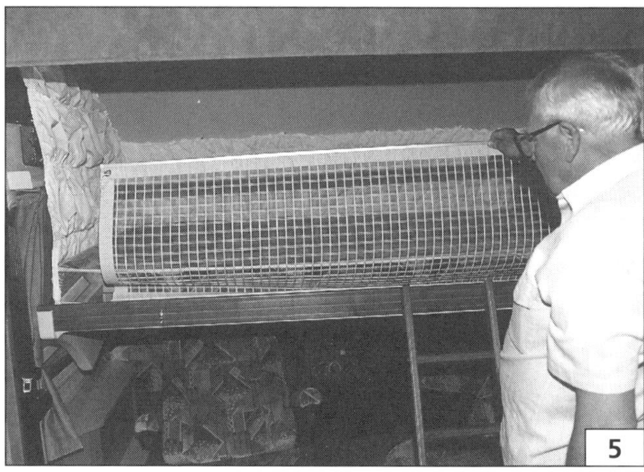

5

☐ 5. ...this Pilote A-class uses nets. Whatever is supplied always use them!

CHAPTER 5 - SERVICING THE LIVING ACCOMMODATION

Most motor caravanners use their vehicles through the summer months and take them out of use for the winter. For the 'caravan' part of the vehicle, this does not present any special problems, provided that the Jobs shown below are carried out. For the 'motor' part of the vehicle, problems can be greater, but see CHAPTER 6: SERVICING THE BASE VEHICLE for more details.

For those of us who enjoy going out and about in the winter months - and there are some great pleasures to be had in getting away from busy times and peak periods - the sections shown below on PREPARING FOR THE START OF THE SEASON and the close-down sequence, PREPARING FOR STORAGE AT THE END OF THE SEASON, obviously won't apply. But intrepid souls may wish to cast their eyes over the Jobs listed there and combine any that are relevant with the complete annual service.

PART I: PREPARING FOR THE START OF THE SEASON

These are the Jobs that need to be carried out before you start using your motor caravan, at the start of the season. While several of these Jobs won't need to be carried out again for another 12 months, some of them also need to be repeated at more regular intervals - lookout for them in later service intervals!

i INSIDE INFORMATION: Carry out these jobs some time before you are due to go on your first trip - there will undoubtedly be repair work needed, so give yourself time to obtain spares and carry out the work. i

☐ **Job 1. Check all hinges and brackets.**

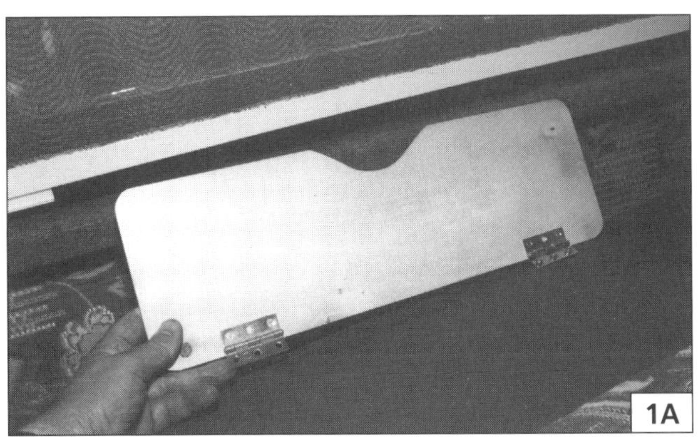

1A

1A. Fold-out shelves and doors quite frequently shed their screws. They're quite frequently expected to carry quite heavy loads with inadequate-sized screws and hinges.

1B

1B. Table supports are particularly prone to coming loose. They are nearly always made to fold away, or double-up as shelf supports, so their fixings are always placed under a lot of pushing and pulling strains.

making it easy! • *Where the old screw thread has stripped, use a slightly longer screw if it's going to be screwed into the end of the panel.*
• *If you're screwing into chipboard, be sure to use coarse-thread chipboard screws, not regular wood screws.*
• *If the thread has stripped in a thinner panel, don't risk causing damage with a larger screw: drill the hole out, if necessary, and use a plastic wall plug - they come in quite small sizes from your local DIY centre - before refitting the screw*

1C. Lubricate any sliding supports with silicone lubricant to prevent sticking and future damage. Try your local hardware store for silicone lubricant - don't use oil or grease because it will stain fabric upholstery and clothes.

Job 2. Check beds and seats.

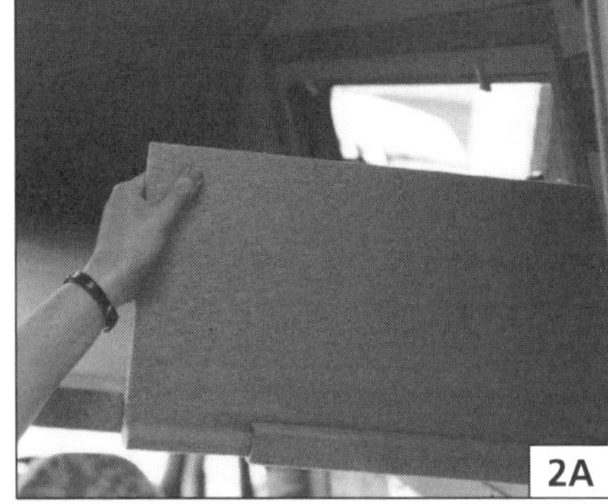

2A. Just as in the previous job, bedding support flaps can come loose: re-fix as necessary.

2B. Remember also to check the cab seats where they form a part of the bedding arrangements. Make sure all the fill-in pieces are available - and that you remember where they all go! (Illustration, courtesy Murvi Motorcaravans)

2C. Also check the seat swivels themselves and lubricate the swivelling mechanisms with silicone lubricant, or light oil used very sparingly, so that it can't get onto clothes.

2D. Assemble the beds so as to make doubly sure that all of the cushions and support panels you need are in the 'van. (Illustration, courtesy Auto-Sleepers)

Job 3. Check upper bunks.

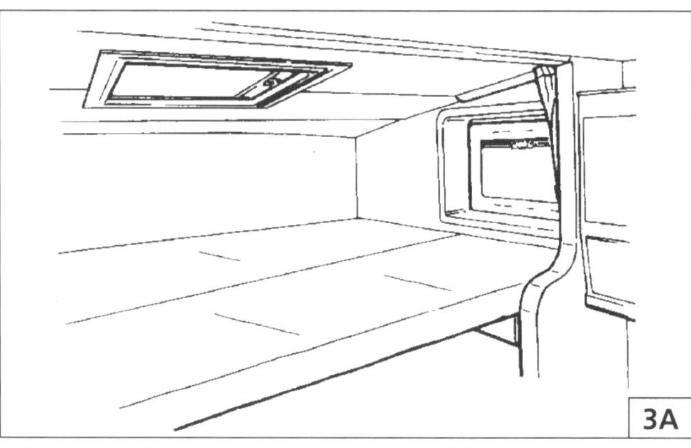

3A. Erect, assemble or pull-down (in the case of an A-Class vehicle) any upper bunks or bedding. Make sure it's all there and that it works correctly. (Illustration, courtesy Swift)

3B. On most motor caravans, straps and fixing are used to keep bunk bed ladders (and seat backrests) in place. Check all the press-studs (or whatever system is used) and replace or repair as necessary.

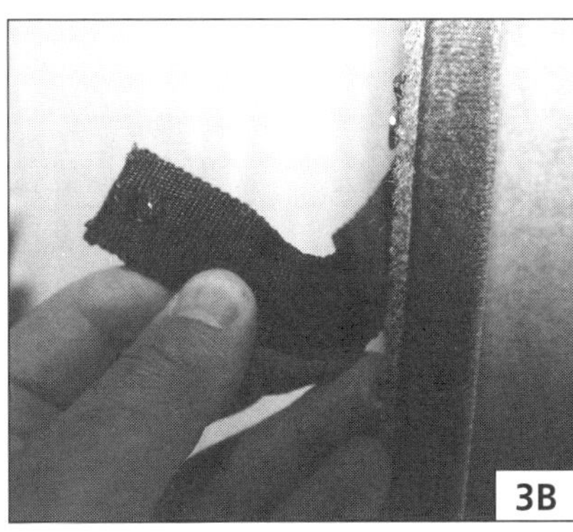
3B

• You can buy press-stud pliers, from your local haberdashery.
• Alternatively, change over to Velcro, available in rolls from the same source.

☐ Job 4. Check curtains, blinds and nets.

4A. Check that all the curtains pull smoothly and that there is no mould on them. Check that blinds and flyscreens unroll and retract satisfactorily, not forgetting the flyscreens in the roof lights and air vents - check the fitted type to make sure that they are clear. (Illustration, courtesy Auto-Trail)

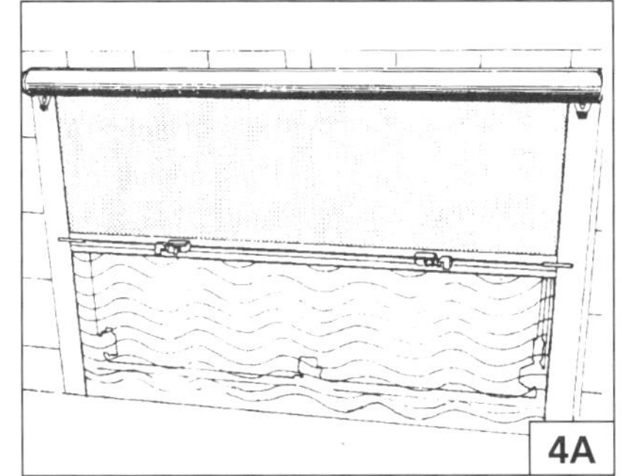
4A

making it easy!

• If the flyscreen or blinds have been left in the "down" position for too long, the spring mechanism may lose its tension.
• To put matters right, gently pull the cross bar downwards and evenly, towards you, and then allow it to retract, still holding onto the crossbar.
• Do this five or six times and the correct tension will normally be restored.

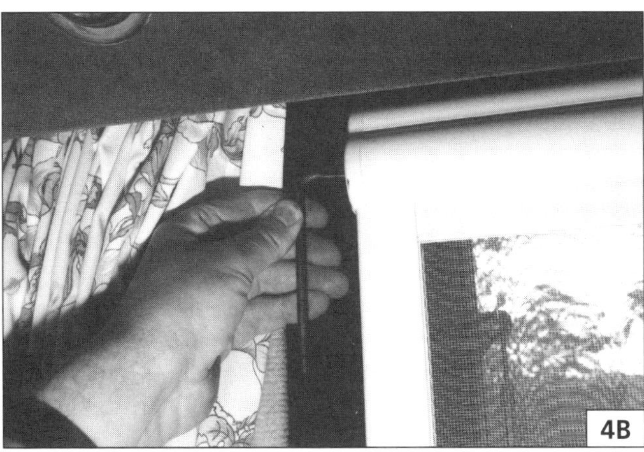
4B

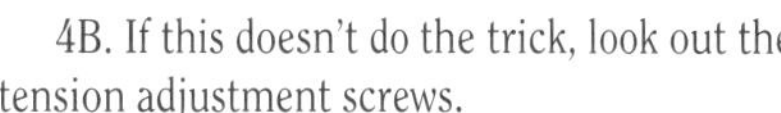

FACT FILE: TENSIONING BLINDS AND FLYSCREENS

4B. If this doesn't do the trick, look out the tension adjustment screws.

• On this model, which has a combined flyscreen and blind, the top one is for the flyscreen and the lower one is for the blind.
• Contrary to appearances, this isn't an Allen key we're using here; it's a screwdriver with a cranked end - there isn't always a lot of room if the blinds are close to an end wall!
• Turning the tensioning screw clockwise increases the tension while turning it anti-clockwise reduces it.
• IMPORTANT NOTE: You must apply gentle inward pressure on the screw to release it from its internal ratchet. When you stop turning, let the screw come back out again, when it will re-engage into the ratchet.
• Adjust the tension of the blind/flyscreen so that there is *just enough* tension to return the blind or flyscreen into its fully retracted position but *don't* over tension the mechanism for obvious reasons!.

☐ Job 5. Have gas systems inspected.

This is a job that should be carried out professionally. See later Jobs for checks that you can, and should, carry out yourself.

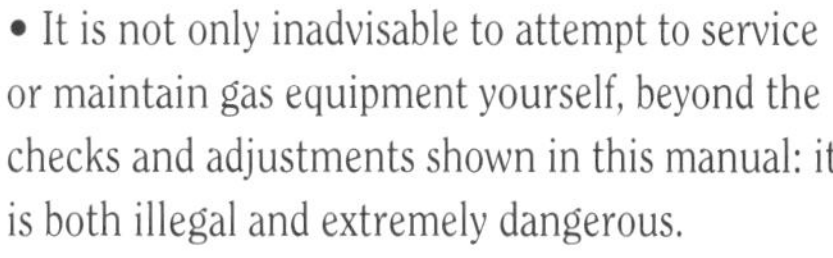

FACT FILE: GAS APPLIANCE SERVICING

• It is not only inadvisable to attempt to service or maintain gas equipment yourself, beyond the checks and adjustments shown in this manual: it is both illegal and extremely dangerous.
• 5A. In the words of Calor Gas themselves: *"Installing [and servicing] a gas appliance is an expert job and, by law, must only be carried out by people who are competent to do so.*
• *A large proportion of accidents involving gas occur because incompetent people have interfered with installations or appliances. Only allow qualified gas installers to install or service gas appliances."*

SAFETY CALOR SAFETY

5A

• 5B. Use gas installers which display the CORGI symbol as they are registered with the council for registered gas installers and undertake to work to the highest standards of safety.
• Amateurs and DIY 'experts' can put you and your family at risk and may face prosecution. Don't take that risk. Use the professionals.

5B

We strongly recommend that you have your certifying engineer check your system annually and that you keep the annual certificate somewhere safe for future reference.

Job 6. Check vents and flues.

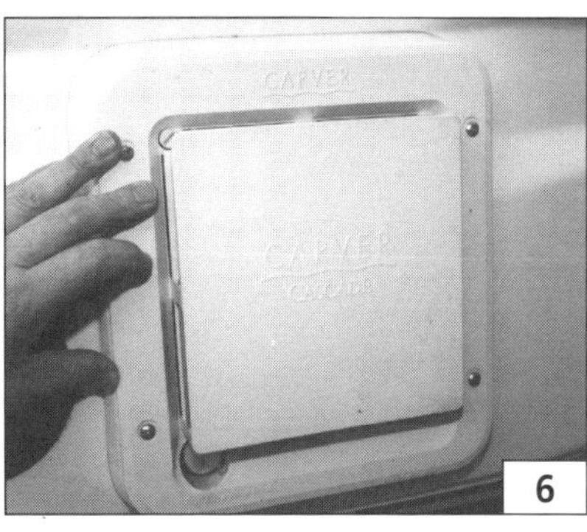

6. It is essential that each vent and flue for each gas appliance is kept clear. Check that each one has not become blocked by leaves or spiders' webs. Check especially carefully the flue pipes from the room heater and water heater, and make sure that they are securely connected at both ends and that there is no damage to the pipes. If any looseness or damage is found, have them secured by an approved gas fitter before using the appliance.

SAFETY FIRST!

Using a gas appliance with a faulty flue could well be fatal! If there is a problem, don't use the appliance until it has been fixed.

Job 7. Check flexible gas hoses and regulator.

In almost all cases, flexible hoses are easily visible, since they connect appliances and gas bottles to the rigid pipe system. You should be able to 'get at' each of them quite easily.

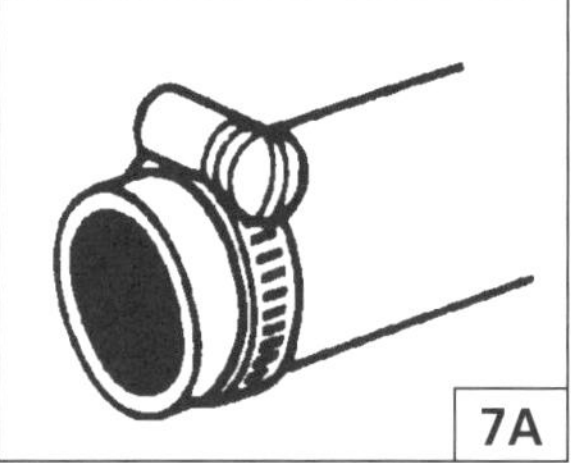

7A. All flexible hoses must be secured with proper hose clips. Make sure that the hoses are kept clear of 'hotspots' and inspect them each year, checking for any splits, chafing or brittleness. (Illustration, courtesy Calor)

making it easy! *• 7B. Try squeezing each hose between thumb and finger especially at each end and near to any 'warm' areas inside the motor caravan. Listen for any crackling sounds which will indicate that the hose is going brittle and should be replaced.*

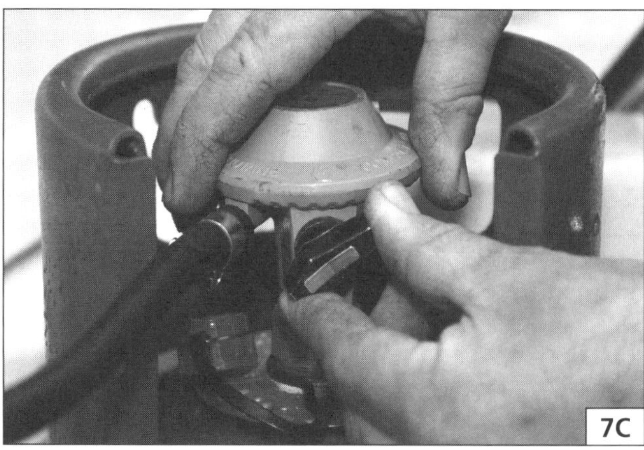

7C, Check that the regulator ON-OFF valve works smoothly and if you ever have the slightest problem with it, replace it straight away.

FACT FILE:
PIPES AND REGULATOR LIFESPANS

- Liquid petroleum gas (LPG) attacks natural rubber and therefore, over a period of time, both hoses and regulators deteriorate to the point where they need replacement.
- As a matter or course, replace all rubber hoses after every five years and renew all regulators after every ten years.
- Be sure when replacing hoses to secure them with proper hose clips and avoid using excessive lengths of hose.
- Rubber is attacked by liquid propane gas and rubber hoses should therefore never be used. Hoses should be made from Neoprene and must conform to BS3212.
- Some hoses are marked with a expiration date and the hose should be replaced by that date irrespective of the age of the hose - especially since you don't know how long the hose had been store before it was fitted to your vehicle.
- You'll know where you are if you mark the hose with the date at which it was last replaced - or a fresh expiration date if none is already fitted.
- You should also make sure that the date of replacement is marked on the regulator.

IMPORTANT NOTE: Some industrial LPG appliances operate at high pressure and require a regulator with an adjusting valve on it. NEVER use such a regulator when motor caravanning, caravanning or camping or for your barbecue.

Job 8. Carry out leak test.

You may laugh but this has been known to happen... DON'T check for leaks with a match! Always use soap solution or a proprietary brand of leak tester which you should paint onto each joint looking for bubbles. Do not operate any electrical apparatus whatsoever if you suspect a leak and if you can smell gas but can't find a leak, turn off the gas system, evacuate the motor caravan and have a qualified gas fitter put the problem right before using the motor caravan again.

Job 9. Check gas appliances.

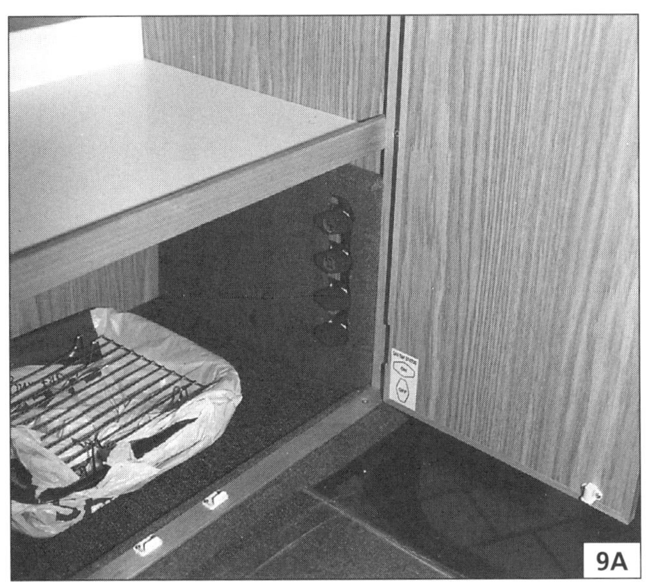

9A

SAFETY FIRST!

9A. Ensure that the gas supply is turned off at the regulator or, if you are only working on one appliance, turn off the isolator supply to that appliance, if fitted. See your handbook - illustrated here is a set of isolator valves beneath the sink unit in an Auto-Sleepers motor caravan.

In this instance, there is a sticker nearby to tell you which is ON and which is OFF. Generally, such taps are ON when the 'ears' on the knob lie in-line with the pipe, and OFF when the 'ears' lie across the line of the pipe.

Read all of Job 5 and act upon it before carrying out any of the work described in this Job.

We have divided up the checking of gas appliances into the following six areas. Much of it is based around the servicing of a Carver heater, but the general principles apply to all types. Do consult your handbook and instruction booklets, which should be supplied with your motor caravan.

I. CLEANING

9B

9B. Room heaters such as the Carver range of caravan heaters have a removable cover, spring-clipped into place, which should be taken off...

9C

9C. ... so that the heat exchanger beneath - the fins that transmit the heat created in the burner into the living space, via the heater body - can be cleaned, removing any fluff, dust or any other foreign matter.

9D

9D. Use a soft brush - or in the case of stuck-on dirt, a damp cloth - to clean the flame viewing window.

9E

making it easy!

• 9E. Don't try re-fitting the cover without repositioning the operating control. It will probably have been pulled away as the cover was removed.

• The operating control is a rod which runs from the operating knob to the control, at the bottom of the heater. You'll have to relocate it at the base before the cover is re-fitted.

9F

9F. INSIDE INFORMATION: Most heater casings can be a source of rattles but, in the case of the Carver, they are easily cured. Make sure that the four spring mounting clips - one in each corner - are pulled outwards efficiently so that the cover clips tightly into place.

II. CHECK/LUBRICATE CONTROLS

9G

9G. Check that all knobs and controls work smoothly and are secure on their spindles. Check that all of the controls do in fact operate the equipment to which they are connected and that any auto-igniter, if fitted, works properly.

Change the batteries, if necessary, in any spark-ignition system fitted, particularly if it is of the automatic type, designed to re-ignite the flame in a heater if it blows out.

INSIDE INFORMATION: If the gas taps become stiff they can be greased BUT ONLY USING AN APPROVED LPG GREASE available from your local caravan or motor caravan dealer.

IMPORTANT

BLOWN AIR HEATING SYSTEM

1. **Ensure all internal and external vents are kept free from obstructions.**
2. **Ensure that adequate ventilation is available at all times.**

9H

9H. If your motor caravan is fitted with a Propex or other type of blown-air heating system, you must make sure that the outlet vents are clear and not blocked in any way. Be sure NOT to put odd items on the floor against the vents and so partially block them off. Also, check that there is ventilation coming in at all times when the blown air system is in use. The warning sign shown here should be on display. If you don't have such a warning sign, you could photocopy this one and fix it in a clearly visible place. (Illustration, courtesy Auto-Sleepers)

9I

9I. The Propex heater's thermostat sensitivity can be adjusted as follows:

If the vehicle is getting too hot before the thermostat turns the heater off and too cold before it turns it on again, the sensitivity is too low. On the other hand, if the heater keeps turning itself on and off too often, the sensitivity is too high.

To adjust the sensitivity, gently pull the knob off the thermostat, undo the screw beneath it and remove the cover. The adjustment may be made by very gently using a small screwdriver. Turning anti-clockwise increases sensitivity, while turning clockwise decreases it. See *page 43* of *Chapter 4, Operating Instructions* for full details and illustrations of how to carry out this job.

III. CORRECT FLAME STRUCTURE

9J

9J. Check that all pilot flames - the ones that are constantly burning when the apparatus is not in heating use - burn quietly and clearly. This is the flame window in the Carver heater and is seen through the heater casing when fully assembled.

Auto-Sleepers usefully recommend the following checks to be made on flame quality. Where appropriate, look through the viewing window to observe the type of flame:

REFRIGERATOR: With a refrigerator gas control turned to maximum, the colour of the flame should be predominantly blue.

INSTANTANEOUS WATER HEATING: This applies to the type of water heater which heats the water as it passes through the heater. The main burner flame should be of even height and blue in colour when the heater is operating. A flame burning yellow will allow sooting to occur and indicates that the heater needs to be adjusted by the specialist.

OVENS: The oven flame should burn quietly and be of even height, mainly blue/green in colour. If the gas is propane, the flame will normally develop yellow tips as the burner heats up. If the gas is butane, a small amount of yellow tipping will be seen immediately after lighting, increasing as the burner heats up.

GRILL BURNERS: It is normal for the flames on this type of burner to develop yellow tips as it heats up, particularly when using butane.

GENERAL: A flame lifting away from the burners is an indication of too high a pressure, although it may happen temporarily with grille burners while the frets are heating up. A yellow flame will cause sooting and is an indication of too low a pressure. Provided that the regulator and pipes have been checked and found to be in satisfactory order, the above faults should not appear. IMPORTANT NOTE: If there are any faults with any of the above, refer to **Job 5**.

IV. FLUES

You should also refer to **Jobs 6**, **Job 27**, and **Job 42** in connection with this area.

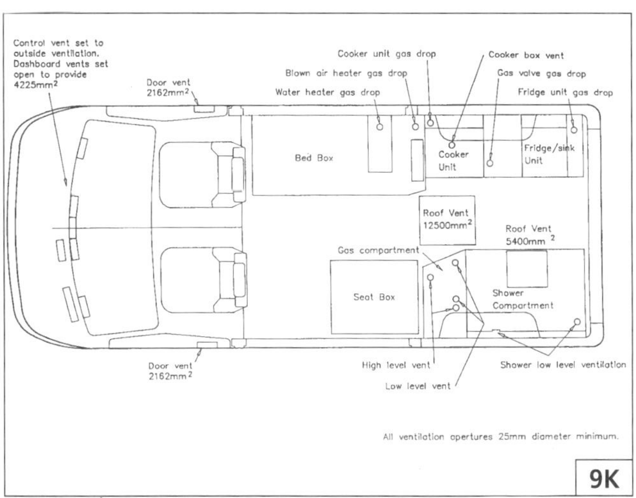

9K. This is the plan shown in the Auto-Sleepers' Peugeot Symphony handbook, showing positions of gas appliances and, most importantly, the ventilation points. Note that cab vents (and in this case, door vents) should also be opened when gas appliances are in use and ventilation is required.

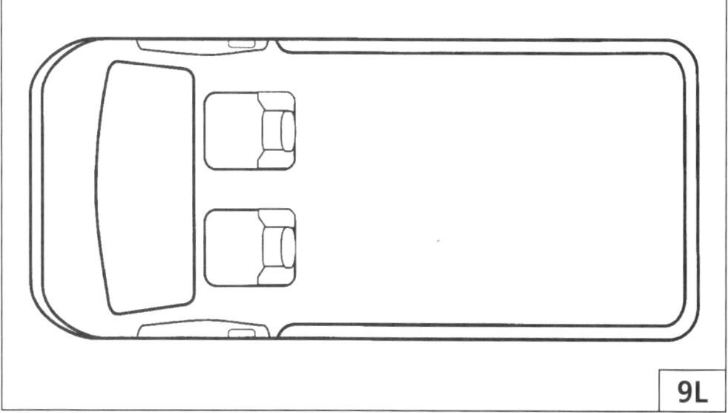

9L. It would be very useful to have a plan showing the positions of gas appliances and the positions of all vents. Add yours to the diagram printed above. Consult your specialist or dealer, if necessary. Then, you can carry out your own servicing in a systematic manner. See **Job 51B** for a similar 'blank' plan for showing gas pipe runs.

9M. All flues must be examined for security and fixing and for correct attachment to appliances and flue terminals. They must be free from damage and corrosion otherwise they must be replaced by a specialist.

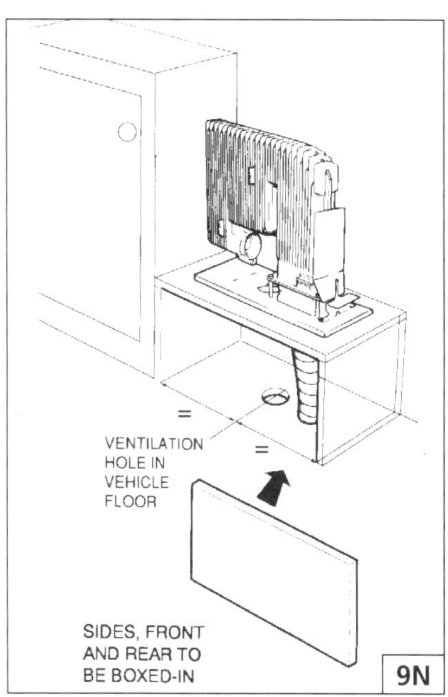

9N. You must also remember to check the air intake which draws air from outside the motor caravan on many types of gas appliance. There is, or should always be, a ventilation hole at the base of the unit to allow any escaped gas to drain out of the vehicle, rather than building up, the gases used being heavier than air. (Illustration, courtesy Carver)

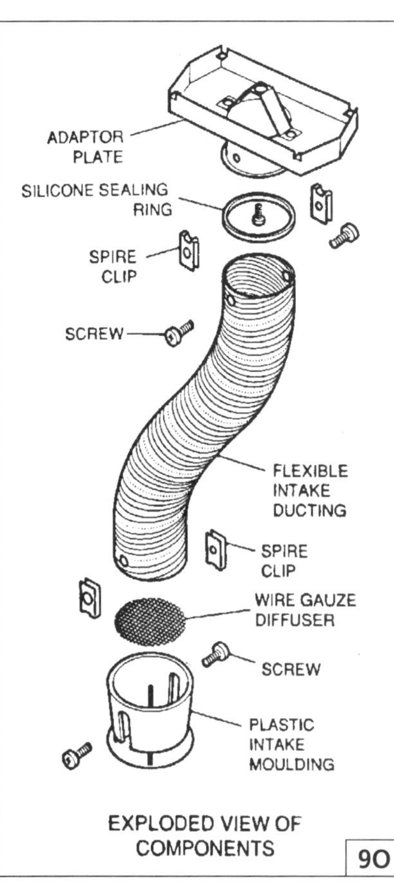

9O. One other area to check is that on some motor caravans, there may be an air intake extension kit fitted at the base of the unit. It is important that if this is fitted, it is properly in place and undamaged and that the wire gauze filter is not blocked. (Illustration, courtesy Carver)

9P. Outside the vehicle, on the roof, check that any external flues are sound, with an adequate rain cover fitted, that they are sealed properly to the roof, with no risk of water leaking in and that there are no blockages.

V. FLAME FAILURE DEVICE

On each appliance check the flame failure device as described in **Job 52**.

VI. SECURITY

Check that each appliance is securely fixed to the vehicle or furniture and that it is free from rattles.

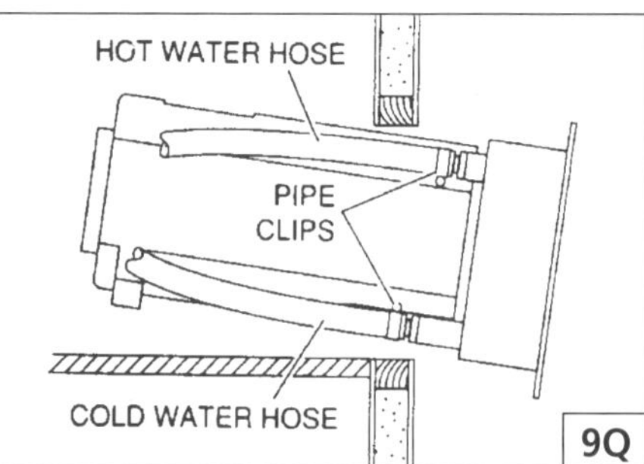

9Q. Where applicable, check that water pipes are properly attached with no sign of leakage. (Illustration, courtesy Carver)

SAFETY FIRST!

• When gas does not burn properly, poisonous carbon monoxide fumes may be produced.

• You cannot see or smell carbon monoxide fumes. They are invisible, odourless, colourless and tasteless - but they do kill!

• Fumes from partially burnt gas kill more people than fires and explosions from unburned gas.

• Faulty gas appliances, poor ventilation and incorrect flues may all produce carbon monoxide. The danger signs on gas appliances are stains, deposits of soot and excessively yellow or orange flames.

• Carbon monoxide can cause drowsiness, dizziness, headaches, watering eyes, chest pains or palpitations, sickness, stomach pains or diarrhoea. Unfortunately these are vague symptoms also produced by many other causes such as influenza and food poisoning.

• You cannot be sure, unless you have taken the precaution of having the gas system properly maintained AND you use a Carbon Monoxide detector in the motor caravan.

• You should seek medical advice if you persistently suffer from any of the symptoms listed above after being in a room where any gas burning appliance is in use, and of course have your gas installation checked by a competent gas installer.

• Remember, gas appliances which are designed, installed and used correctly, regularly serviced, and properly ventilated and flued, are completely safe.

☐ **Job 10. Replace CO and smoke detector batteries.**

If the vents or flues should become damaged or blocked, carbon monoxide (CO) can gather and in the enclosed confines of a motor caravan, this would rapidly be fatal. You are strongly recommended to fit both a CO detector and a smoke detector into your motor caravan and to renew the batteries every year, whether you think they need it or not.

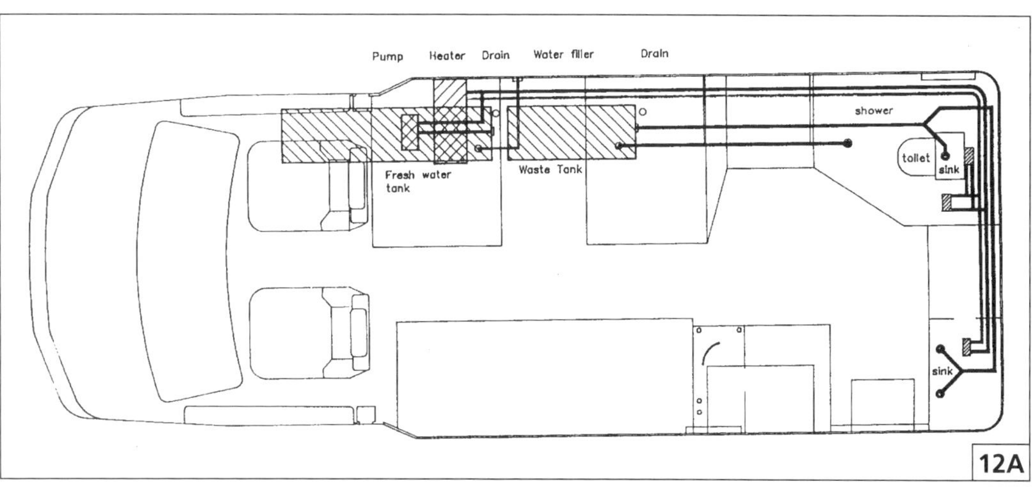

12A

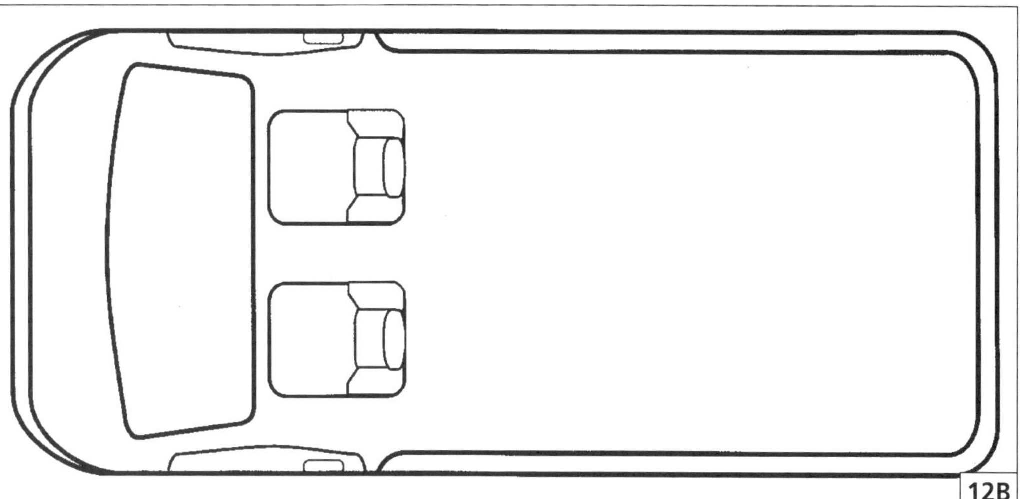
12B

Job 11. Prepare refrigerator.

11. It is likely that the fridge will require a good clean-out and this is certainly something that you don't need to be an expert to do! You will no doubt do this as part of your domestic chores, but it should certainly be done before your motor caravan is stored over a long period and then again before it is used after being brought out of storage. It may also be necessary if there are spillages from food and drink stored in the fridge - not unknown as things topple over *en route*. Generally, all that is needed to clean the fridge out is the use of plain warm water with a teaspoon of bicarbonate of soda in a bowl of water and a clean cloth. Be sure to wipe off thoroughly using only plain water afterwards.

11

Job 12. Check fresh water system.

Check that the water pump/s work with the 12 volt supply turned on and be sure to flush the water system with fresh water.

12A. These are the water components and pipe routes in an Auto-Sleepers' Amethyst model. (Illustration, courtesy Auto-Sleepers)

12B. It is extremely useful to have your own plan of where all the pipes run so that you can check them without having to remember anew each time, and so that any specialist carrying out a service or repair can save time (and save you money) by not having to play hunt-the-pipework. You could fill in the 'blank' plan shown here, if your motor caravan doesn't have one.

making it easy! *• If the fridge has a persistent smell, something that can happen if it is left turned off with the door closed for any period of time, mix in a teaspoon of bicarbonate of soda with a cup of warm water and use that to clean out the fridge. This is an excellent way of getting rid of most odours.*

• Use a proprietary mould remover, or bleach, for stubborn mould marks: never abrasives. Once you've washed the fridge out, be sure to dry it well with a clean cloth.

• If you're not planning to use the motor caravan for some time always make sure that you leave the fridge door in the storage position. This means positioning the retaining pin into the outer of the two holes in the top of the door.

• In this way air is allowed to circulate through the fridge preventing odours forming and stopping any condensation turning to mould.

Job 13. Renew water filter.

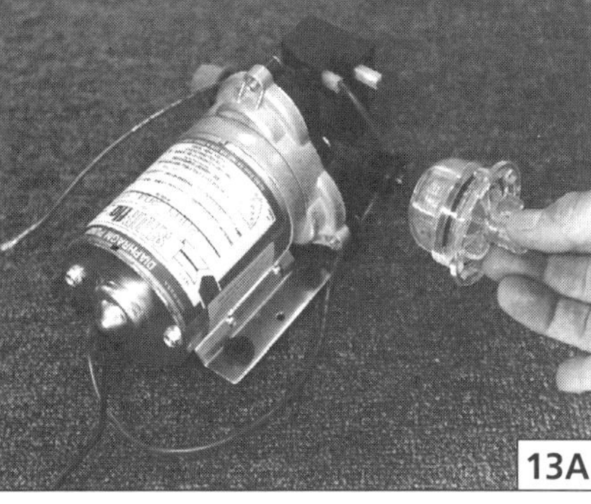

13A. Throw away the old water filter, if you didn't take it out at the end of the previous season, and fit a new one at this stage. You should replace the water filter at the start of every season and then as often as the manufacturers recommend. This type is mounted on the water pump...

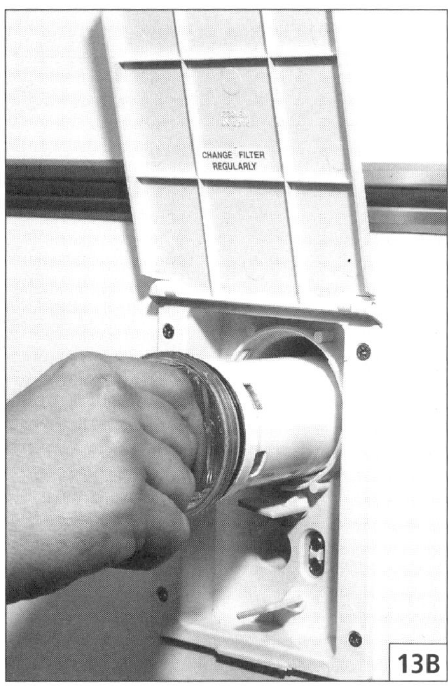

13B. ...while this one, fitted usually where there is no storage tank, is fitted remotely. (Illustration, courtesy Carver)

making it easy! • *Before finally draining the fresh water storage tank, fill up with an appropriate dilution of Milton's fluid, or a supermarket own-brand equivalent. Follow the directions for use on the container.*

- *Flush all of the pipes and taps with the diluted fluid.*
- *When the tank is empty again, be sure to flush the system through extremely thoroughly with fresh water so that there is no taste or tainting from either brackish water or Milton's fluid left in the system.*

INSIDE INFORMATION: Some motor caravans are fitted with underfloor water tanks which can relatively easily be unclipped and removed from the vehicle. It is well worthwhile, once a year, removing these tanks so that they can be thoroughly flushed.

Job 14. Check waste water system.

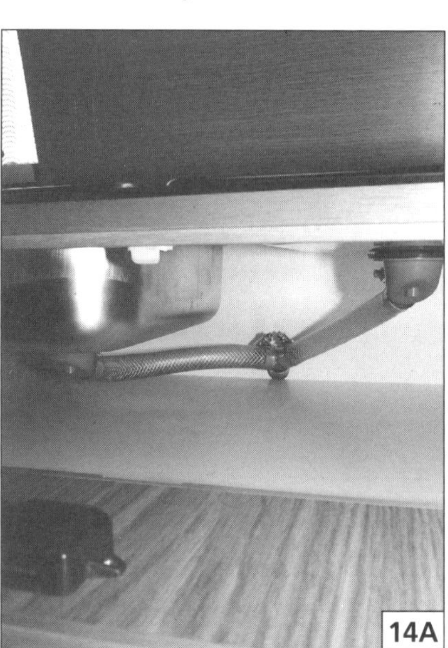

14A. While flushing through the fresh water system, take this opportunity to check that the waste water system doesn't have any leaks inside the vehicle and make sure that the drain tap both seals and opens easily.

INSIDE INFORMATION: If your motor caravan has a shower, make sure that you have a plug for the shower tray plug hole. You will be able to obtain a replacement from your local caravan/motor caravan store.

If the plug keeps popping out, roughen the plastic edges of the shower tray outlet lightly with very fine sandpaper and push the plug in before setting out. Result: no more waste water slopping back through the shower outlet!

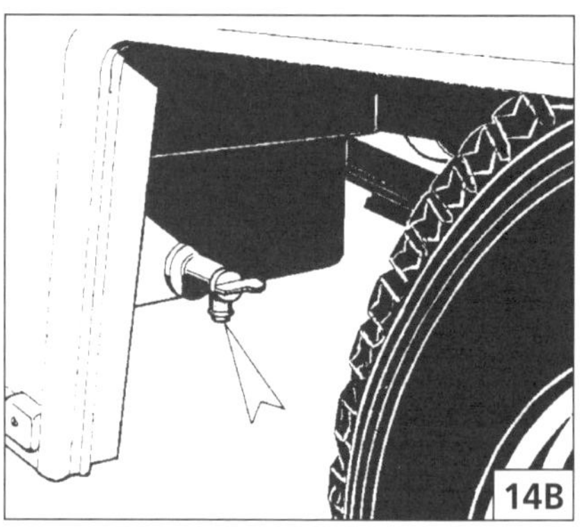

14B. Ensure that the waste water tank drain tap is free, that it doesn't leak and that the pipe you use for draining the tank into the appropriate drain is with the vehicle and pushes easily over the end of the tap. (Illustration, courtesy Auto-Trail)

Job 15. Clean out waste water system.

It is best to flush out the waste water system at the end of every trip, but if you have forgotten to do it or if niffy smells have started to arise, flush it out now.

INSIDE INFORMATION: Add a charge of chemical toilet fluid before filling and flushing the tank as a way of getting rid of unwanted gremlins, hobgoblins and smells.

Job 16. Check level indicators.

16. Check that the level or full indicator on the water storage tank, w.c. and waste water tanks (if fitted) work properly. Try filling each tank with water to check that the gauge reads accurately. There is invariably a 'SET' or adjuster screw on the unit.

16

Job 17. Prepare w.c..

17

17. Make sure that the w.c. is properly prepared. In the case of cassette types, add a charge of flushing water in the tank, and with all of them, add the appropriate chemical in the soil tank. Also, make certain that the flushing mechanism operates satisfactorily.

If you are not carrying out a full service at this stage, be sure to service the flushing mechanism as shown in **Job 48**. Also, see *Chapter 4, Operating Instructions* for information on preparing and emptying the w.c..

Job 18. Prepare heating system/s.

18. Before you set out, turn on the gas and check that each of the heating systems works satisfactorily. Ensure that the vents are clear. This is the Maxol Malaga's input and output vent covering. Be sure that the water heater (where fitted - flue inlet/outlet illustrated) has water in it before turning it on! (Illustration, courtesy Maxol)

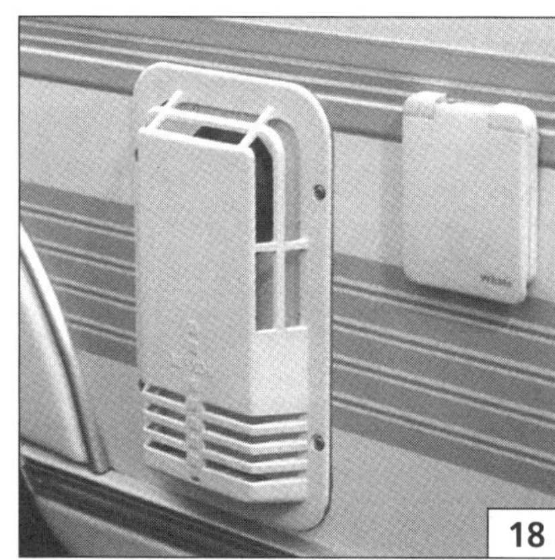
18

Job 19. Check extractor fans and air conditioning.

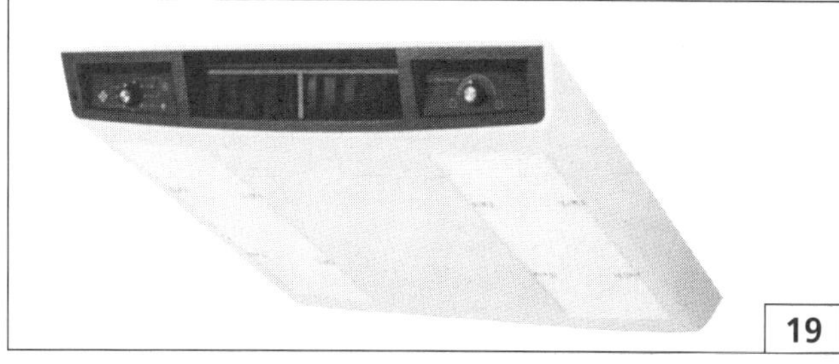
19

19. If fitted, plug in the mains electricity supply and make sure that the air conditioning works satisfactorily. If it doesn't work, try it three or four times and then seek specialist advice. (Illustration, courtesy Electrolux)

INSIDE INFORMATION: Air conditioning systems don't like to be left unused for long periods of time so you should try to remember to operate the system at least once a month when it is not in use.

Far more common are cooker and fresh-air extractor fans. Replace the filter in the former, if necessary, and try them both to check that they work properly.

Job 20. Remove portable heater.

Some people place a portable heater inside the motor caravan to help air it and warm it through. This should NEVER be left in place so take it out before you leave. You should also NEVER use a heater of the open-flame type or with an exposed electrical element. An electrical convector heater would be okay, but only on a low setting, with the heater well away from anything flammable, and while the vehicle is in storage, NOT when in use.

Job 21. Check compatibility of cylinders and regulators.

Many motor caravanners use different cylinders at different times of the year and in different countries. *(See Chapter 3, Using Your Motor Caravan.)* Be sure, before setting out, that you not only have gas in your cylinders, but that the regulators and cylinders actually match each other!

Job 22. Check 12 volt system.

22. Make sure that you also carry spare fuses for the main fuse box which is on the Zig control unit in the great majority of motor caravans. (Illustration, courtesy Zig)

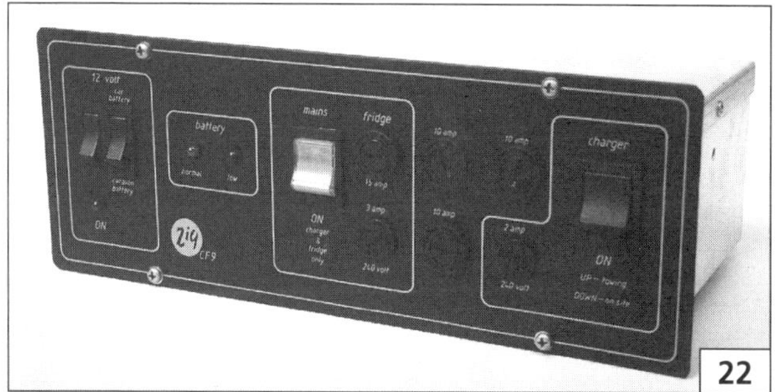

22

☐ Job 23. Check wiring and connections.

Examine all the visible 12-volt wiring and check that all connections and joints are sound and satisfactory. Wiring that is becoming flimsy, especially where it is connected to components, cannot possibly carry a sufficient load and you might find that equipment operates below par. Remake connections wherever necessary.

It pays to know where your 12-volt wiring runs and to understand the fundamentals but you are strongly recommended only to have anything other than the most basic work carried out by a qualified electrician because of the risk of fire which is both significant and extremely dangerous in a motor caravan. 12-volt wiring is at least as capable of bursting into flame as mains voltage wiring if it shorts out or if there is any other fault introduced into it.

☐ Job 24. Have mains electrics inspected.

Examine the cable used to connect the motor caravan to the on-site mains supply and pay special attention to the connector on each end. Ensure that only the outer sheathing is visible where it enters each plug, not the inner cables and that the cable is clamped tight and cannot move in and out of each plug. Check that the cable itself is not abraded or split - if it is, renew it; DON'T tape it up!

Look inside the motor caravan to make sure that all of the electrical connections appear sound, that all of the fixed appliances and the internal supply and trip unit (the RCD unit) are securely mounted.

It is recommended that the inspection and certification of the mains voltage systems is carried out only by a qualified electrician who is an approved contractor of the NICEIC (National Inspection Council for Electrical Installation Contracting) or a member of the Electrical Contractors Association.

We strongly recommend that you have your certifying engineer check the system annually and keep the annual certificate somewhere safe for future reference.

☐ Job 25. Check hook-ups.

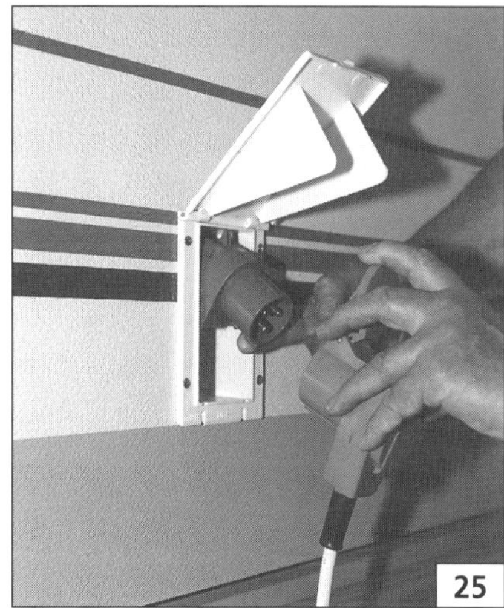

25. Make sure that you have the correct hook-up cable or cables with you before setting out.

☐ Job 26. Check mains voltage system.

If you have the means of doing a hook-up at home, try out the mains system to make sure everything works satisfactorily. See **Jobs 24 and 26** for essential safety checks to be carried out.

☐ Job 27. Check external low-level vents.

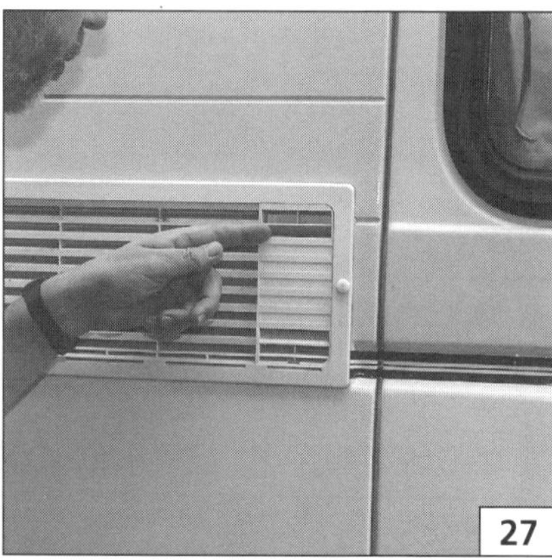

27. Check all the external vents on the sides of the bodywork, such as those to the refrigerator, room heater or water heater. Both high and low level ventilators must be free from obstruction and allow a free flow of air.

If the ventilator can be adjusted manually, ensure that the mechanism is free and operates correctly.

Double-check that the vents to the gas locker from outside the motor caravan are clear and that the vents in the base of the gas locker are also clear. Although this is covered as part of an earlier job, make sure that any internal doors to the gas locker seal the gas locker from the inside of the vehicle.

☐ Job 28. Check awning rail seal.

Some motor caravans use a 'drive-away' awning, held on with flaps, clips and ropes while the majority have a pull-out canopy-type awning. With the latter type, check that the elements cannot get in where the awning cassette is fitted.

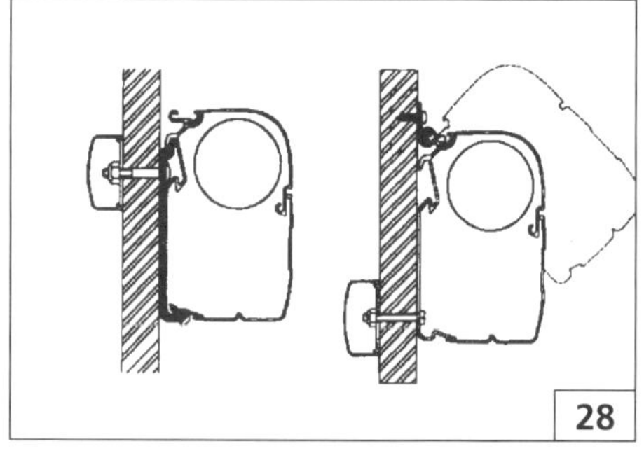

28. Find the positions of the mounting bolts for pull-out awnings, inside the motor caravan. Prise off any plastic cover caps that maybe fitted and make sure the bolts are tight. Look around the anchorage plate for any signs of water staining. Check on the outside that the awning is weather proof where it fits against the vehicle. If necessary, slacken all of the mounting bolts (remember that the awning box is very heavy!). Clean off all traces of mastic around the mounting holes and apply fresh sealer before tightening the awning box back up again. (Illustration, courtesy Omnistore)

Job 29. Check/lubricate corner steadies.

29. Check each of the rear corner steadies, if fitted. Ensure first of all that each one is securely mounted to the vehicle and tighten up any bolts that may have come loose. Clean off any dirt that might have been thrown up from the road and lightly grease the threads... and all the moving parts of the mechanism.

Job 30. Check/lubricate folding step.

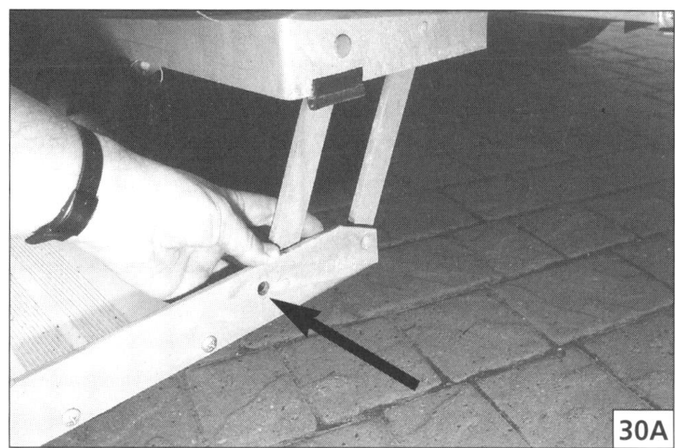

30A. It is not unknown for folding step pivot arms, or rather their mounting pins, to break away - they do take rather a hammering! Check for any looseness, excessive wear or missing pins and replace or renew as necessary.

30B. Thoroughly lubricate each of the pivots. Be sure to keep oil away from any of the electrical components when an electrically operated folding step is fitted. Note that there are also plastic steps and those with nylon bushes. Both types may positively be harmed by lubricating them with oil. With all types, wash the undersides of the step making sure that no dirt is trapped around the pivots.

Job 31. Check underfloor tank mountings.

31A. Check that underfloor water tanks, both for fresh and waste water, are securely fixed to the vehicle's body. Mounting straps, if made of thin steel, are prone to rusting and could well break at an inconvenient moment. Clean off and treat with underbody wax if necessary.

Some tanks are fitted with a releasing mechanism so that the tank can easily be removed. Check that the mechanism is free of rust and that it operates freely and, once again, treat with underbody wax protection.

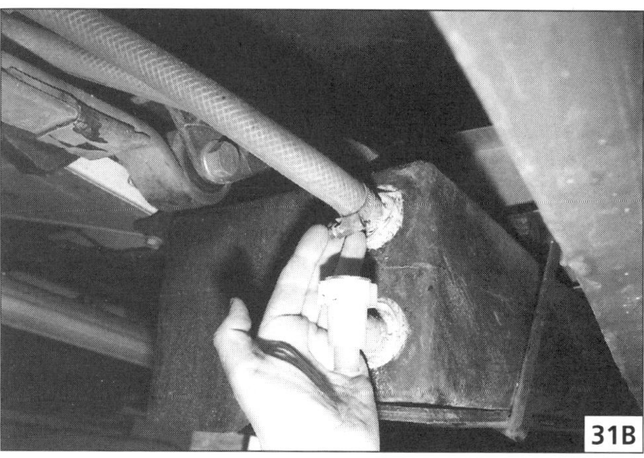

31B. Check the pipe mountings to the tank. Look for corrosion in the tank, if it is a metal one, or for cracks in plastic. Ensure that pipes aren't split and that jubilee clip connections are tight.

☐ Job 32. Check wheelarches/wheelboxes.

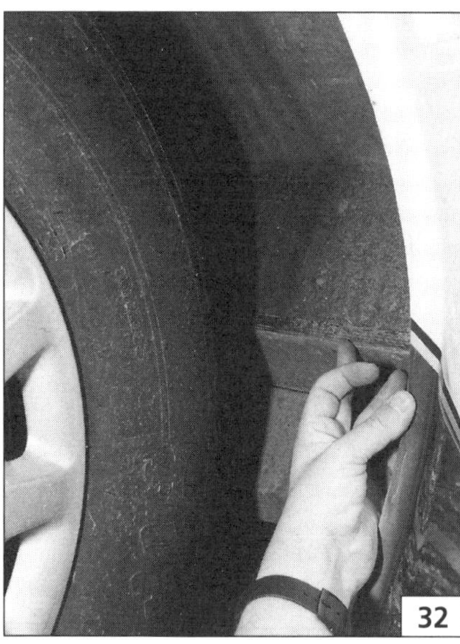

32. From underneath the vehicle, clean off and check that there is no damage, corrosion or tyre rubbing in evidence around the wheelboxes. On coachbuilt caravans, the wheel arches are usually made of plywood. Check that joints are tight and that there is no rot present.

From inside the vehicle check that no water has been getting in - this is a common water ingress point on Coach-built and A-class models, so get out that damp tester again!

INSIDE INFORMATION: On van-conversion models, this is a common place for rust to set in, especially where the wheelarch joins the van body. Clean any mud from around the wheelarch and treat the wheelarch with underbody wax treatment both inside and outside.

☐ Job 33. Clean bodywork.

Over the winter months, some mould and discoloration will undoubtedly have taken place, particularly on the "out of site, out of mind" tops of coach built models. Wash off with bicarbonate of soda in water - leaving the stuff to soak in a while sometimes helps - and apply a good quality silicone-based polish to keep discoloration and mould at bay.

INSIDE INFORMATION: From your car accessory store, you will be able to buy a liquid treatment that is claimed to prevent rubber and plastics from going brittle and cracking. Apply this to all of the window rubbers - and even the vehicle tyres - and the risk of perishing from the effects of UV and ozone should be diminished.

☐ Job 34. Check awning.

34. If you have an awning, whether of the pull-out type or stand-alone type, erect it fully and make sure that you have all the bits! Clean off any corrosion from holes and mould from canvas; lubricate sliders with silicone grease and, if necessary, adjust the tension on the pull-out type. (Illustration, courtesy Omnistore)

☐ Job 35. Prepare generator.

At the close of the previous season, you should have drained the fuel out of the generator. Refill it now and make sure it starts and runs correctly. Try out the electrical part of it, too. Leave yourself plenty of time to have any necessary repairs carried out before you set out and also change the oil and have the 'genny' serviced if necessary.

INSIDE INFORMATION: If your generator is still on last season's fuel and won't start or runs badly, drain the fuel (SAFELY, OUT OF DOORS, AWAY FROM SOURCES OF IGNITION) into a safe container and recharge with fresh fuel. The safest way to dispose of the old fuel is by adding it to half a tank or more of 'fresh' fuel in your (petrol-engined!) car - it won't be noticed.

☐ Job 36. Check audible and visual warning systems.

Check the step-down warning, reverse buzzer, and/or reverse sensors, according to which you have fitted to your vehicle, to ensure that the relevant warning sound or light works properly. The step-down warning, when fitted to coachbuilt motor caravans with electrically operated steps, should sound with the step in its lowered position and with the ignition turned on.

making it easy!

- *If your vehicle has a reversing warning buzzer, check that it works properly.*
- *If it is fitted with the reversing sensor, have someone walk slowly towards the back of the vehicle with the reverse gear selected and the ignition turned on.*
- *This will establish that the sensors are picking up objects in a) the right positions and b) at the correct distances.*
- *Adjust the angles of the sensors and clean their rearward-facing surfaces, if necessary.*

☐ Job 37. Check cycle rack.

37. When fitted, ensure that the cycle rack mechanism operates correctly and that the cycle or cycles will clamp securely in place. Lubricate all of the pivot points. (Illustration, courtesy Simpsons Motor Caravan Centre)

Job 38. Check towing equipment.

If your motor caravan is fitted with a towbracket - some people take a small trailer for extra equipment; some tow a small car while others even take a small caravan with them - check that the towbracket is securely fitted to the vehicle and lubricate the towball.

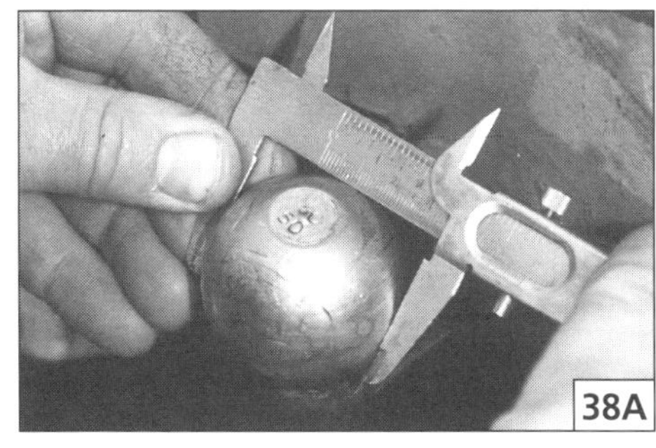

38A. SPECIALIST SERVICE: Unless you possess appropriate measuring equipment, have your specialist measure the towball for you. AL-KO Kober recommend a minimum diameter, at any point, of 49.61 mm. If the ball is worn below this point, REPLACE IT BEFORE TOWING!

38B. Always ensure that the towball is lubricated before use.

38C. Apply water repellent spray to the 12N and 12S plugs and sockets to stop them corroding.

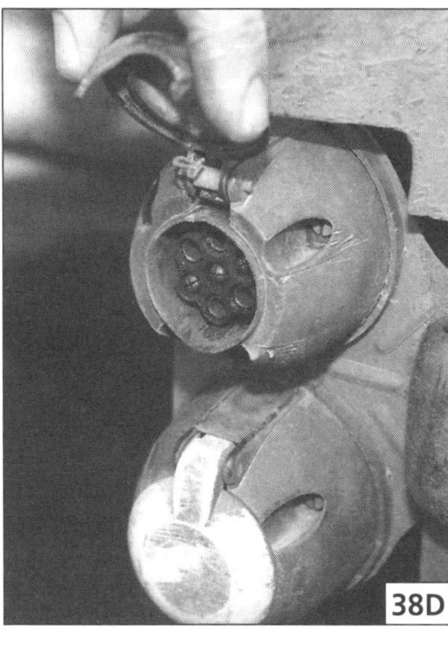

38D. Ensure that the seals on the 12-volt sockets on your motor caravan are sound and that the springs holding the lids closed are working.

38E. If you use your motor caravan to tow a small car, the **Car-a-Tow** frame will also need regular attention. The pivots mounted on the car will need to be greased regularly.

INSIDE INFORMATION: Use brake grease; ordinary grease rots the rubber stops on the pivots.

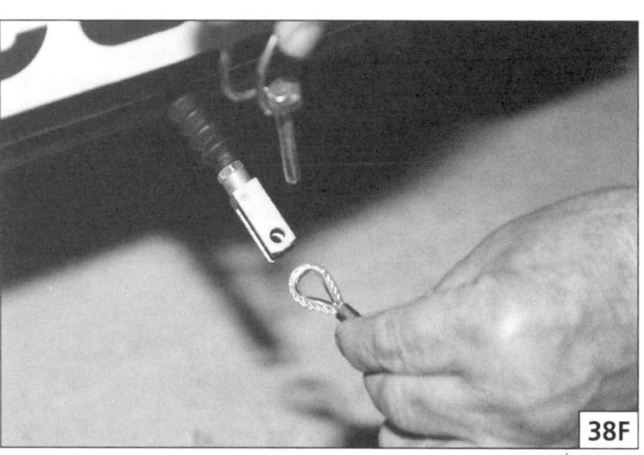

38F. Check the brake linkage particularly carefully. Ensure that the connector eye and the cable itself are in good condition. Apply a blob of brake grease (see above) to the end of the rubber sleeve, where the cable enters the car and also grease the handbrake mechanism, including the ratchet, on the tow frame itself.

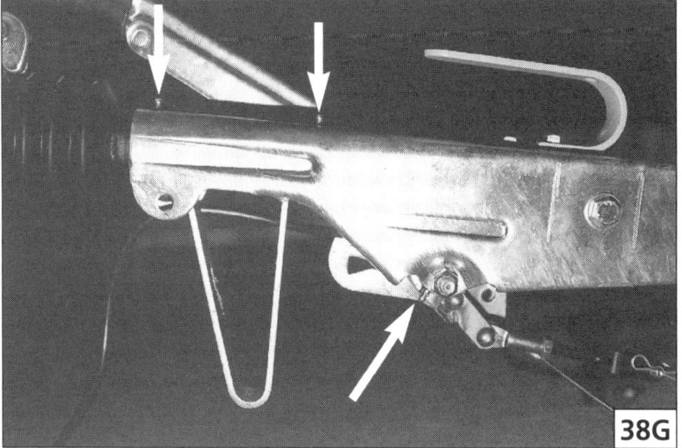

38G. There are three grease points (arrowed) on the tow frame over-run mechanism. Use a grease gun on them.

PART II: BEFORE EVERY LONG JOURNEY

Job 39. Check auxiliary battery fixings.

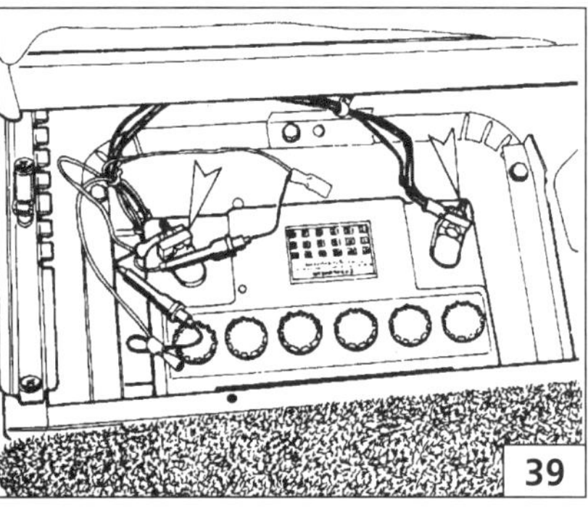

39. Check that the battery mountings and the electrical connections (arrowed) are securely in place before setting out. (Illustration, courtesy Auto-Trail)

Job 40. Clean out/prepare cassette w.c..

Refer to **Job 17** and *Chapter 4, Operating Instructions, Part II* and prepare the w.c. for use.

Job 41. Replenish fresh water system.

Top up the fresh water system before you set out and ensure that you have the appropriate food-quality water hose with you for topping up while you are away.

> *making it easy!*
> • *Water is extremely heavy stuff - carrying more water than you will need until you reach your destination means lugging loads of unnecessary weight around with you!*
> • *Thanks to consistencies of the metric system, water weighs one kilogram per litre, and (a gallon weighs approximately 10 pounds).*
> • *For the same reason, ensure that the waste water system is drained before setting out.*

Job 42. Check roof vents.

42. While you are going round closing all of the roof vents, check them for security, make sure that they will close down securely and check visually for leaks.

Job 43. Check for flammable surfaces.

Just before you set out, look around to check that no fixtures, fittings or upholstery have been added, either permanently or temporarily, adjacent to any of the heaters.

Job 44. Check bedding arrangements.

This is an extension of **Jobs 2** and **3** and could save you several uncomfortable - not to say unsafe! - nights.

Job 45. Check inventory.

Take a look at *Appendix 2 - What to Take* and go through your check-list item by item.

PART III: REGULAR CHECKS

These are jobs which have to be carried out regularly but at a number of different recommended service intervals, according to the manufacturers of the components concerned.

Job 46. EVERY WEEK - Check electrical trip unit.

46. Your electrical trip unit will have a test button fitted to it. Once a week (and every time you hook up to the mains on-site), you should test the residual current device (RCD) which is fitted to provide protection against earth faults and possible electric shock. With the RCD in the ON position and with the electricity connected, press the TEST button marked 'T'. The unit should immediately switch to the OFF position. If it does so, the unit is working correctly and the switch can then be returned to the ON position so that the electricity supply is returned to normal. If it does not, have a qualified electrician to find the fault and put things right before you use the vehicle.

IMPORTANT NOTE: Unlike most household 13A electrical switches, the mains and MCB switches on your control unit are UP for ON and DOWN for OFF. (Illustration, courtesy Auto-Trail)

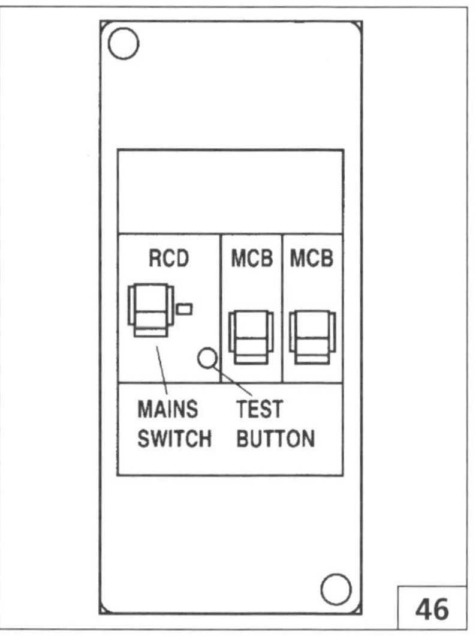

FACT FILE: ELECTRICAL MAINS UNIT

Modern motor caravans are fitted with an electrical control unit containing an RCD and MCBs. Its a good idea to know what these are for!

RCD = RESIDUAL CURRENT DEVICE:

- If the RCD detects an earth fault, causing a leak of current to earth, either directly or via the human body, the unit is designed to immediately trip and switch OFF the supply before any damage can be done.
- If this should happen, the supply can only be re-set once the fault has been eliminated.
- If your RCD should trip, try switching it back ON again and if it won't immediately switch back into the ON position, i.e. if the switch refuses to stay on or rapidly jumps back off again, there is a fault in the mains electrical system and you should disconnect the mains electrics until a qualified electrician has found the fault and put it right.
- The RCD is a life-saving device and should never, under any circumstances, be ignored or over-ridden.

MCB = MINIATURE CIRCUIT BREAKER:

- MCBs are designed to operate if a circuit is over-loaded. They protect the motor caravans circuits against over-load damage and will automatically switch to the OFF position if an over-load takes place.
- An over-load could be caused by simply using too many appliances or appliances with an excessive current requirement, or it is possible that a faulty appliance could cause an over-load to take place.
- In the majority of cases, it will be simply be a matter of reducing the load on the circuit but it is important that you find out the true cause for the MCB to trip before switching it back on again (against the spring pressure) in an upwards direction.

☐ Job 47. EVERY WEEK - Check fire extinguisher.

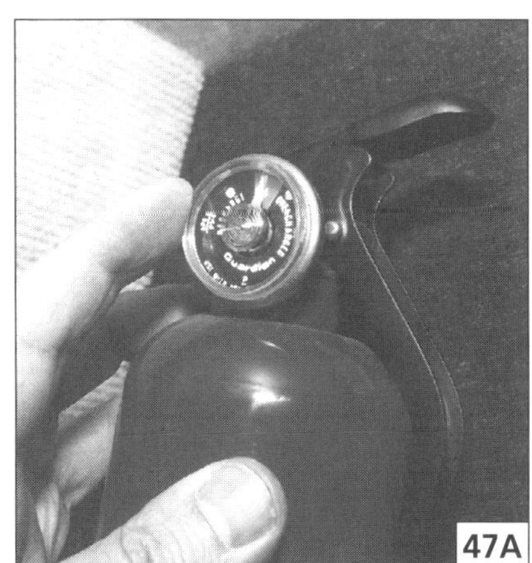
47A

47A. Every week, you should look at the gauge on your fire extinguisher to make sure that it is still charged. If the needle drops into the red, take it to your local fire extinguisher specialist (see your local Yellow Pages) and have the extinguisher recharged.

IMPORTANT NOTE: Do not test-fire the fire extinguisher to make sure it works. All this could mean is that it won't work when you need it!

47B

47B. You should also check that the security seal - sometimes paper, as shown here - and coming loose!; sometimes thin wire - is in position. This indicates that the unit has been used and if it's not in place, it tells you that someone has been fooling with the extinguisher, in which case you should get it checked.

INSIDE INFORMATION: Before taking your fire extinguisher in to have it recharged, check on the price of having the work done and compare it with the cost of buying a new one. You may find that you can buy a reputable make for no more or maybe for even less than the cost of having the extinguisher recharged. Whatever you do, don't make the mistake of trading down to a make you have never heard of (made in China perhaps?) or to a smaller size, or to a water-based extinguisher. You MUST use a powder-based or CO_2 fire extinguisher.

47C

47C. Check the nozzle, to make sure it's clear.

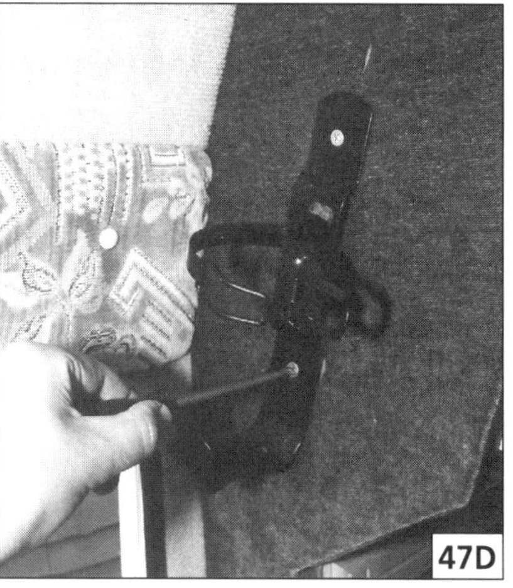
47D

47D. Check that the clips and fittings securing the extinguisher to the wall are tight. They can - and do - vibrate loose under the movement of the motor caravan and the weight of the extinguisher.

SAFETY FIRST!

Understand how to use your fire extinguisher so that you don't panic should the need arise. Remember, that fire extinguishers should always be directed at the BASE of the fire and not at the tops of the flames.

Job 48. EVERY 2 - 4 WEEKS - Service w.c. flushing mechanism.

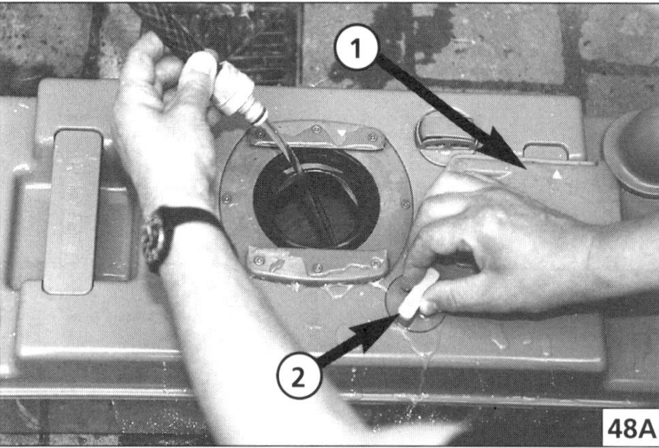

48A. Thetford recommend that the seals in the cassette w.c. are cleaned once or twice a month. Slide the access door out of the way (arrow 1) and turn the soil tank opening knob (arrow 2) to open up the top valve. You can now wash this out.

48B. Use silicone spray on the large seal, rotating the flap control knob so that all of the seal is lubricated...

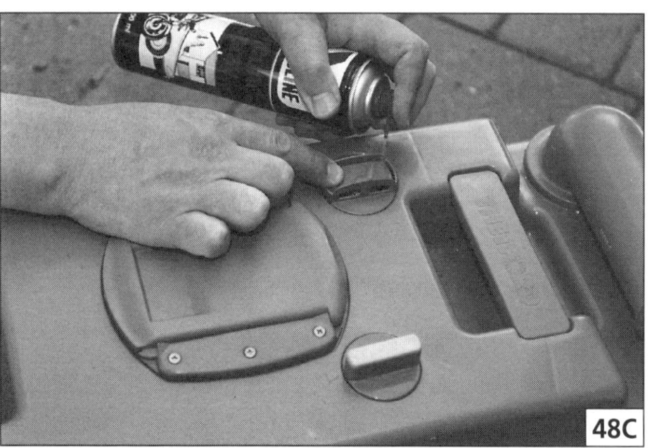

48C. ...and also remember to use silicone spray on the ventilator seal shown here.

48D. Also, remember the air release button - the one you press when draining the tank (see the relevant section in *Chapter 4, Operating Instructions*).

48E. Thetford recommend that the toilet bowl, seat, the cover and the toilet itself are cleaned with a little washing up liquid on a damp cloth. DO NOT use strong household cleaners or any solutions containing chlorine, acids, solvents or bleach as these might well damage the toilet.

making it easy! *If you want to sterilise the surface, use Milton 2, Chempro SDP or a similar alternative sterilising fluid in an appropriate solution of warm water.*

Job 49. ONCE A MONTH - Check accessible gas pipes and connections.

At least once a month, visually check all the easily accessible gas pipes and connections, visible in storage areas and on and around all the gas appliances and cylinders. If you find any loose jubilee clips on the ends of rubber hoses, tighten them up again. If any of the other connections look loose or the rubber hoses appear to be cut or chaffed, have a CORGI qualified gas fitter carry out the necessary repairs. See **Jobs 5** to **10**, inclusive.

☐ **Job 50. ONCE A MONTH - Check auxiliary battery.**

One item which is essential to keep well maintained is the 12-volt leisure battery. Forgetting or ignoring to maintain the battery could well cause it to fail, potentially leaving the motor caravan without power for the items such as the light and water pump.

SAFETY FIRST!

When servicing the battery:

- ***Always switch off the battery charger and disconnect the main's electrics hook-up and 12N/12S cables.***
- ***Make sure all the electrical components in the motor caravan are turned off.***
- ***Always disconnect the battery's negative terminal (earth) first and, when the servicing is complete, reverse the procedure by re-connecting the negative terminal last.***
- ***Never smoke or allow a spark anywhere near a battery, especially when it is being charged, as it gives off explosive fumes.***
- ***Wear gloves and goggles when handling non-sealed type batteries and if any battery electrolyte (acid) is spilled onto skin or eyes, wash off with copious amounts of cold, running water and immediately seek medical advice.***

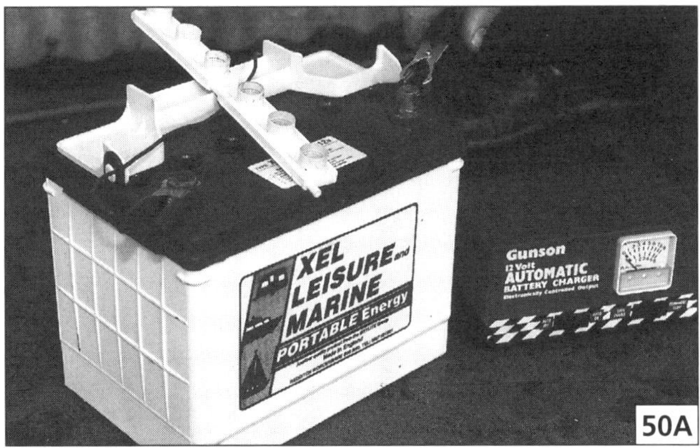

50A. If the motor caravan does not have its own battery charger, the battery should be removed every three months, or in the winter every month, and recharged outside of the motor caravan.

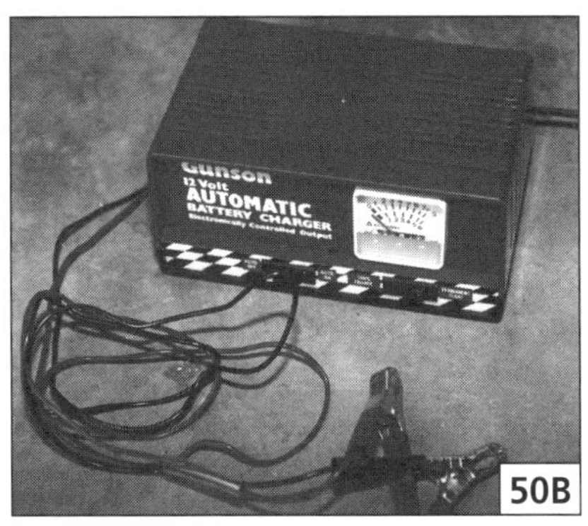

50B. For this purpose, use only a battery charger designed for the job and preferably one that sets its own, correct charging rate automatically. Not all car-type chargers are suitable. This Gunson's battery charger is designed to give several options which are perfect for leisure batteries. It can be left permanently connected while the motor caravan is not in use, utilising the charger's 'Permanent Float' setting, and it can be used to charge sealed batteries without any risk of gas build-up - the clever little devil regulates itself to prevent such a thing from happening!

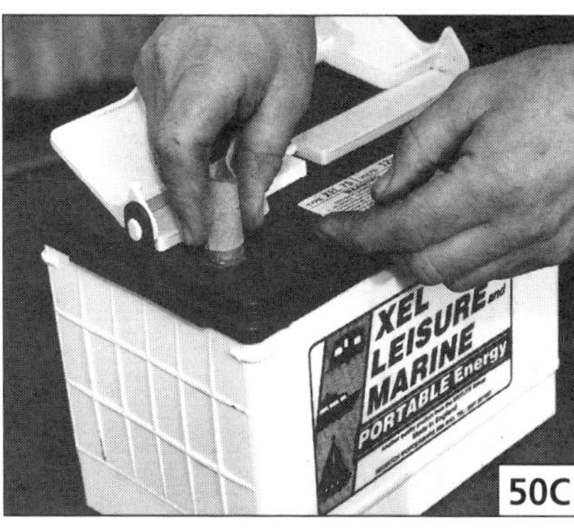

50C. While the battery is disconnected, make sure that its terminals are clean, secure and in good condition. If not, clean them off with sand paper, back to a shiny surface, both on the battery and the terminals. Protect the surfaces with copious amounts of Vaseline. Similarly, check the battery leads and connectors in the motor caravan for signs of wear, damage or corrosion and check the battery casing for signs of cracks or damage.

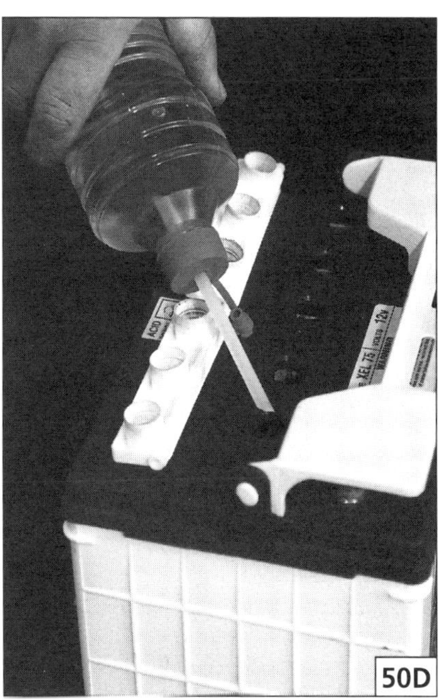

50D. If the battery is of the non-sealed variety, check the electrolyte levels and, if necessary top them up with distilled water. Distilled water is generally available from car accessory shops. This won't be necessary if the battery is of the sealed variety. Wipe the top of the battery casing - dirt or grease on the top of the casing can help 'furring' to occur.

making it easy!

- *You don't need elbow grease to remove battery 'furring'!*
- *Simply boil the kettle, remove the battery somewhere where water can run away safely, and pour a kettle of just boiled water over the 'furry' terminals. It will come off as if by magic!*
- *Take care to keep the battery cell covers (if a non-sealed battery) firmly closed.*

50E. Make sure that the vent in the battery box is clear and, if the battery is fitted with one, that the breather pipe is clear. When the battery is returned to the storage locker make sure that it is strapped or clamped securely into place so that it can't move about when the motor caravan is on the move.

SAFETY FIRST!

SAFETY FIRST! and INSIDE INFORMATION:

- **Always keep a battery safely out of reach of children and somewhere that it's unlikely to get knocked or dropped.**
- **Don't store it on the floor as a battery stored on a concrete floor will slowly discharge itself.**
- **If the battery is removed from the motor caravan for any length of time, for example, while the motor caravan is stored over the winter period, make sure that it is never left in a discharged condition.**

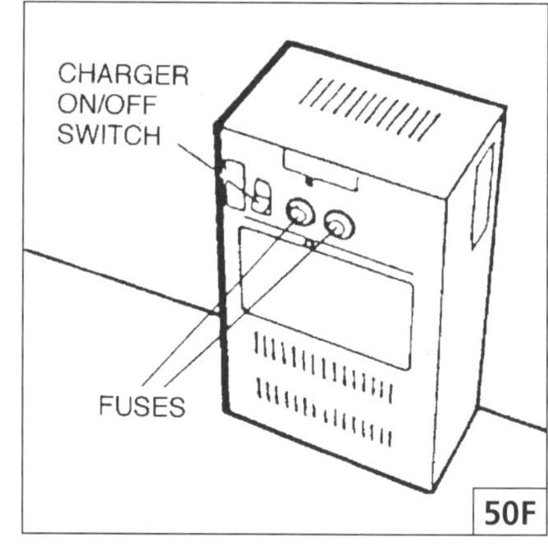

50F. Check that you have spare fuses for the 12-volt power and integral battery charger system, when fitted. On most motor caravans, this is designed to provide power to the motor caravan even if a battery is not fitted (although it is always recommended that you do have one in place) and to re-charge the leisure battery when in place. (Illustration, courtesy Swift)

INSIDE INFORMATION: 'Leisure' batteries are not the same as ordinary car batteries. They are designed to give a smaller load over a longer period of time, whereas car batteries are designed to provide a very high load (such as when starting the engine) in short bursts. In theory, leisure batteries should last a lot longer than car batteries although in practice, some motor caravans have found the reverse to be true! It might be worth checking out the prices of each and taking a chance on a car battery if you feel that you can save yourself a very significant amount of money.

PART IV: EVERY THREE MONTHS

☐ **Job 51. Check all gas pipes/connections.**

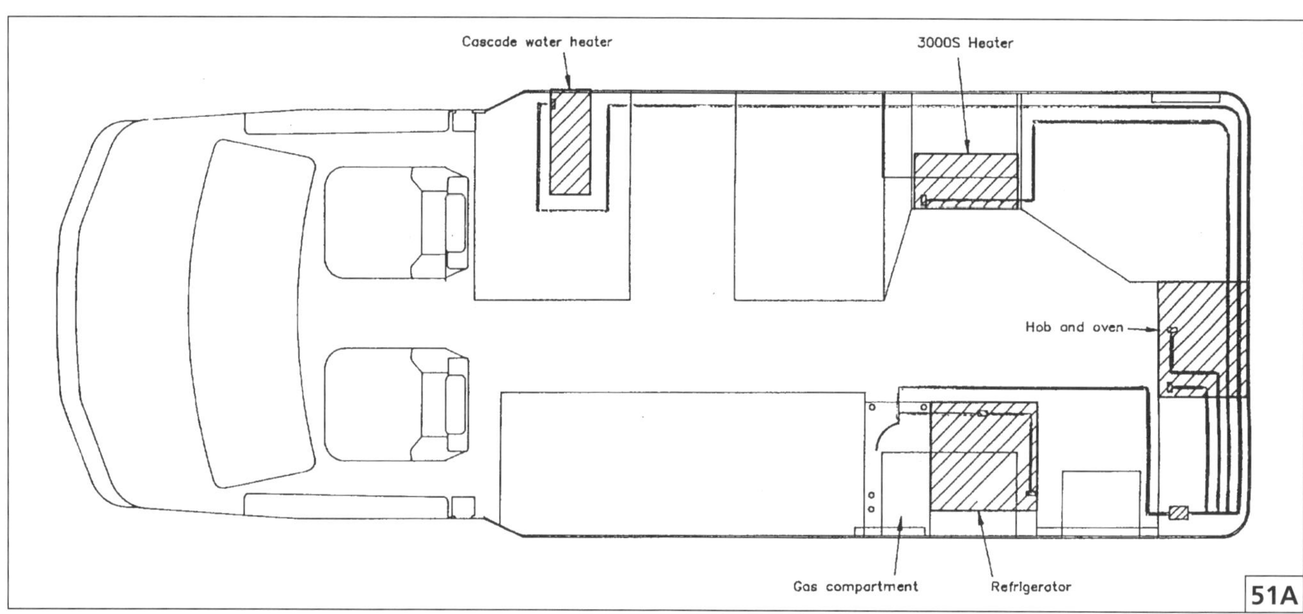

51A. This is the layout of the gas components and pipe routes in an Auto-Sleepers Amethyst, as reproduced from the relevant handbook. (Illustration, courtesy Auto-Sleepers)

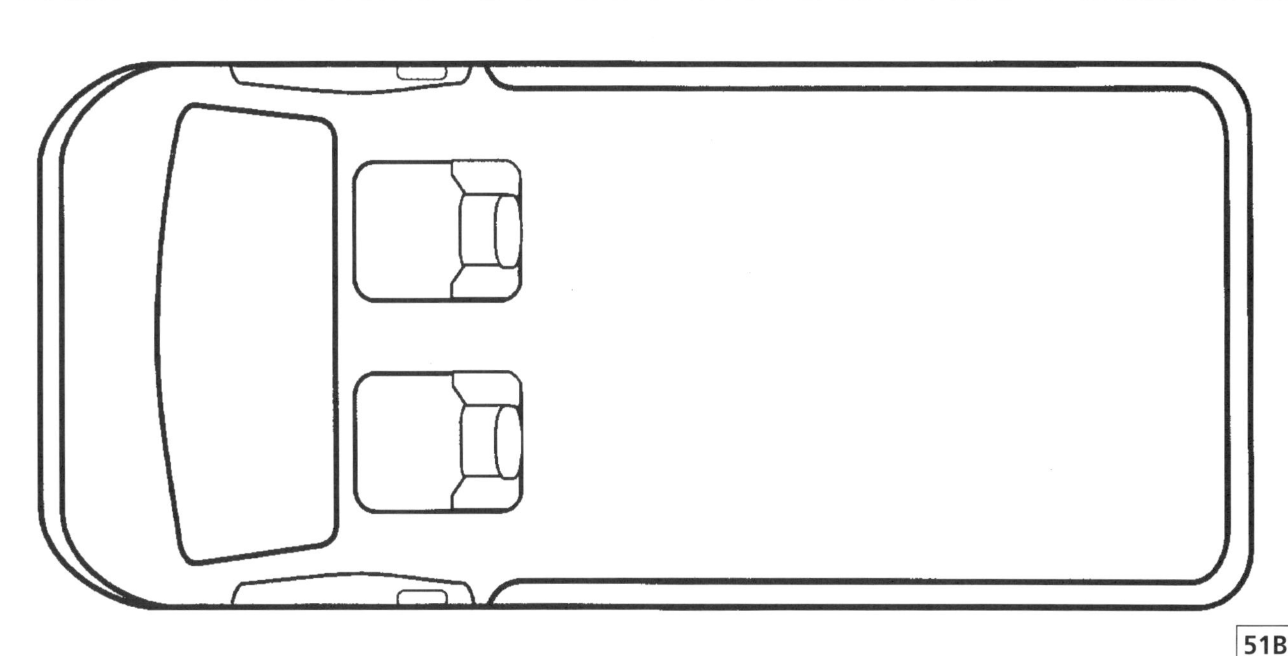

51B

51B. If you don't have such a similar schematic drawing of your motor caravan, you are strongly recommended to fill in the drawing above, perhaps with the assistance of your dealer. In this way, you, or your service engineer, won't have to search them out every time you want to carry out the necessary checks.

Every three months (or three times a year if the motor caravan is not used in the winter) make a systematic check on all of the gas pipes and connections, including those that may need removal of panels or bedding to get at.

51C

51C. You should also check that any external or (*especially!*) internal door fitted to a gas cylinder cupboard has an effective seal on it...

51D

51D. ...and that the vents and the gas drain hole in the gas cylinder compartment are both free from obstruction.

IMPORTANT NOTE: Under no circumstances should any holes in the bottom of the gas cylinder cupboard be filled in: they're there for a reason! Butane and propane are both heavier than air and if there should be a leak, they need to have somewhere to 'drain away'. With no drain holes, any such gas could gather with potentially catastrophic results.

51E

51E. Ensure that the straps and clips designed to hold the (heavy!) gas cylinder/s are sound. Check all flexible hoses for cracking and for overall condition, check all the pipe connections, both rubber and metal hoses and make sure that all metal pipes are free from corrosion and are properly clipped to the vehicle's body or chassis. Any exposed piping underneath the vehicle should also be checked to make sure that it hasn't been damaged.

☐ **Job 52. Check flame failure device.**

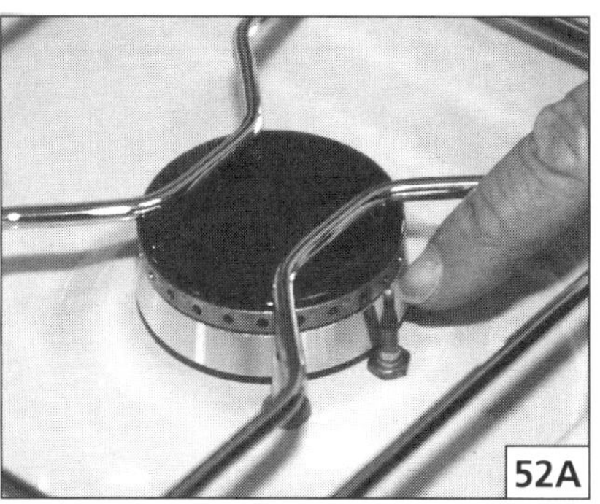

52A

52A. The flame failure device should be checked on every appliance to which it is fitted. You'll see that, on each appliance, the flame failure device sits in the flame of the pilot light, sensing the presence of the flame. The job of the flame failure device is to ensure that, if the pilot light flame is blown out, the gas supply is shut off. So, if your flame failure device fails to work properly, you could have an accumulation of unburned gas - and a huge explosion!

TESTING: Make sure that the appliance works by lighting it in the normal way and then turn it off again, allowing time for the heat-sensor in the flame failure device to cool.

52B. Now attempt to relight the appliance in the normal way except that you must not push in the gas control knob shown being pressed here, on this cooker. (This normally overrides the flame failure device for as long as it takes the appliance to light up). With the gas control knob turned to the "on" position, use the usual igniter and see if the appliance lights. If it does not do so, the flame failure device is satisfactory. If it does light, the flame failure device, or its sensor has failed and you must have it repaired by a qualified gas fitter before using the device again.

☐ **Job 53. Check appliance security.**

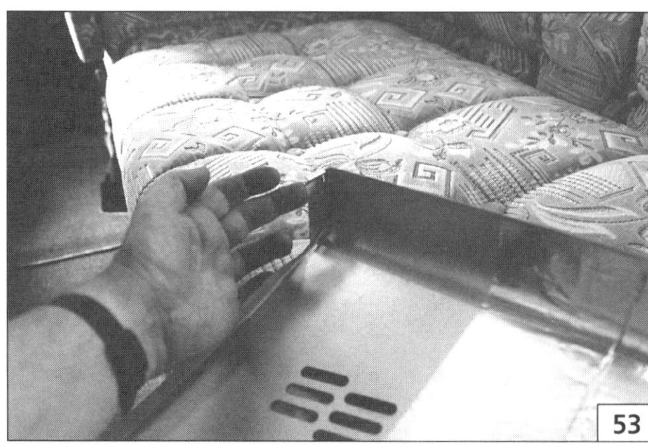

53. Check that all gas appliances - and the gas cylinders! - are securely fixed to the vehicle and/or its furniture and that they are free from rattles when the vehicle is being driven. Where applicable, check that water pipes are correctly attached and that there are no signs of leakage.

INSIDE INFORMATION: Rattles from appliances are often due to loose or missing spring clips. Make sure that any clips holding cooker components in place, or covers onto heating units, are all gripping tightly.

PART V: ONCE A YEAR

The following jobs must be carried out once a year, although it is not important when in the year these jobs are carried out. Jobs which are annual, but which really do need to be carried out at a specific time are shown under the relevant sections. In practice, you may wish to carry out this section along with the *PART I: PREPARING FOR THE START OF THE SEASON* jobs shown at the start of this chapter.

These jobs will ensure that your motor caravan is maintained in safe, reliable condition and that it will continue to be a pleasure to use. Carrying out all of them could take some little time but will save you a good deal of money and no little frustration in the long run, as well as maintaining the value of your motor caravan. If you ensure that the service history is kept up-to-date in the back of this book, that will go even further to maintaining your motor caravan's value when it comes time to sell.

☐ **Job 54. Check interior for damp/leaks.**

All types of motor caravans are prone to leaks, especially the more traditional coach-built models and those with elevating roofs, although A-class models are often prone to leaking in around the windscreen rubbers.

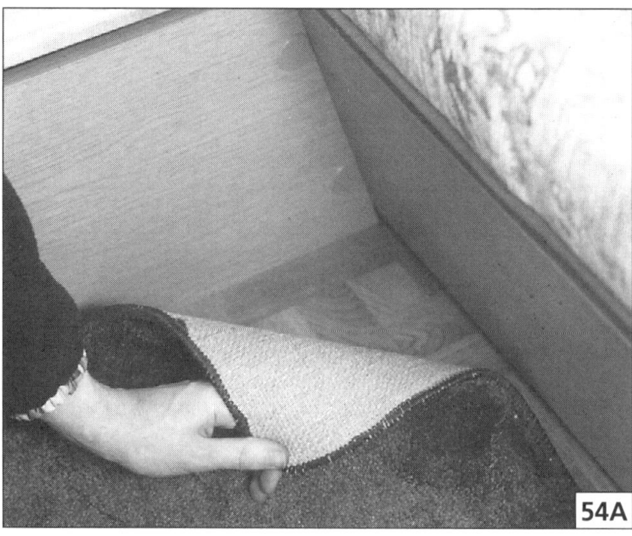

54A. Water leaks can be ignored for several years without too much apparently going wrong, but the damage water leaks will cause are insidious and are probably the cause of the demise of more motor caravans than anything else, other than body or chassis rust. Use the evidence of your eyes - look under carpets and inside cupboards, especially in the corners - use your nose (beware the sweet smell that indicates that rot has already taken a hold) and be sure to invest in a damp detector.

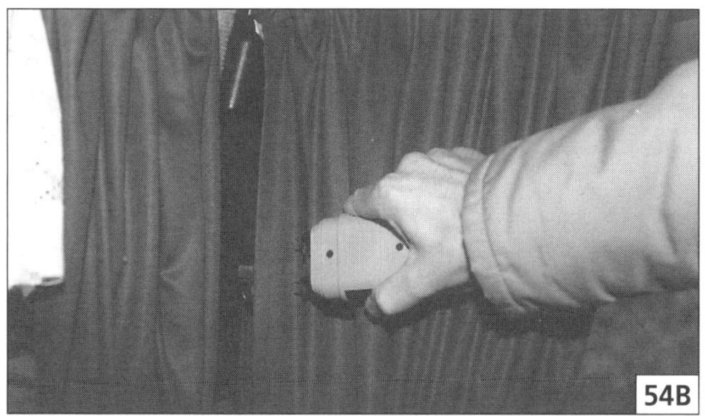
54B

making it easy! • *54B. This Plasplugs unit costs less than a tank of petrol or diesel but could save you thousands of pounds - but only if you find the source of any leaks and act upon them.*

• *This particular tester emits a range of sounds from a low clicking sound, rather like a Geiger counter in the movies, up to a high pitched shriek when it detects something that is wringing wet.*

• *This is quite a useful feature since it saves you having to use your own breath when you come across such a dreadful discovery!*

Job 55. Check fire blanket.

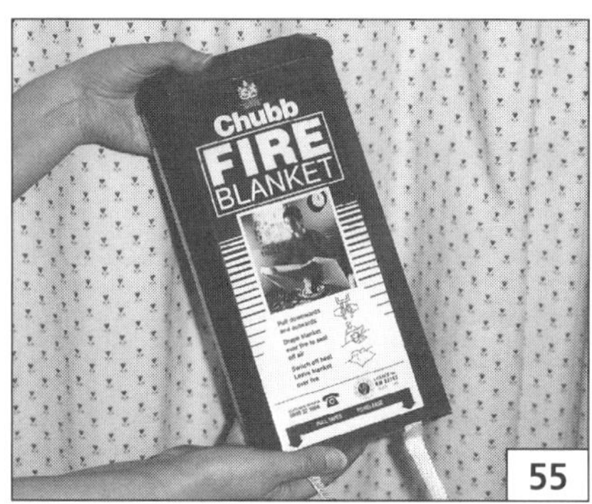

55

55. Make sure that the fire blanket is in its correct position, that it is easy to remove when you need it and that it is mounted securely to the vehicle.

Job 56. Adjust water pressure.

If your motor caravan is fitted with a pressure water system, it might need adjusting occasionally. If it does, this is usually due to variations in the power source, generally caused by a drop in battery power. If this is the case, refer to the specific instructions in your motor caravan's handbook. With most models, there is a simple procedure to follow:

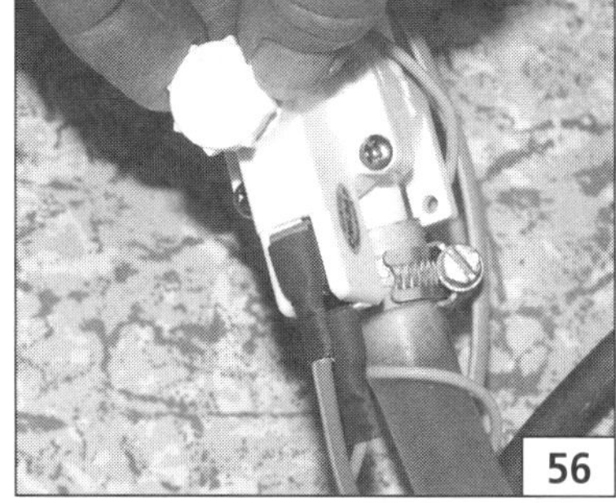
56

56. Locate the adjusting nut. This is usually to be found on the back or the top of the pressure switch, depending on model. Turn one of the motor caravan taps on and turn the adjusting nut slowly in an anti-clockwise direction until you hear a click. Then turn it a further half-turn in the same direction, and the setting should be correct.

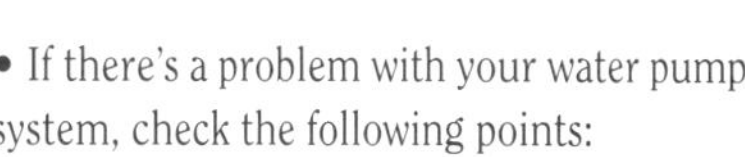

FACT FILE:
PROBLEMS WITH SWITCHES

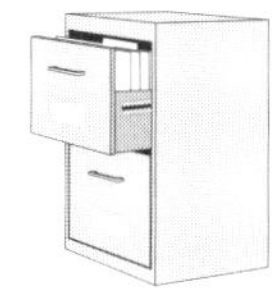

• If there's a problem with your water pump system, check the following points:

• Most motor caravans equipped with pressure switches will have an isolation switch fitted. This is used as a safety precaution to stop the pump running dry and burning out, should the pump develop a fault, such as a leak. Check out the isolation switch.

• If your motor caravan has a microswitch attached to the tap, this will occasionally fail and need replacing.

• Signs of switch failure are commonly: that the water pump fails to cut out even though the tap has been turned off; or there is a notable delay between the tap being turned off and the pump cutting out.

Job 57. Replacing a microswitch.

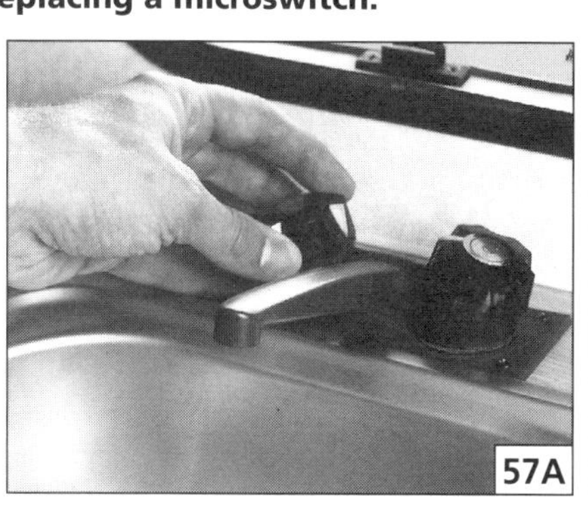
57A

57A. Because so many different types of tap have been fitted to motor caravans over the years, it is impractical to detail the procedures for replacing all of the varieties of microswitch fitted. Probably the commonest type to be found is made by Whale and, in those cases, it makes sense to refer to the detailed instructions that Whale supply with their replacement microswitches.

making it easy! • *Because of the great variety in types of switch available, you should always take with you the old switch when buying or ordering a replacement.*

• *Also, quote the make, model and year of your motor caravan to help in narrowing down the possibilities - take with you the appropriate Motor Caravan Data-Base information from the front of this book.*

Although the following is based mainly on Whale-type switches (the most common), there is much that is common to the majority of non-Whale switches, as detailed below.

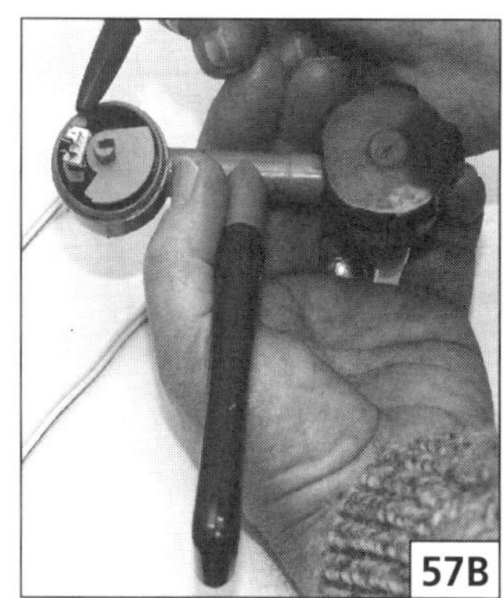
57B

57B. After disconnecting the auxiliary 12 volt battery, carefully remove the control cap on the top of the tap to gain access to the microswitch assembly. Disconnect the microswitch wires from beneath the tap mounting and remove the microswitch.

After fitting the new microswitch and reconnecting the wires, the tap control cap can be refitted and the motor caravan battery can be reconnected.

☐ **Job 58. Clean folding wash basin.**

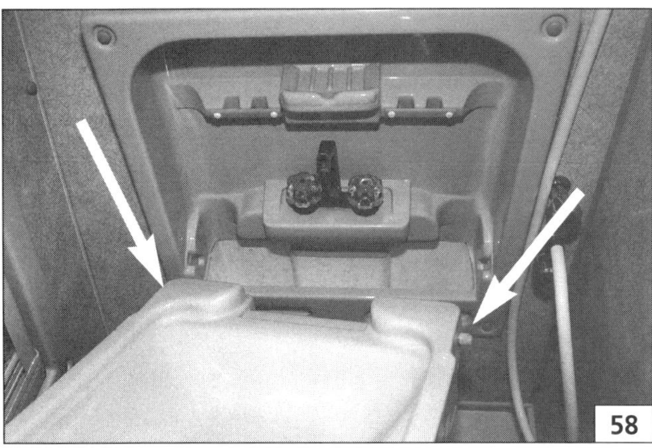

58. Every now and again, the folding wash basin (when fitted) should be removed and the water exit, at the rear of the wash basin, cleaned out. With the basin tilted to about 45 degrees, the two retaining pegs (arrowed) are simply pulled up and out of their slots in the housing. The drain outlet at the back of the unit can now be reached.

☐ **Job 59. Check body/chassis mountings.**

COACH BUILT AND A-CLASS ONLY

59A. There are no hard and fast rules about where the body will be mounted to your vehicle chassis. If the chassis extension (arrowed) is galvanised, you will eventually see some 'white rust' - furry white deposits on the galvanising. Lightly wire-brush off and paint on a coating of waxy underbody seal.

INSIDE INFORMATION: If your exhaust needs replacement work out which bits are 'standard' and try the cost of having a simple extension made up for you by your local exhaust specialist - it might work out cheaper.

59B. Most larger motor caravans have extensions to the original manufacturers' chassis and the motor caravan body is bolted to a mixture of the original mounting points and new ones. From underneath the vehicle, provided that it is reasonably clean, all of the mounting points should be easily visible. Check for tightness with suitable spanners and look out for corrosion, especially on the base vehicle's non-galvanised steel. You are strongly advised to have your motor caravan's body and chassis treated with rust proofing fluid, sprayed into all of the enclosed cavities, and to repeat the treatment every two years at most.

59C. While you're in the area, check the condition of the exhaust system, especially any non-base-vehicle part. An exhaust extension may have to be specially ordered from your motor caravan dealer.

☐ **Job 60. Check body retention.**

DISMOUNTABLES ONLY

The body retainers for dismountables can come loose where they bolt to the dismountable's body work. Tighten them up and if this by itself doesn't do the trick, you may have to carry out more extensive repairs.

INSIDE INFORMATION: If any of the mountings are loose and it isn't obvious how to replace them, have the work carried out by a specialist. In extreme cases, you may have to replace any coach screws with suitable bolts, going right through the body and supporting timberwork and with a very large washer underneath the new nut, so that it doesn't bite into the vehicle's wooden framework.

☐ Job 61. Remove window and body scratches.

There is very little you can do with minor scratches or dings on aluminium panels since the paint covering is rarely thick enough to enable you to polish it out in the same way as you can with scratches on the cab body. At the same time, aluminium is not particularly prone to corrosion and so minor scratches are not very important. However, scratches to fibreglass bodywork and to acrylic windows can be dealt with in accordance with the following information supplied by Auto-Sleepers:

CLEANING FIBREGLASS BODYWORK:

At regular intervals, you should wash the fibreglass bodywork with a recognised detergent sold for use on fibreglass gelcoats.

Should marks remain, use a cleaner with chemical and abrasion agents formulated for use on gelcoats such as Boat Pride Hull Cleaner. This is designed for cleaning large areas of fibreglass surfaces in a fast and economical way. It removes grime, oil, stains, and old polish restoring the surface and colour to its original state.

DISCOLORATION:

Fading or discoloration of the gelcoat is a natural ageing process caused by ultraviolet light.

To overcome this, use a mild abrasive which removes a thin layer of the discoloured surface. This will restore the bodywork to its original colour and surface lustre. Since discoloration develops gradually it should not be necessary to carry out this procedure more than every three years.

Frequent use of abrasive materials can reduce the thickness of the gelcoat, to a potentially harmful extent. Depending on the severity of the discoloration use either Boat Pride Hull Cleaner, or in extreme cases Boat Pride Rubbing Compound.

REMOVING SCRATCHES FROM BODYWORK:

Scratches can be removed from both gelcoat and painted hull surfaces. The method depends upon the depth of the scratch, as care has to be taken to avoid penetrating the paint or gelcoat.

Very fine, hairline scratches can be removed by rubbing across the line of the scratch with rubbing compound. Slightly deeper scratches should be lightly wet sanded first using very fine (1200 grit or finer) abrasive paper. Rubbing compound will then remove the flatting marks created by the abrasive paper.

For deep, gouge-type scratches, where the paint or gelcoat may have been penetrated, you should first seek the advice of your local dealer.

REMOVING SCRATCHES FROM ACRYLIC WINDOWS:

Apart from the chassis cab windows and the luton windows, all remaining windows (on most modern motor caravans) are manufactured in acrylic. Over time these become scratched and their clarity becomes impaired.

Minor scratches can be polished out directly. Some deeper scratches can be removed by wet sanding with a fine grade of abrasive paper (1500 grit for example) first, and then polishing with Boat Pride Acrylic Window Polish.

Some care should be exercised since it may not be possible to remove severe damage without seriously weakening the acrylic. For scratched acrylic windows, Boatpride Acrylic Window Polish removes unwanted scratches and blemishes and leaves a clear, haze free finish.

FACT FILE:
RECOMMENDED MATERIALS:

• Auto-Sleeper recommend Farecla Boatpride Materials for both fibreglass maintenance and for the removal of scratches from acrylic windows.

• The following materials are readily available from boat chandlers or similar outlets, or through your nearest Auto-Sleepers Dealer:

• CLEANING FIBREGLASS BODIES AND ROOFS: Farecla Boatpride Hull Cleaner.

• DISCOLORATION: Farecla Boatpride Rubbing Compound.

• REMOVING SCRATCHES FROM BODYWORK: Farecla Boatpride Rubbing Compound or Farecla Boatpride Acrylic Window Polish.

• REMOVING SCRATCHES FROM ACRYLIC WINDOWS: Farecla Boatpride Acrylic Window Polish.

☐ Job 62. Check windows.

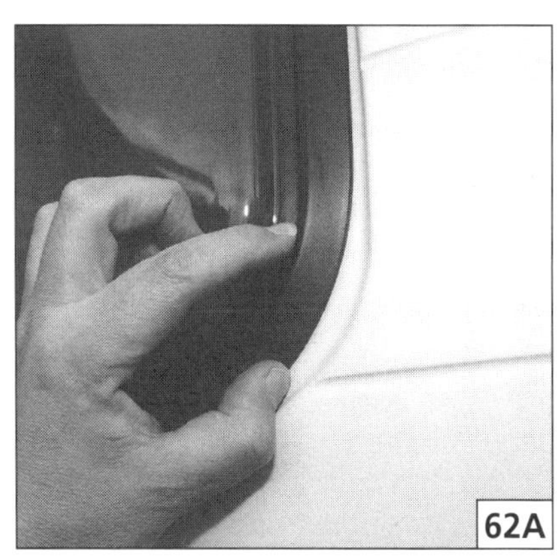

62A

62A. Check the window glazing rubber or sealing for cracks and for general condition. Check for a good weather seal when the window is closed and latched. Perished glazing rubber can usually be changed for new. Check with your motor caravan manufacturer to see if the profile (shape) used on your motor caravan is still available. Otherwise, check with your local motor caravan parts supplier.

62B

62B. Check that the window opens and closes correctly and that the catches hold in all positions. Take a close look at where catches are mounted on the perspex. Cracking often takes place in this area and if it is too bad, the only solution will be to replace the window. Lubricate any hinges or catches where this is appropriate - but DON'T use oil on plastic components. Use silicone lubricant rather than oil so that clothing can not be marked.

62C. Check the fixing of the top hinge rail on top-hung windows and check especially carefully on those windows which can slide on their hinge rail to ensure that they are located correctly and no damage has taken place.

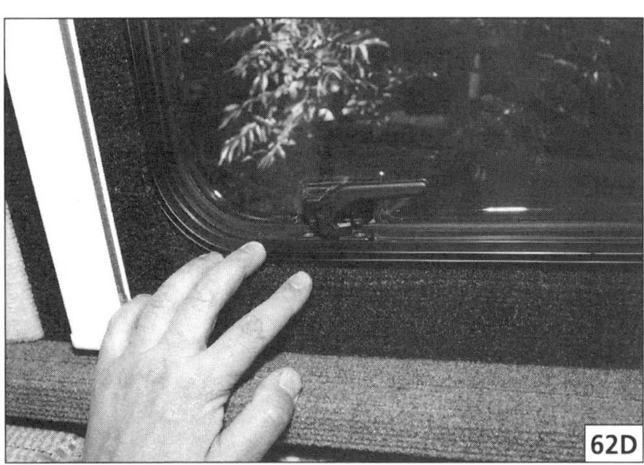

62D. INSIDE INFORMATION: Condensation can often form inside double glazed plastic windows. This is because the acrylic plastic is pervious and allows moisture to pass through it. By the same token, the moisture can be encouraged to pass out of it again and a spell of hot, dry weather usually does the trick. However, things get out of hand, it could be because the acrylic has cracked. You could try using a suitable acrylic adhesive, or windscreen repairer meant for cracked motor vehicle windscreens but if all else fails, the window will have to be replaced.

Job 63. Check/lubricate external doors.

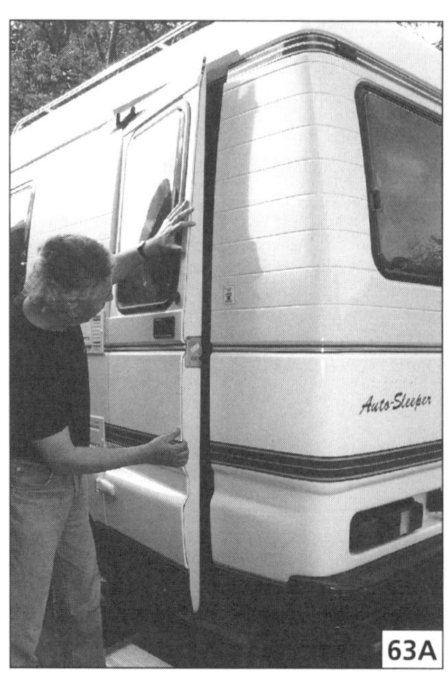

63A. Check that the hinges and catches work properly and that when latched, the door or doors are held securely shut. With the vehicle parked on level ground, check that the doors shut with a fairly even gap all round. Bad misalignment could be worn hinges but, on a coachbuilt motor caravan, it is more likely to be evidence of sagging framework. Consult your dealer if necessary.

63B. Make sure that keys or internal latches lock the doors correctly and that if a device is fitted to hold the door in the open position, that it is aligned with the door and works properly.

63C. As well as lubricating all the door hinges and catches (use silicone lubricant where there is a chance of it getting onto clothing) lubricate the door locks to prevent stiffness or seizure.

63D. Check all door seals for cracking and general condition, just as you did for the window seals. Check that when the door is closed it is weather tight. You could try playing a soft spray from a hose all around the door to see if water is let in.

SAFETY FIRST!

63E. Where a door is fitted with a child-proof lock, check that an appropriate warning notice is fixed adjacent to the door.

Job 64. Check/lubricate locker doors.

External doors often become difficult to open, when all you need is to...

64A. Check that all external locker doors seal correctly and that stays and catches are present and correct.

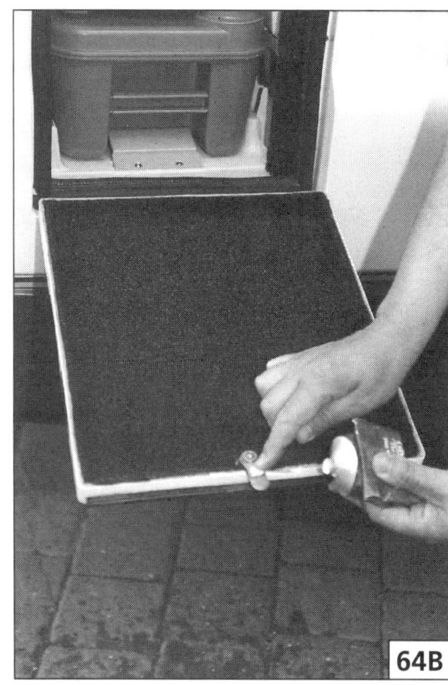

64B. Lubricate the locking mechanism...

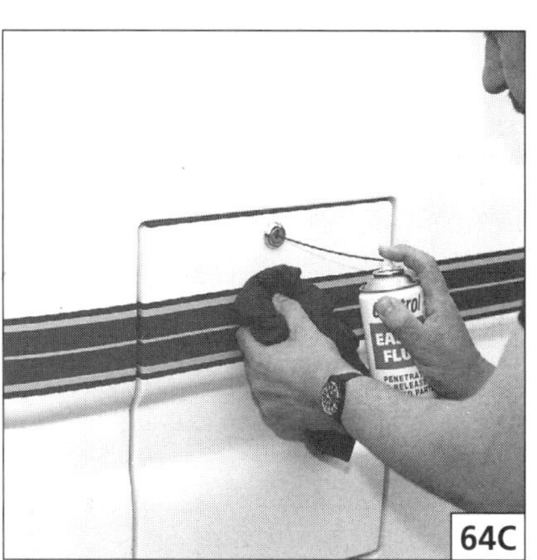

64C. ...and also the lock internals using an aerosol spray can with a nozzle.

64D. Also ensure that an appropriate warning notice is fixed to any external gas locker door.

☐ **Job 65. Check/lubricate filler caps.**

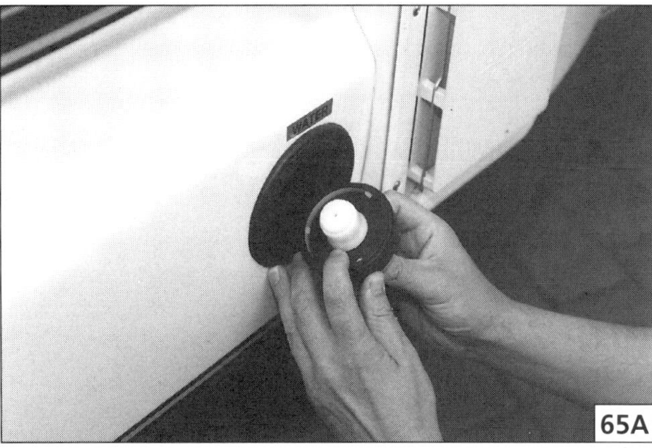

65A. Check that the drinking water filler cap seal is in good condition and lightly lubricate the lock so that it operates freely.

65B. Check that a warning notice is in position alongside the drinking water filler cap so that it is not accidentally confused with the fuel filler cap!

☐ **Job 66. Check elevating roof.**

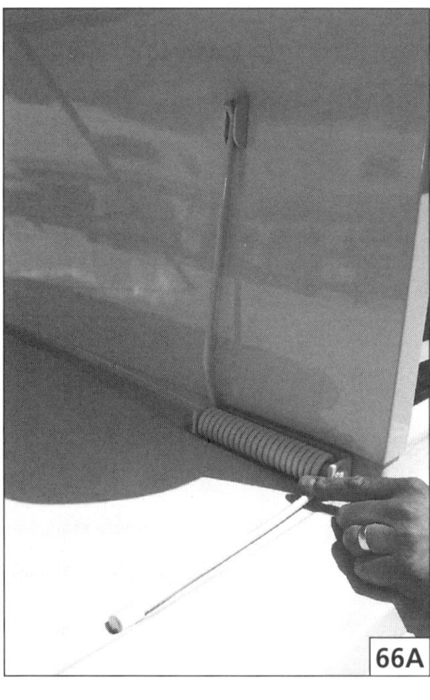

66A. LIFTING MECHANISM: Gas struts or spring struts should be checked for corrosion (particularly on the piston rods of gas struts). Smooth operation when operating roof up and down and to ensure that they support the roof when fully up. Check attachment points of struts to body and roof.

66B. CANVAS SIDE OR END WALLS: Check for satisfactory attachment to body and roof. Check for splits or holes, particularly at fold lines and that all opening flaps or vents are waterproof. Check that the canvas stowed satisfactorily when roof is lowered. (Illustration, courtesy Bilbo Trading Co.)

making it easy!

- *Use a soft spray from a garden hose and check that the canvas side walls are waterproof.*
- *You could use a canvas tent waterproofing agent if the side walls are made of canvas and if the canvas has become porous.*

66C. SOLID SIDE WALL: Check sides and end panels fold up and down correctly, that they seal against each other where appropriate and that retaining mechanisms are satisfactory. Check all hinges for security and freedom from strain.

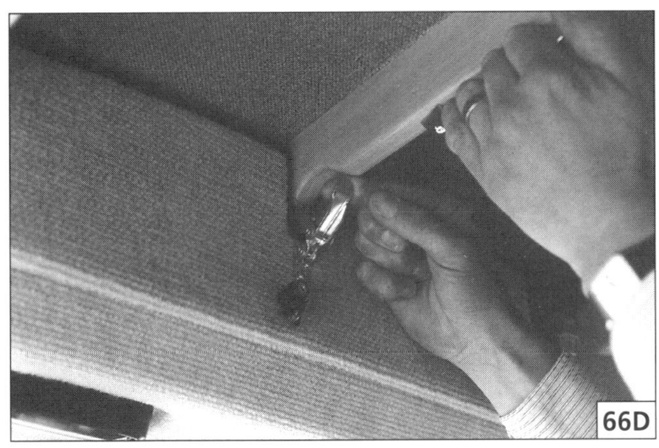

66D. ROOF LOCKING: It is important to ensure that, when the roof is in the travelling position, it is safely and positively locked down.

66E. Any locking retaining mechanism should be carefully examined.

Job 67. Check roof vents.

Check the roof vents for cracking of the acrylic at the mounting points and make sure that they are sealing correctly. Also check that they hold in the lock-down position. Get up onto the outside of the vehicle and check that the roof vent mountings to the vehicle body are properly sealed and replace any cracked or missing seam sealer so that no water can get in.

Job 68. Check roof racks and ladders.

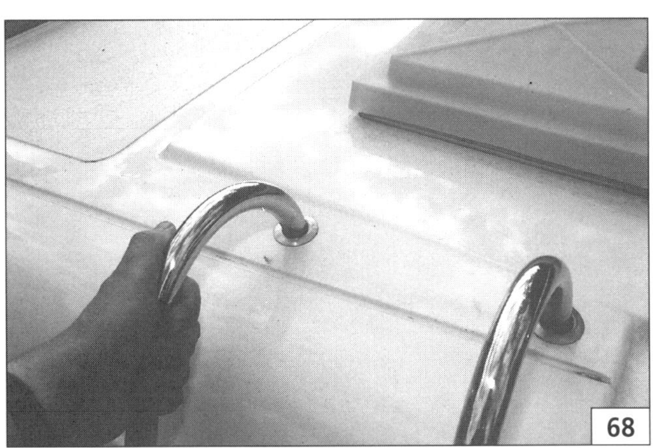

68. Give any roof racks or ladders a good tugging at each mounting point to make sure that none have come loose. Also check the roof for damage in the area of any roof rack that may be fitted. Any damage that could cause a leak should be attended to immediately.

Job 69. Check/clean furniture.

Systematically go around all the items of furniture in the motor caravan and make a note of any repairs that need to be carried out. Cleaning the upholstery in your motor caravan is very much the same as cleaning the upholstery at home, although obviously on a much smaller scale. One problem that you might encounter is that the seat covers aren't always detachable. In this case there are a number of upholstery cleaners similar to those available for cleaning the interior of cars, suitable for use with the upholstery *in situ*.

If the upholstery is covered with cotton print outers, then it is often necessary to have these dry cleaned. If in doubt, consult your dealer or local dry cleaner.

As for the carpets in motor caravans, any proprietary carpet cleaner should do the job, along with regular attention from a vacuum cleaner. Some modern motor caravans are now fitted with removable carpets allowing them to be taken out of the motor caravan and given a more thorough cleaning.

For light marks and smears on general surfaces, the walls or the roof lining use a damp cloth and a mild general purpose cleaner. For plastic or aluminium surfaces make sure that only a very small amount of non-abrasive cleaner is used with tepid water and a soft cloth.

Job 70. Lubricate hinges and catches.

70A. While cleaning the furniture, apply a small amount of silicone lubricant to the hinges and on any doors, drawers and lockers and check that all are working satisfactorily catches. (But DON'T use oil on plastic!). Nylon catches do break and replacements are generally available.

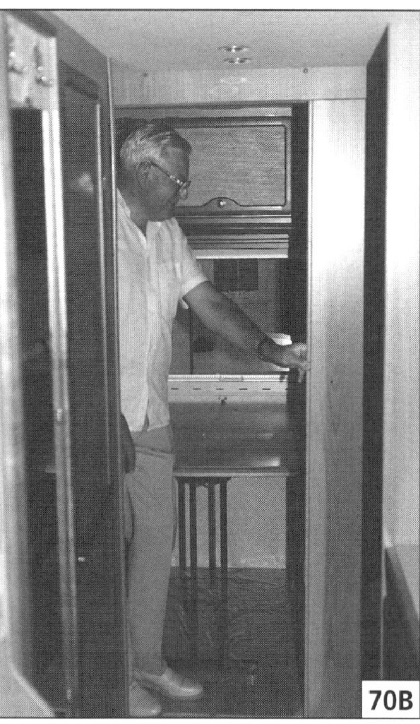

70B. Where sliding doors are fitted, make sure that runners are free from dust and grit and, once again, lubricate with silicone.

70C. IMPORTANT NOTE: You should also check that all locking cupboard latches do in fact lock and hold in position so that doors cannot swing about while the vehicle is in motion. Replace any that fail to do their job properly.

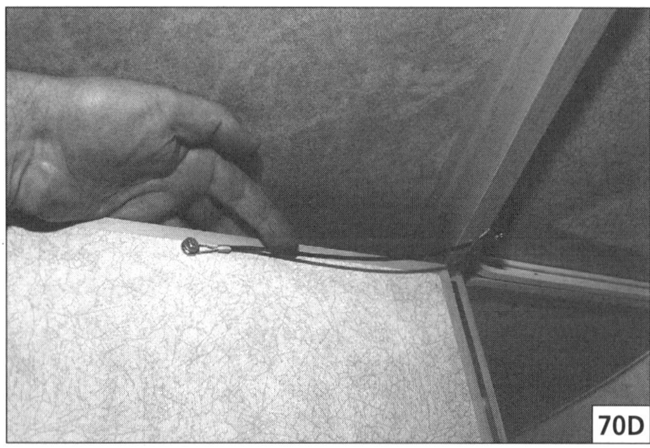

70D. Also check that any cords or rigid stays have not broken or come adrift and, once again, renew wherever necessary.

☐ Job 71. Check internal doors.

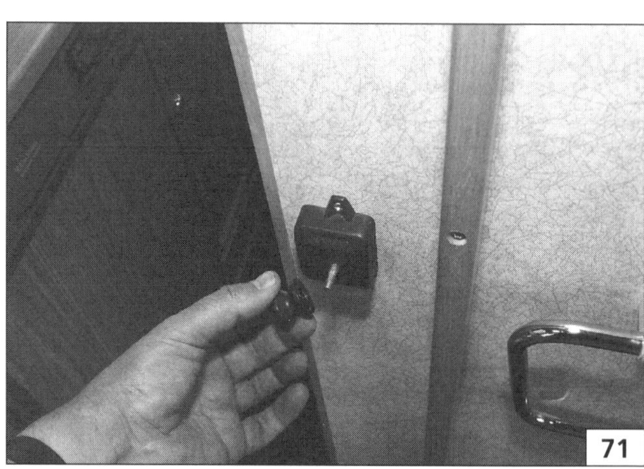

SAFETY FIRST!

• 71. Check that any closing mechanism fitted to hold a door in the closed position can be operated from both sides to open the door in an emergency, in those cases where the door can be accessed from both sides.

• Obviously, this requirement applies particularly to w.c. doors. We all know the old ditty, "Oh dear, what can the matter be ..." Fortunately, this knob just screws back on, but whether Gran. would work that out before next Saturday is anybody's guess!

☐ Job 72. Check 'advice' notices.

Check that all of the necessary advice and safety notices are in place on your vehicle. As a short-term measure, you could photocopy any of the relevant notices shown in this book and Blu-tack them in place on an internal door (DON'T use sticky tape - it will probably peel any finish off your attractive fitted surfaces!) But the 'proper' versions of these notices can be obtained from any of the reputable motor caravan manufacturers or converters.

☐ Job 73. Check fluid couplings.

Check that the appropriate markings are used - blue for fresh water, grey for waste water. Ensure that a sealed-off cover is supplied for each coupling. Also check that all of the filler positions are correctly designated 'petrol', 'diesel' or 'water' as appropriate.

PART VI: PREPARING FOR STORAGE AT END OF SEASON

These are jobs that need to be carried out at the end of the season or, in some cases, in order to prepare the motor caravan for winter storage or winter use. In a number of cases, these are jobs that you will need to carry out once a year, before the onset of winter, whether you use the caravan all-year round or not, and whether the motor caravan is kept in a winter climate or not.

☐ Job 74. Check insurance policy!

Take a look at your insurance policy to make sure that your vehicle is covered while off the road, especially if stored away from your home. Also make sure you don't leave anything in the vehicle that might not be covered by your policy.

☐ Job 75. Prepare storage site.

75

75. INSIDE INFORMATION: Do not store your motor caravan under trees. Not only is there the added risk of storm damage, the resin from some types of tree can cause permanent damage to paintwork.

There are a number of options for storing your motor caravan over the winter:

Keep it at home on your driveway. This is a common enough solution and as long as your driveway is wide enough, you should have no problem. However, before you do this, check with your local council (and in your house deeds) to see if they allow motor caravans to be stored on driveways. Some require that you apply for permission first.

Store it at a local site or farm. Often larger sites and farms will put areas aside for storing caravans and this is certainly one way of keeping your van well out of the way. However, there are problems. Caravans and motor caravans are often stored close together which would be disastrous in cases of fire. Security is extremely difficult. It can also be rather expensive!

Specialist storage facilities. Although relatively uncommon, there is a growing number of specialist motor caravan storage facilities, some of which even offer undercover storage. These are certainly safer than some farms but will undoubtedly cost more and places may be restricted.

To find your local farm, site or specialist motor caravan storage, consult Yellow Pages or give either The Caravan Club or the Motor Caravanners' Club a call. Alternatively, ask at your local motor caravan dealership.

☐ Job 76. Check security.

Ensure that your motor caravan is stored as securely as it can be.

making it easy!

- *If yours is a petrol engine, try swapping plug leads numbers one and three or two and three (check that it won't run like this - some will, albeit badly!).*
- *Be sure to make a note and keep it safe so that you know what you have done!*

76

76. You could try fitting wheel clamps or caravan-type 'winter wheels', which means removing one or both of the front wheels (provided they are not held by the handbrake) and fitting wheel supports in their stead.

INSIDE INFORMATION: If your motor caravan is fitted with an alarm, don't turn it on unless you are prepared to go and run the motor caravan and/or recharge the battery every couple of weeks. Otherwise, the battery will simply run flat and the alarm, if it has its own internal back-up battery, will go off as soon as the vehicle's battery has run down - and this is sure to be at 3 o'clock in the morning, which won't make you very popular!

☐ Job 77. Drain fresh water system.

Just as in your home, if water is allowed to freeze in the pipes of a motor caravan, the pipes can crack and, when the frozen water thaws, there'll be a flood in your motor caravan. Therefore it's necessary to drain the water system:

Open the drain tap at the base of the water tank and open all the taps with the power supply to the pump turned off. This should allow any water in the system to drain out. Make sure there are no sagging pipe runs in which water may have gathered.

Before finally draining the fresh water storage tank, fill up with an appropriate dilution of Milton's fluid (see the directions on the bottle), flush all of the pipes and all of the taps with the diluted fluid and this will help to keep the system sweet while the motor caravan is in storage.

77A. In addition, don't forget the water heater tank. The most common of these is a Carver Cascade type of water heater. Draining this is a simple matter of locating the drainage screw next to the vent...

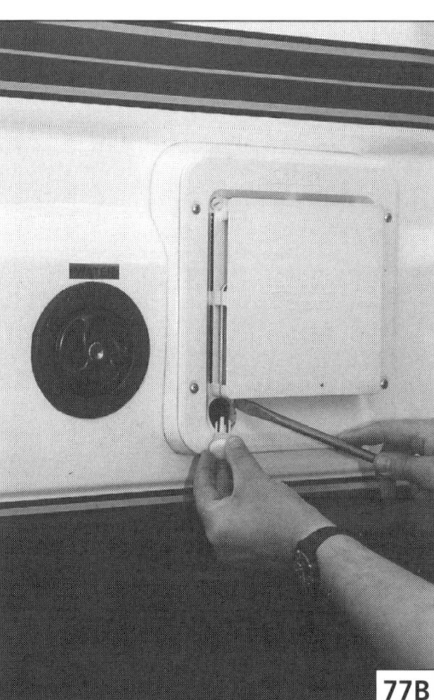

77B. ...removing it and allowing the tank to drain.

77C. This might well take as long as an hour but will be considerably speeded up if you remove the air screw shown here, and the taps in the motor caravan. Once it's finished draining, replace the plugs.

Ensure that you cover up all the water inlets and taps to stop insects crawling in and blocking up the pipes.

☐ Job 78. Remove/drain water filter.

Because the water filter has been busy removing all sorts of impurities from the water, it could be a good breeding ground for bugs over the winter months. Take it out, throw it away at the end of the summer and fit a new one at the start of next season. (See **Job 13**.)

☐ Job 79. Drain waste water system.

Connect the drain hose to the waste water tap and train out to a suitable foul drain.

> *making it easy!* *Simple ways to keep smells at bay:*
>
> *• Leave the plugs in the kitchen sink, washroom basin and shower tray (see **Job 14**) to stop any smell from water left in the pipes - or creepy crawlies! - from getting into the living accommodation.*
>
> *• Place a small quantity of water with w.c. fluid into the waste water tank to keep it sweet.*
>
> *• However, if you want to ensure that frost can't cause damage to the tank (a very small amount of water certainly won't allow ice to cause damage to the tank itself) you could try topping up the waste water tank with a charge of chemical toilet fluid in it, then draining it away so that the residue keeps the insides of the tank as fresh as possible.*

Job 80. Service w.c. and shower

One important area that's often forgotten when servicing a motor caravan is cleaning the cassette toilet. In fact, little work is required, as the toilet's own chemicals help to keep it clean when the motor caravan is in use.

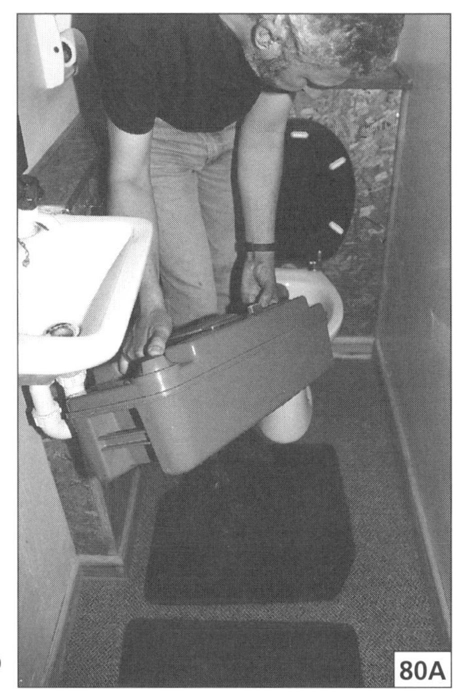

80A. Even so, it's not a bad idea to rinse out the toilet and waste tank at home, washing it through with warm water and Milton 2 or Chempro SDP sterilising fluid. DO NOT use strong household cleaners or anything containing bleach, chlorine, solvents or acid, as these might well damage the toilet. A mild soap solution can be used to clean the toilet bowl, seat and cover, as well as the outside of the toilet and cassette.

80B. On some models, the toilet roll holder fits into the main w.c. housing, so that it doesn't get wet when you take a shower. The toilet roll holder fits into the housing with a waterproof rubber seal. Lift out the housing and check that the seal is okay.

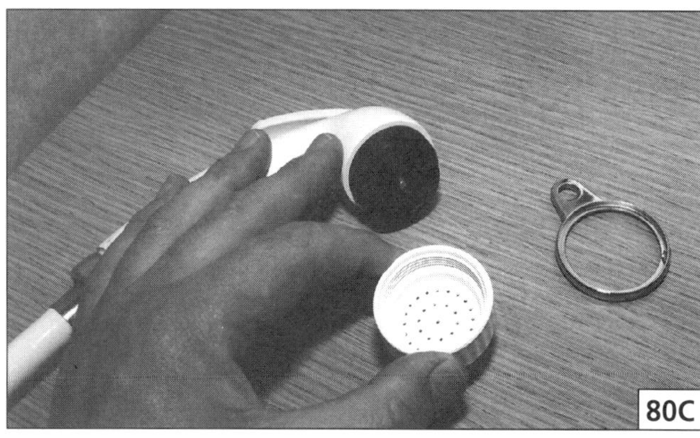

80C. Don't forget that shower heads invariably clog up over a period of time. Unscrew the head and clean out the head. A kettle scale cleaner may be needed, but a pin and patience could also do the trick!

Job 81. 'Winterise' the w.c..

Don't forget that, in order to prepare the toilet for winter frosts, it also needs draining and that includes both the waste and water feed tanks.

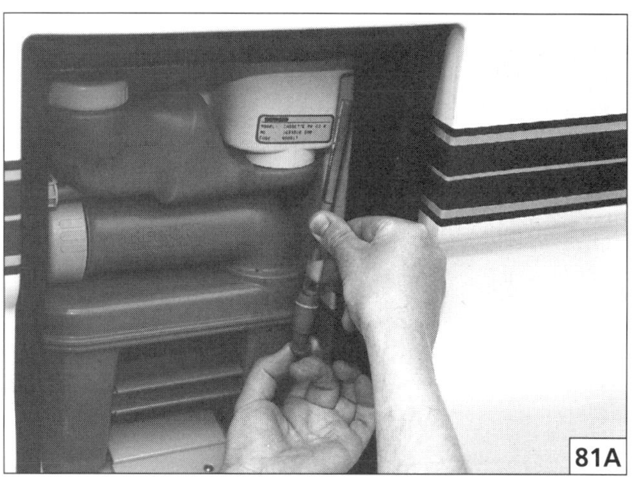

81A. Empty a cassette toilet's fresh water tank using the drain tube. Pull the drain tube down and outward through the door opening...

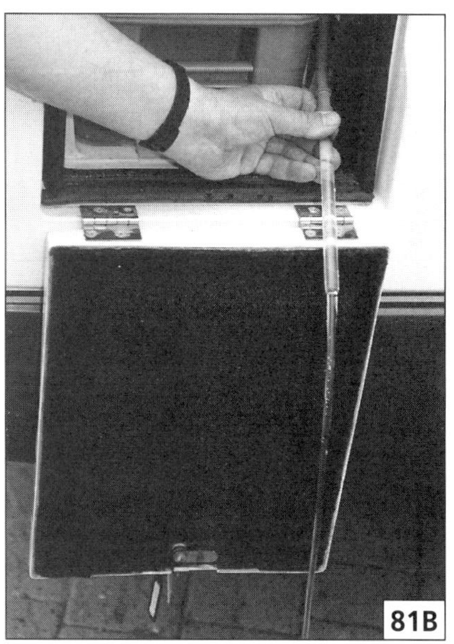

81B. ...which allows water to drain from the tank. In the case of manual flush models, turn the flush knob a few times to drain the pump assembly.

81C. Empty the water fill funnel by swivelling the filler away from the tank. Remove the small water cap at the bottom of the filler which allows water to drain from the filler.

IMPORTANT NOTE: When you put the caps back on leave them loose, which helps to allow a little air to circulate and thus to keep the unit dry.

Be sure to service the w.c. unit to keep the seals in good condition. See **Job 48**.

☐ Job 82. Clean out refrigerator.

82A. You'll no doubt clean the fridge's storage area as part of your domestic chores, but it should certainly be done before a motor caravan is to be stored over a long period and before it is used again after being brought out from storage. It may also be necessary if there are spillages from food and drink stored in the fridge. Generally all that is needed to clean the fridge out is the use of plain warm water with a teaspoon of bicarbonate of soda in a bowl and a clean cloth.

82B. If you're not planning to use the motor caravan for some time always make sure that you leave the fridge door in the storage position. This means positioning the retaining pin into the inner of the two holes in the top of the door. In this way air is allowed to circulate through the fridge preventing odours forming and stopping any condensation turning to mould.

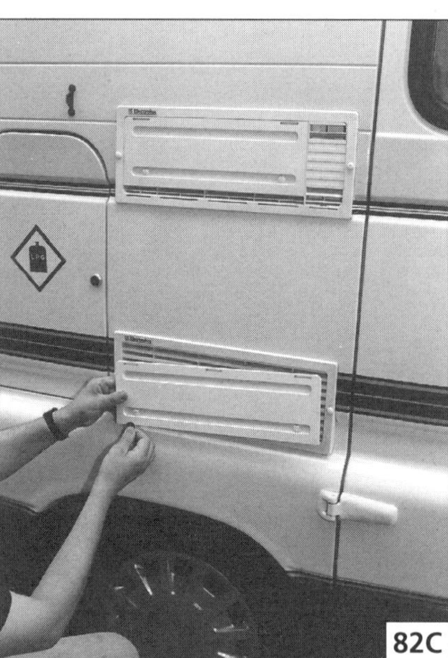

82C. 'WINTERISING' THE FRIDGE: On the other hand, if you intend using the motor caravan through the coldest weather, you can place covers over the refrigerator inlet and outlet vents to stop strong wind from gusting through.

☐ Job 83. Prepare curtains, blinds and screens.

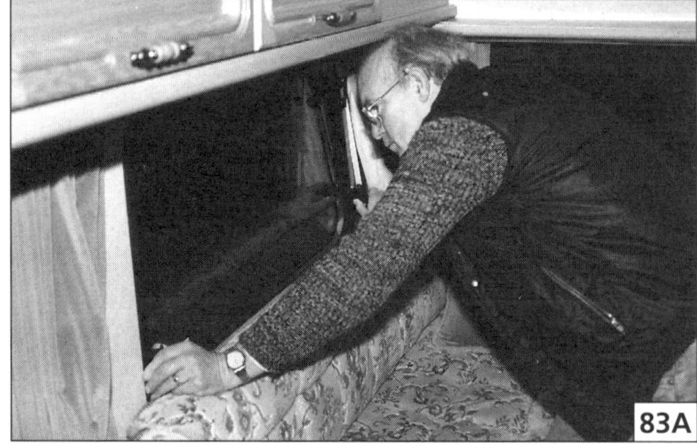

83A. Don't leave the flyscreens and blinds in their down position. This can actually put a strain on the roller mechanism and when you go back in the spring to release them, the result might be that they won't roll back into their cassette.

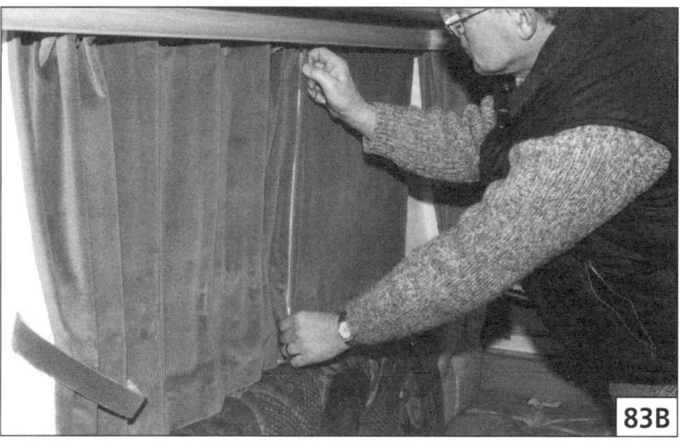

83B. Draw the curtains to prevent creasing and vertical 'stripes' of fading and reduce the risk of mould forming.

Job 84. Remove/clean upholstery.

If you've got the space to store it, remove the upholstery and cushions and store them in the house, somewhere dry.

Now would be a good time to clean off any stains from the upholstery, using a proprietary brand of upholstery cleaner. Make sure that the fabric is thoroughly dry before storing it.

INSIDE INFORMATION: Putting your motor caravan's upholstery in the loft is probably a bad idea. Not only will it be quite damp, you will also run the risk of providing a friendly home for visiting mice, who will probably go on to make a meal of your seating arrangements!

Job 85. Prepare interior.

Leave a simple dehumidifier in the motor caravan to take out any moisture in the air. If you are fortunate enough to own an electric dehumidifier, let it run inside your motor caravan for, say, a day a week to keep damp at bay. (You can often hire locally, for the occasional weekend 'drying out' session.) Also, remember to remove any valuables from the motor caravan and store them somewhere secure.

Job 86. Maintain auxiliary battery.

Remove the motor caravan's battery (or batteries, in most cases) so that they are not left to discharge. Over the winter be sure to regularly charge the batteries to keep them up to peak condition. Do not store directly placed on a concrete floor because - believe it or not! - this will cause a battery to discharge itself.

making it easy! • *Leaded fuel does not go off anywhere near as quickly and so if you are not sure whether you will be using the generator during the winter months or not, make sure that your last fill-up was with leaded petrol.*
• *Leaded petrol will not cause harm to a generator engine designed to run on unleaded. (It damages the catalytic converter on cars, not the 'unleaded' engine itself.)*

Job 87. Store gas cylinders.

87. Remove the motor caravan's gas cylinders and store them somewhere safe: ALWAYS upright; never on their sides; with the regulator thread cover in place. Store out of doors, well away from heat or anything flammable. While you're at it, cover the gas pipes and regulators to stop any insects getting in.

For identification Butane is supplied in BLUE cylinders and Propane in RED cylinders. 87

Job 88. Dry and store awning.

Before putting the awning away for the winter, make sure that - if it is of the canvas type - that the fabric is completely dry. Open it out to dry in your garage if necessary. Store it somewhere warm and dry, perhaps with the upholstery which you may have removed earlier.

Job 89. Drain generator fuel.

Unleaded fuel 'goes off' as the volatile elements evaporate away over the winter months. This will cause the carburettor to gum up and the petrol to go stale, preventing you from restarting the generator. The best bet is to drain the petrol out of the generator (work out of doors and keep well away from anything flammable or that creates sparks), tipping the fuel into your motor caravan's (if it has a petrol engine) or your car's petrol tank.

Job 90. Maintain air conditioning.

INSIDE INFORMATION: Air conditioning gas contains a lubricant. Without it, the 'innards' of an air conditioning unit will seize. Be sure to run your air conditioning unit, preferably once a week, even if just for a few minutes, throughout the winter storage period.

Job 91. Check seams and seals.

"Leaking seams" are two words that send fear through the heart of any motor caravanner! Nothing makes a motor caravan deteriorate faster than moisture getting in through the outer panels and, because of the unavoidable flexing of a motor caravan's body as it is being used, leaks may be inevitable sooner or later.

There is, however, no reason why you shouldn't be able to keep your motor caravan well sealed and cared for, through regular maintenance. It is therefore important to keep a regular check on external body seams.

When choosing which sealant to use, go for the non-hardening, silicone, exterior type or better still a motor caravan body mastic, such as that made by Bulldog. Other types dry out, crack and are a waste of time, although they are much less expensive.

There are a number of different makes on the market and your local motor caravan accessory shop should be able to supply you with a product specifically for caravans and motor caravans. Whichever type you try, do be careful to pick a colour that matches the motor caravan's body colour.

IMPORTANT NOTE: Make sure you use a sealant recommended by the motor caravan manufacturer. Not all chemical compositions suit all construction types.

Check all the seams on a coachbuilt motor caravan minutely for cracking and replace sealant where necessary. If the sealant along the exterior seams of a motor caravan appears to be cracked or flaking, it's essential to reseal those seams. Although this is a pretty simple job, don't be put off if the first few attempts turn out untidy, because the sealant is messy to use and has a tendency to be on the sticky side. Just have plenty of rags available to clean it off and try again.

i INSIDE INFORMATION: Before starting, find out which solvent will be needed to clean off the sealer. Try white spirit first, then methylated spirit. If cellulose thinners is needed, use a different sealer, because there is the risk that you will wipe paint off your motor caravan as you wipe off the excess sealer. i

IMPORTANT NOTE: This is a job that should only be carried out under cover and preferably after several fine days to dry things out. The last thing that you want is for rain to get in as you're cleaning the old sealant out of the seam. If you find moisture trapped in the seam, dry it out thoroughly with a hair dryer on a cool setting before starting work. DON'T use the hairdryer too hot or dwell too long in one place because you could blister the paint.

91A. Scrape out the old sealant that has become loose, taking care not to scratch the motor caravan's paintwork.

91B. Clean off the surface immediately around the seam with white spirit and a clean cloth.

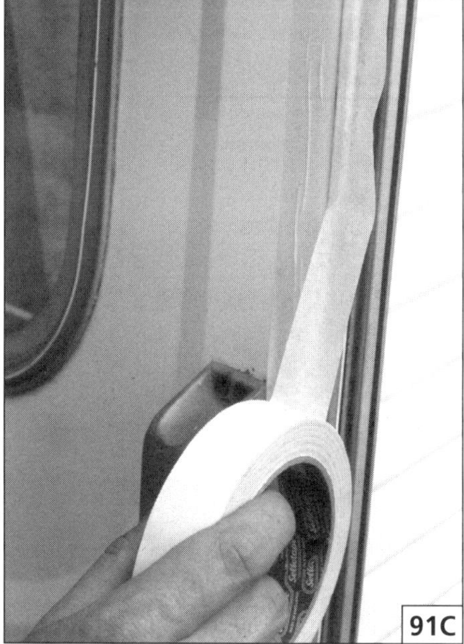

91C. Place masking tape down either side of the seam to stop any excess sealant sticking to the motor caravan.

91D. Using the correct sort of sealing gun, carefully and smoothly apply the sealant down the length of the seam.

Familiarise yourself with the working of the gun before you start. As soon as you finish a 'run', take the pressure off by pressing the release lever on the gun, otherwise sealer will continue to emerge for some time. Do no more than about a meter (one yard) at a time.

making it easy! • *When you cut the end off the applicator nozzle, cut off as little as you can reasonably get away with.*
• The further down the tapering nozzle you cut, the larger the hole - and the more that sealer will go everywhere!
• A small hole will also make it easier to inject the sealer deeper into the seam.

91E. Using a spatula, carefully smooth down the sealant. To help give a smooth finish it can help to wet the sealant by dipping the end of the spatula in water.

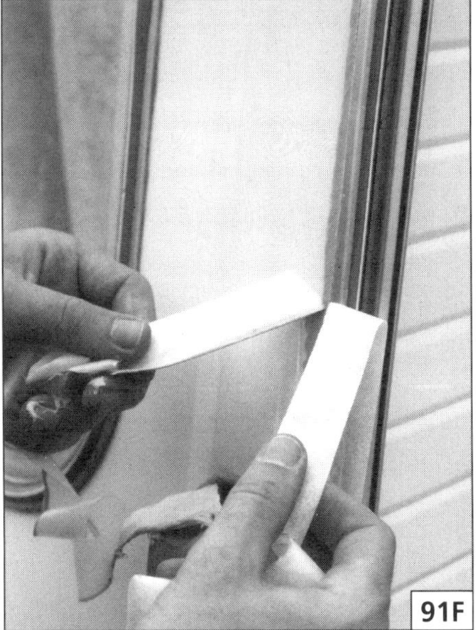

91F. Remove the masking tape and clean off any excess sealant with white spirit. Although this type of sealant will not harden completely, it should be left for a while to set slightly.

☐ **Job 92. Check body/cab joints.**

92A. This is really an extension of the previous Job except to say that body to cab joints are among the most vulnerable of all and almost never have the kind of exterior seals shown in the previous Job. As an example of how the better manufacturers treat sealing in this area with the utmost seriousness, here is an Auto-Sleepers fitter applying sealer to a new vehicle in the factory.

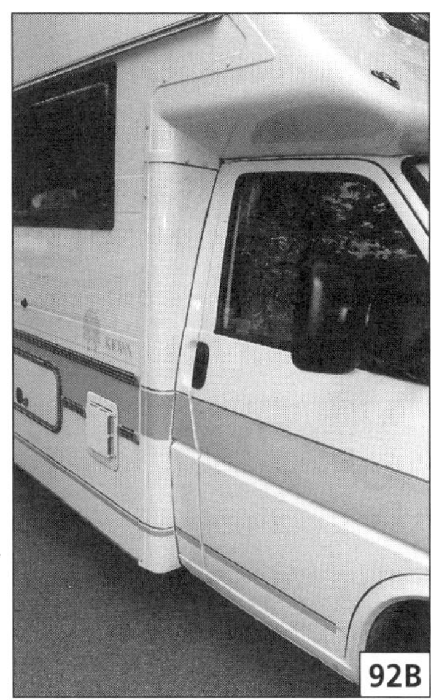

92B If you find any minute cracks in the sealant between body and cab, scrape out all of the old sealant and replace with new. Use masking tape along both sides of the joint so that you don't accidentally damage the paintwork.

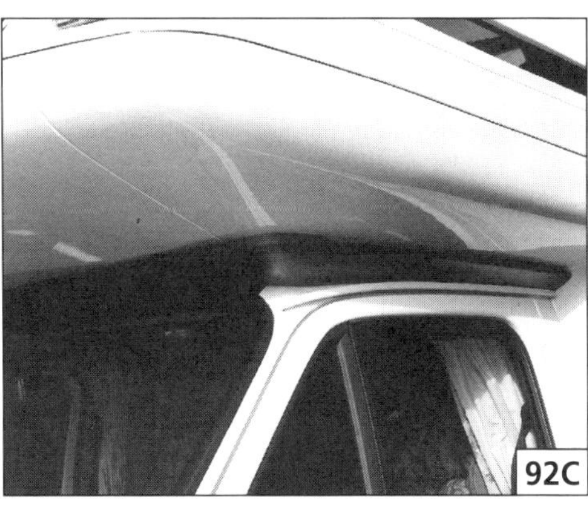

92C. Where a rubber membrane is used between body and cab, there is usually no need to use sealer unless the rubber has become cracked or brittle but if in doubt, consult your local motor caravan specialist.

☐ Job 93. Check top-box mountings and seals.

A top-box mounting point is another place where water will tend to get in. Look inside the vehicle to see if there is any evidence of water staining in the area in which the top box is mounted. See below.

93. INSIDE INFORMATION: The best way of mounting top boxes on mounting blocks. IDL Mastic tape should be used between the mounting blocks and the motor caravan body and between the blocks and the top box itself. It would pay dividends every now and again to unscrew your top box, check that your mounting points are properly sealed with mastic (clean off the old mastic and renew it) and consider fitting the correct type of mounting blocks to give some clearance between the bottom of the top box and the motor caravan roof. (Illustration, courtesy Swift)

1

VIEW FROM INSIDE OF TOP BOX SHOWING SCREW POSITIONS

2

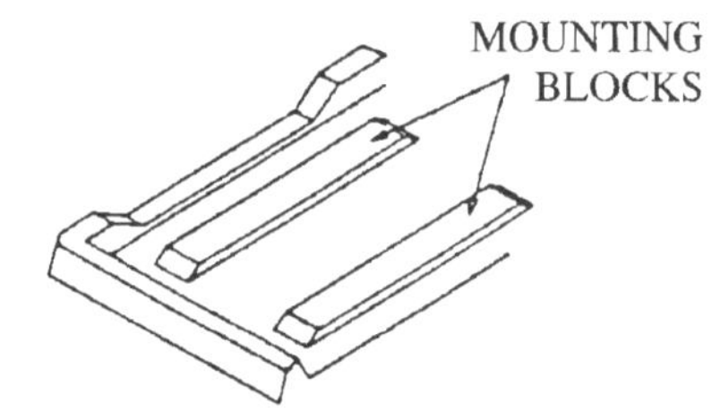

POSITION TOP BOX SUPPORT RIBS CENTRALLY ON RAISED MOUNTING BLOCKS

3

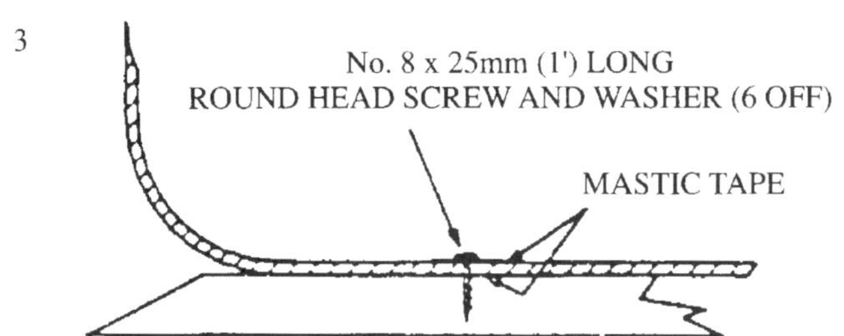

IDL MASTIC TAPE MUST BE ROLLED DOWN BETWEEN MOUNTING BLOCKS & TOP BOX, AND WASHERS & TOP BOX

CROSS-SECTION THROUGH TOP BOX/MOUNTING BLOCK SHOWING APPROVED METHOD OF FIXING

93

☐ Job 94. Clean bodywork.

94

94. Mould may form on the paintwork over the winter months. You can deter it by making sure that the motor caravan starts the winter clean, using a car wash/wax to give extra protection. If you're feeling extra enthusiastic, you can go over the whole motor caravan with car wax polish. Don't leave it on unpolished because it's unlikely ever to come off again if you do so!

☐ Job 95. Lubricate cycle rack.

So that your cycle rack's joints don't seize up over the winter months, make sure that all the pivot points are well lubricated.

☐ Job 96. Maintain tyres.

96

96. Most very low-mileage motor caravans' tyres need to be replaced well before their treads are worn out. This is because a combination of UV (from sunlight) and ozone (from the air) attacks rubber and causes it to disintegrate. Covering the tyres up only provides a partial solution. You could try spraying on one of the several brands of tyre rubber preservers - visit your local auto accessory store - using it on both sides of all the tyres to see if it helps.

Don't leave your motor caravan standing in one place. Make sure that you rotate the wheels periodically to keep the wheel bearings lubricated and prevent the tyres from becoming misshapen, otherwise, come next Spring, you'll be driving a motor caravan with 'square' tyres!

CHAPTER 6
SERVICING THE BASE VEHICLE

Every motor caravan owner wants his vehicle to run reliably and to last as long as possible in good health. And we believe a good few of you are also keen to keep your garage bills to a minimum. That's why we've devised this home-

maintenance plan that will allow you to take the burden off garage bills, and keep a regular eye on the essential aspects of your motor caravan's underbonnet to make sure that nothing goes wrong.

With the following information you can keep on top of vital fluids, drive belts, lighting and wipers, and identify whether your brakes are due for specialist attention by the professionals. We don't detail anything that's complicated or requires special equipment, so you can feel confident to carry out EVERY task we cover, or just the ones you fancy. It's entirely up to you!

Don't forget that many adjustments and component replacements are nonetheless included in service schedules, so they MUST NOT be forgotten. If you feel you're a competent enough DIYer to take on ALL aspects of maintenance, then we recommend you use this manual in conjunction with our **Absolute Beginners, Diesel Car Engines** and **Auto Electrics** Service Guides. With these you'll be fully equipped to tackle virtually any servicing aspect of your motor caravan! If you're intent on keeping DIYing simple, though, make sure you get the remainder of the servicing jobs attended to whenever necessary by a reputable garage or mechanic. Please don't ever skimp on any aspect of maintenance!

IMPORTANT NOTE: Before you start, it's imperative that you get hold of the specific service schedule for your motor caravan, and that you use this as the definitive guide to the jobs that need doing, and to their time or mileage intervals. In *Appendix 3, Service Schedule* you'll see our own time/mileage interval recommendations for the Jobs we tackle in this chapter. These are a good guide to typical requirements, but they don't take priority over your vehicle manufacturer's specific schedule.

How To Use This Chapter

The information in this chapter is of a generic nature, as this isn't a book about any one particular motor caravan, but the most popular chassis used for them. The principle of everything we discuss here is much the same from one vehicle to another though, and by selecting the most popular underbonnet configurations and components as examples, we've covered the vast majority of eventualities.

The servicing Jobs we cover are grouped into ENGINE BAY, AROUND THE VEHICLE, and UNDER THE VEHICLE categories for convenience.

ENGINE BAY

SAFETY FIRST!

Some servicing jobs in the engine bay involve opening the fuel system. Naturally this is very dangerous if there is a source of potential sparking present. Such a source is the vehicle's electrical systems, which should be disconnected before working on the fuel system. As well as the risk from volatile fuel, there is also a risk of accidentally short circuiting electrical sources. For these reasons it is best to disconnect the vehicle battery before commencing work.

FACT FILE: COMPUTER PROTECTION

Many modern vehicles depend on a constant power supply from the battery and you can find yourself in all sorts of trouble if you disconnect the battery on those vehicles. You might find that the vehicle alarm will go off. You could find that the engine management system, if fitted, forgets all it has ever 'learned' and the vehicle will feel different to drive until it has reprogrammed itself. Or you could find that your radio refuses to operate again, unless you key in the correct code.

So, you must ensure that the vehicle has a constant power supply even though the battery is removed. To do so, you will need a separate 12-volt battery supply. You could put a self-tapping screw into the positive lead near the battery terminal before disconnecting it, and put a positive connection to your other battery via this screw. But you would have to be EXTREMELY CAREFUL to wrap insulation tape round the connection so that no short is caused. The negative terminal on the other battery will also have to be connected to the vehicle's bodywork.

Fluid Levels

☐ Job 1. Check/top-up engine oil.

Before you check the oil level, the engine should be switched off and left standing for a while to ensure that all oil has returned to the sump - first thing in the morning after garaging overnight could be the ideal time.

1A. Obviously, too, the vehicle should be on level ground

when you check the dipstick. The shallow sump of the air-cooled VW Transporter engine makes this vital.

Your handbook should identify the stick's location, but if not, look for a 'ring pull' disappearing into a tube or hole on the side of the engine.

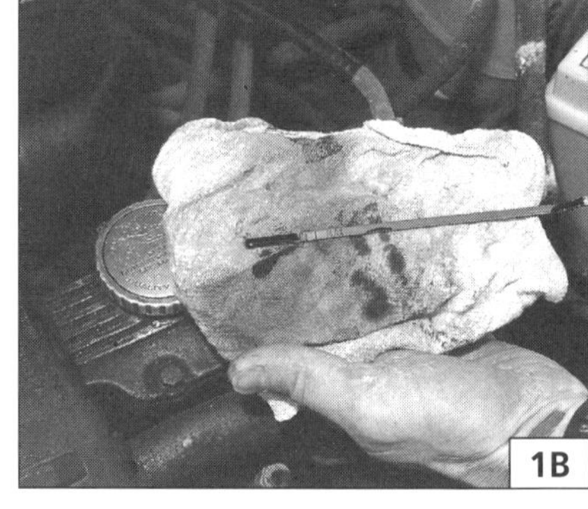

1B. Withdraw the stick and wipe it dry on lint-free cloth. There will usually be MAXIMUM and MINIMUM marks on the stick and some handbooks will quote a specific quantity of oil for the difference between the two (often one litre).

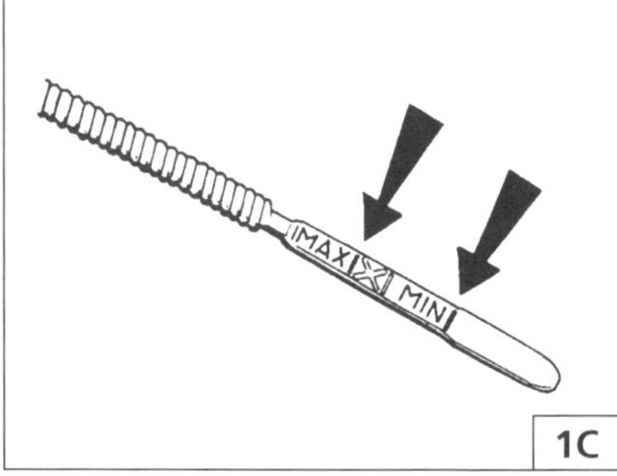

1C. Reinsert the dipstick then withdraw it again - the oil level will be seen on the dipstick and should be on or pretty close to the MAXIMUM (or MAX) mark, not close to the MINIMUM (or MIN) mark. The lower mark is, of course, the danger level. But it could also be unwise to exceed the maximum mark - a shade over won't matter, but substantial over-filling can also lead to over-heating and other problems. (Illustration, courtesy Ford Europe Limited).

INSIDE INFORMATION: If your dipstick has to snake along a curved tube, and especially if the oil is fresh and clear, you might have difficulty in seeing the oil level. Dip, wipe and re-dip several times, turning the stick so that it goes into the tube from different angles, if possible - sometimes oil is wiped on or off the dipstick as it is withdrawn and replaced, but only on one side. If it's the side with the markings on, put the stick in the other way round.

1D. If you do need to top up, do so a little at a time, through the oil filler normally found on the valve cover at the top of the engine, or in front of the valve cover. Allow time for the new oil to reach the sump before you re-check the level, not forgetting to start with a clean dipstick again.

Most oil filler caps unscrew 1/4 turn and lift off, but a few screw all the way in and out. Don't force them down too tight when refitting.

☐ Job 2. Check/top-up coolant.

SAFETY FIRST!

- ***The coolant level should be checked WHEN THE SYSTEM IS COLD.***
- ***If you remove the pressure cap when the engine is hot, the release of pressure can cause the water in the cooling system to boil and spurt several feet in the air, with the risk of severe scalding.***
- ***Take precautions to prevent anti-freeze coming in contact with the skin or eyes.***
- ***If this should happen, rinse immediately with plenty of water.***

Again, this is a check that should be made first thing in the morning, before the engine has been run. There are two reasons for this: (i) Hot coolant expands, so you'll only get a true level reading when it's cold; (ii) Hot coolant (like a boiling kettle) can be extremely dangerous, and removal of the filler cap can release a scalding blast of steam and liquid. See *Safety First!* above, and *Chapter 1, Safety First!*.

2A. NEVER ATTEMPT TO REMOVE THE FILLER CAP WHEN THE ENGINE IS HOT. If, in an emergency, the cap needs to be removed before the engine has completely cooled, wrap a rag around both the cap and your hands, and open the cap in two stages, the first quarter-turn to release any remaining internal pressure.

2B. When cold, the coolant level in an old system should be just below the radiator filler neck...

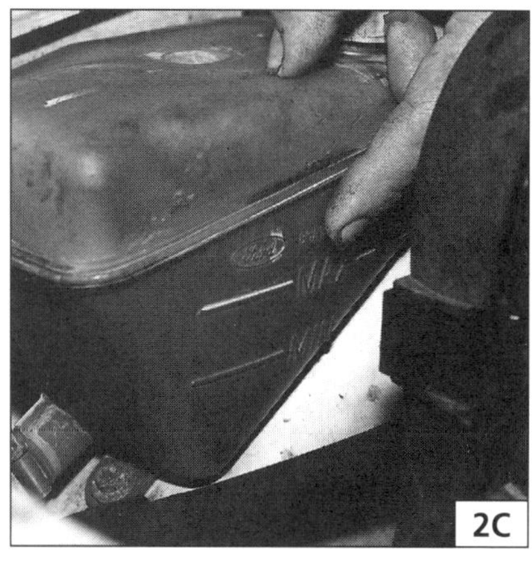

2C. ...or up to the level mark on the expansion tank of a modern system. Some coolant 'expansion' tanks have a raised post inside them, which, when just covered by coolant, indicates the correct level. Where necessary, top up with clean, distilled water mixed with the percentage of anti-freeze (usually 50%) as recommended in your handbook.

☐ Job 3. Check/top-up battery.

SAFETY FIRST!

- ***The gas given off by a battery is highly explosive.***
- ***Never smoke, use a naked flame or allow a spark to occur in the battery compartment.***
- ***Never disconnect the battery (it can cause sparking) with the battery caps removed.***
- ***Batteries contain sulphuric acid. If the acid comes into contact with the skin or eyes, wash immediately with copious amounts of cold water and seek medical advice.***
- ***Do not check the battery levels within half an hour of the battery being charged with a battery charger. The addition of fresh water could then cause the highly acid and corrosive electrolyte to flood out of the battery.***

The battery location in some motor caravans may not be obvious, and there will, in most cases, be more than one battery, so if there is any problem, refer to your owner handbook and to *Chapter 5, Servicing the Living Accommodation*.

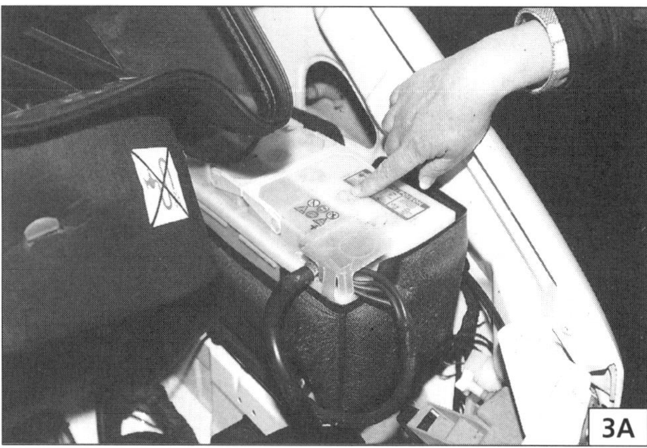

3A. Some vehicles are fitted with sealed batteries and these can't be topped up.

Where the battery is provided with screw caps to the individual cells, as on this Mercedes Sprinter, or obviously removable strips which plug into or over a number of cells at a time, it is obviously intended that its electrolyte content should be topped up as and when required.

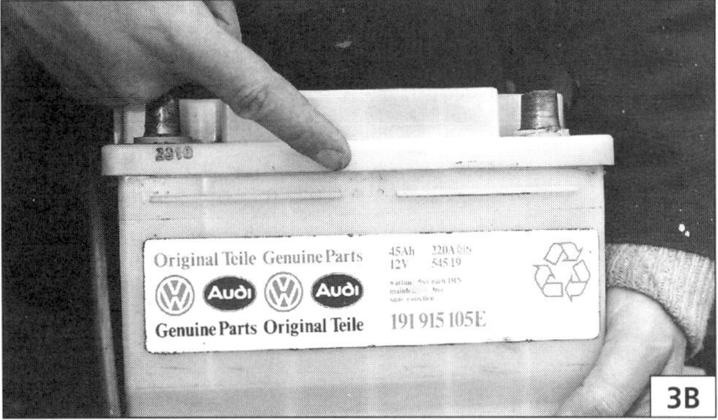

3B. If the battery case is translucent, look for a level mark on its side, otherwise a general recommendation is that the electrolyte level should be just above the tops of the plates which you can see with the cell caps or strips removed.

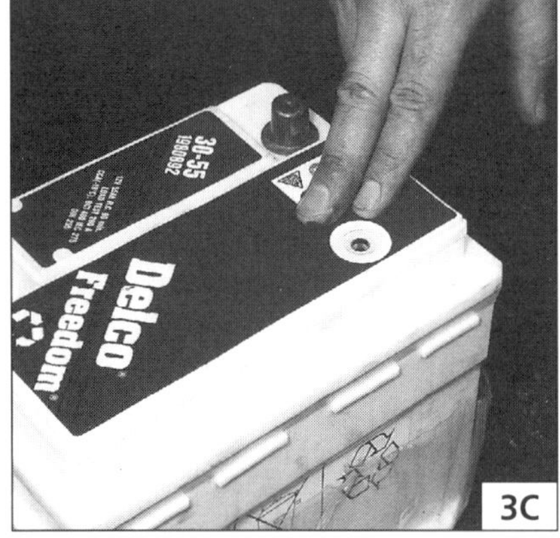

3C. Some batteries have a 'magic eye' which changes colour to indicate the battery's state of charge, or to warn that it is low on fluid.

INSIDE INFORMATION: Note that here is an instance where it is preferable that the battery is warm, such as after a run, before checking the level, since the electrolyte expands with heat. If it is topped up while cold there is a danger that later the fluid might overflow, leading to corrosion of the terminals and the battery tray.

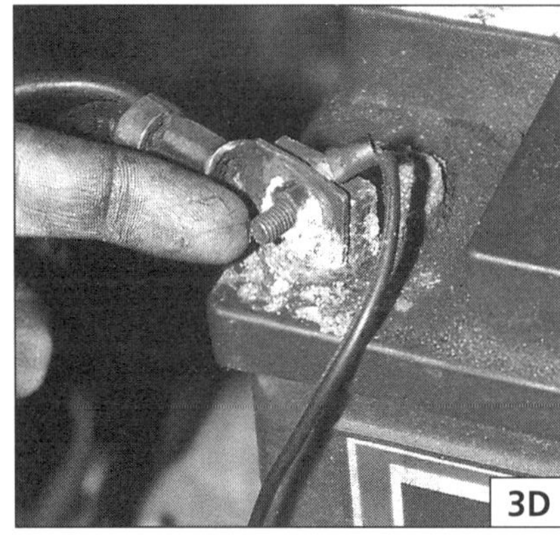

3D. If checking reveals corroded terminals (typically, a white, powdery growth) this is due to electrolyte spillage or excess gassing from the battery cells (possibly indicating too high a charge-voltage). It is very acidic/corrosive and must be removed by pouring hot water over the terminals and any other affected parts. Protect the terminals and terminal clamps with petroleum jelly once clean.

3E. Top up only with distilled (de-ionised) water, never ordinary tap water, which may contain impurities which would damage the plates and shorten the battery's life. Mop up any accidental spillage immediately, and make sure the entire battery exterior is clean and dry. You can buy de-ionised water from motor accessory shops.

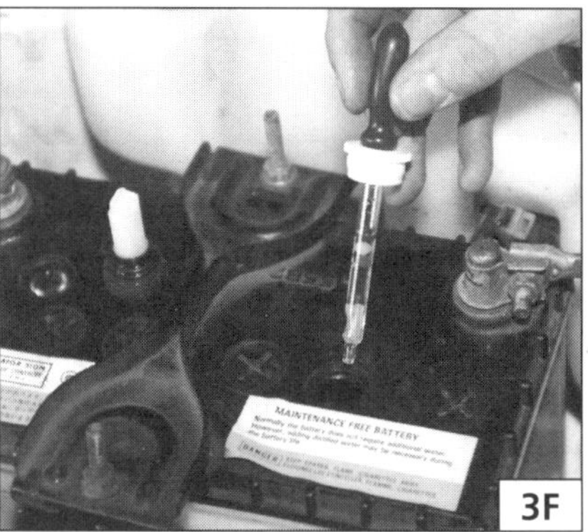

3F. Here's how to check the strength, or specific gravity, of the battery electrolyte. You place the end of a hydrometer into the battery electrolyte, squeeze and release the rubber bulb so that a little of the electrolyte is drawn up into the transparent tube and the float or floats inside the tube (small coloured beads are sometimes used) give the specific gravity. Check each cell and if one (or more) is significantly lower than the others, with battery topped up, the battery is probably on its way out.

Check the tightness of the battery clamp. A loose, rattling battery will have a shorter life than one that is held down securely.

☐ Job 4. Check/top-up power steering fluid/steering box oil.

A steering box (rather than the more common steering rack used on most vehicles) is often found on motor caravans, where it is often power assisted. If your vehicle has power assisted steering, it will almost certainly have an oil reservoir remote from the steering rack or box, maybe even mounted away from the belt-driven power steering pump itself.

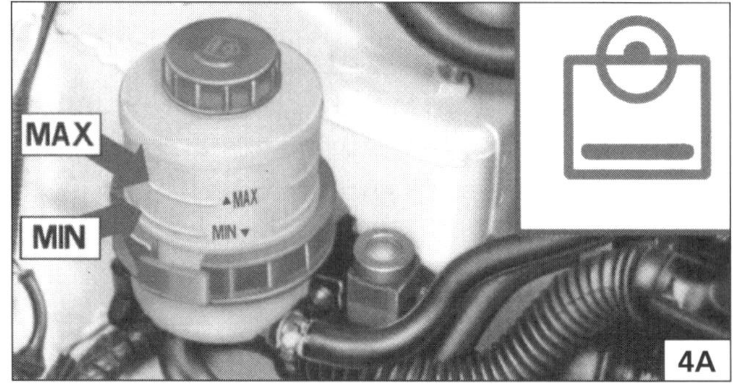

4A. Unscrewing the lid (first clean away any surface dirt) should bring with it an integral dipstick, marked with maximum and minimum levels. Sometimes the reservoir may be translucent, with the levels marked on its exterior. (Illustration, courtesy FIAT Auto UK)

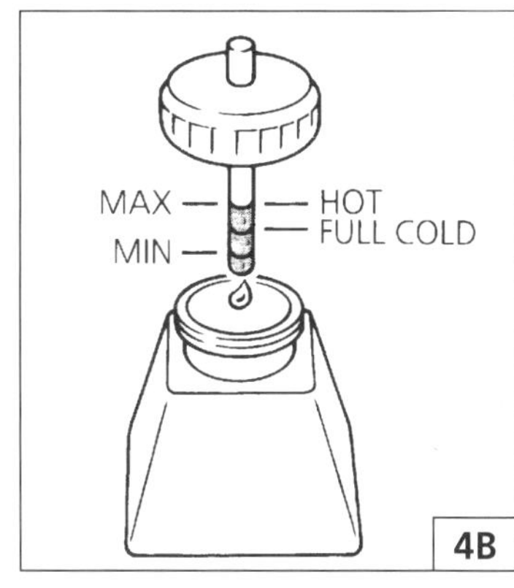

4B. If not, you'll have to rely on the integral dipstick markings. (Illustration, courtesy Ford)

Note that these level marks may be duplicated for 'HOT' or 'COLD' conditions: the former might apply if, for instance, the vehicle has just been driven for 20 minutes or so at around 50mph, the latter if the engine is completely cold. Beware of burns if you are making a 'HOT check. Top-up as necessary, using the oil specified in your handbook.

4C. The steering box (look for it literally at the end of the steering column) is generally filled with SAE 90 oil, and this should last for ever unless leakage occurs. It is still a good idea to remove the filler plug at regular intervals to check that the oil level is up to the bottom of the plug hole.

☐ Job 5. Check/top-up automatic transmission fluid.

The automatic transmission fluid (ATF) is normally checked after a run, when the fluid will have reached normal operating temperature, with the engine idling and the gear selector lever in Park (P).

SAFETY FIRST!

• The engine will be hot and running. Take great care not to be burned.
• Do not allow clothing, hair, jewellery or parts of your body to be trapped or harmed by moving parts.
• The cooling fan, if electric, may suddenly start to work.

5A. Look for a dipstick similar to that for the engine oil. On a rear-wheel drive vehicle it is usually set in a long tube disappearing backwards from the engine, towards the transmission unit behind the engine, while on a front-wheel-drive vehicle it will usually be mounted on the transmission unit itself, in the engine compartment. A typical procedure might be to pull the handbrake firmly on then, with the engine idling, hold the brake pedal down while you shift the selector lever from P through each gear range, and then back to P.

With the engine still idling, withdraw the dipstick and wipe it clean. Examine the marks on the bottom end - there may be just MAXIMUM and MINIMUM level marks, like the engine oil dipstick, or these may be duplicated and marked 'COOL' and 'HOT.

i INSIDE INFORMATION: The 'COOL' check (engine hasn't been run for about five hours) gives reasonable indication of the fluid level, but should you make an accurate 'HOT' check as soon as possible. i

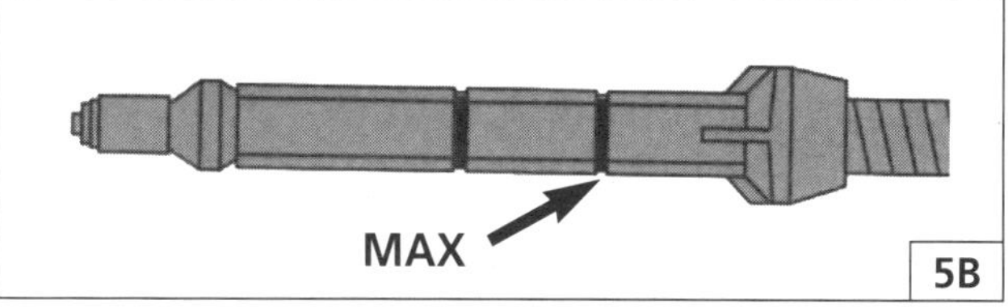

5B. Re-insert the stick, and withdraw it again. If the fluid level falls markedly short of the MAXIMUM mark, the recommended brand of ATF should be added to bring the level up. Usually, the fluid has to be added into the dipstick tube, which, given the narrow bore of the tube, can be a tricky operation! (Illustration, courtesy Mercedes Benz)

making it easy!

• Some main dealers are recommended to use a special anti-blowback device when refilling with ATF.
• The bore of the filler tube is invariably small and ATF will 'glug' back out if you try to fill up using a funnel.
• Some brands of ATF are sold with a specially small dispensing tube made to be inserted right into a dipstick tube.
• Make sure that you use this type of dispenser - and when empty, save the container for future use.

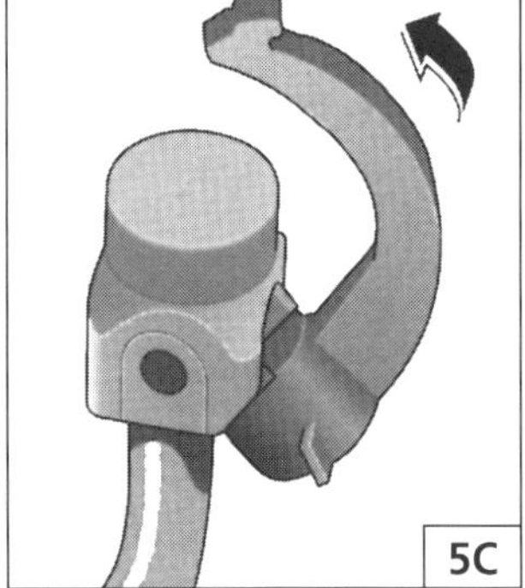

5C. On some engines, such as the Mercedes Sprinter, there is a catch which should be used to close off the level/filler tube when the dipstick is removed with the engine running. (Illustration, courtesy Mercedes Benz)

IMPORTANT NOTE: Whether just checking the level or adding fluid, it is essential to maintain absolute cleanliness, since any dirt entering the system can seriously affect its operation.

Job 6. Check/top-up brake/clutch fluid.

IMPORTANT NOTE: Brake fluid is hygroscopic (meaning it absorbs humidity). This is why the fluid should be changed every two years, or more frequently if the vehicle is mainly driven in areas with a high percentage of humidity in the air. Brake fluid with water vapour in it will corrode brake components and can fail under heavy braking.

SAFETY FIRST!

• If brake fluid should come into contact with the skin or eyes, rinse immediately with plenty of water.
• The brake fluid level will fall slightly during normal use, but if it falls significantly, stop using the vehicle and seek specialist advice.
• If you get dirt into the hydraulic system it can cause brake failure. Wipe the filler cap clean before removing.
• Use only new brake fluid from an air-tight container. Old fluid absorbs moisture and this could cause the brakes to fail when carrying out an emergency stop of other heavy use of the brakes - just when you need them most in fact!

BRAKE FLUID LEVEL

On older vehicles without a translucent reservoir, the fluid level should be up to the bottom of the filler neck.

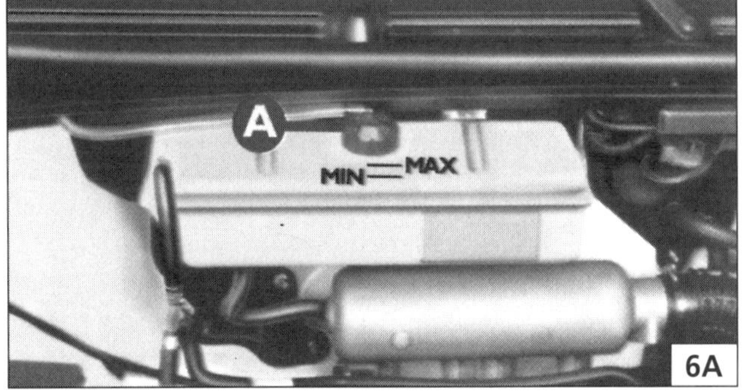

6A. On modern vehicles look for a separate plastic reservoir. Sometimes the assembly will be combined with the brake servo unit at the back of the engine bay. See your handbook for details. There should be a recommended level mark on the reservoir, which is normally translucent so you can see whether the fluid is up to the mark without having to remove the cap.

6B. If you do need to remove the reservoir cap on a modern system, note that it will have electrical connections to it and a float or valve beneath the cap. This is the switch mechanism to the 'low-fluid' warning light found inside the vehicle. Be careful not to damage or accidentally disconnect the wiring.

6C. Top up only with approved brake/clutch hydraulic fluid, fresh from a newly opened container, and have a rag handy to catch any accidental spillage - apart from the mess, brake fluid is an excellent paint stripper!

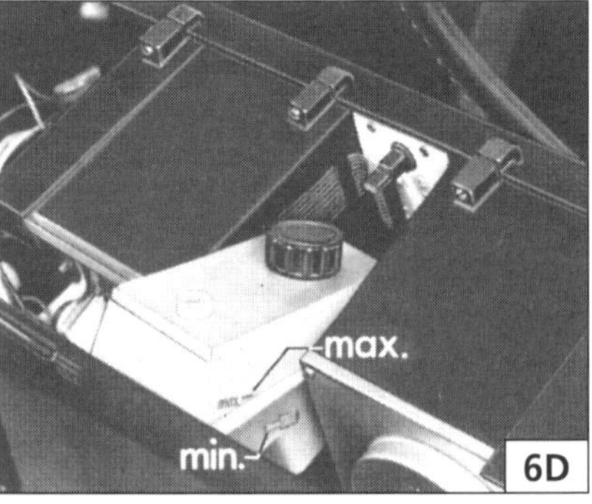

6D. Some reservoirs on motor caravans are so awkwardly positioned that spillage is almost unavoidable! Note that on VW Transporter motor caravans, the fluid reservoir is situated in the dash under the dash cover panel. (Illustration, courtesy Volkswagen)

SAFETY FIRST!

• If the fluid level drops rapidly you must immediately find the cause.
• It could be dangerous to drive the vehicle until the fault is found and rectified.

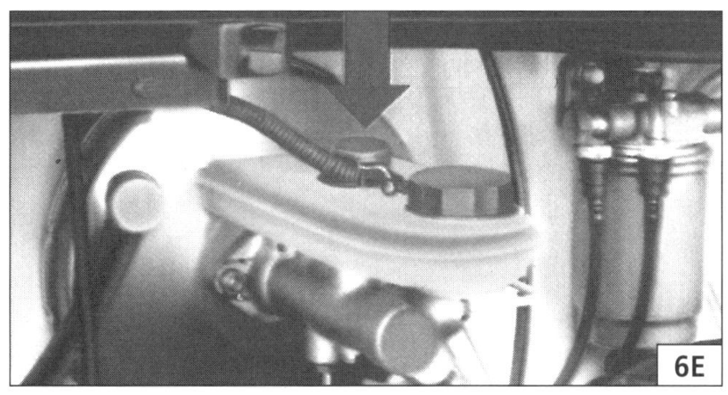

6E. On most modern vehicles, there's also a switch (arrowed) to test the dashboard brake fluid warning light. Turn on the ignition and press the switch to see if the warning light works. On those with no test switch, lift the float high in the reservoir (ignition ON) and check the light. (Illustration, courtesy FIAT Auto UK)

CLUTCH FLUID LEVEL

6F. Most modern motor caravans have a simple cable-operated clutch mechanism, but you will also find some with a hydraulic system. If your motor caravan has a hydraulic clutch system, look for a similar master cylinder and reservoir as for the brakes, but without the servo. Topping-up procedure is the same and the same hydraulic fluid is used.

Renew Fluids

SAFETY FIRST!

• If you remove the pressure cap when the engine is hot, the release of pressure can cause the water in the cooling system to boil and spurt several feet in the air with the risk of severe scalding.
• Take precautions to prevent anti-freeze being swallowed or coming in contact with the skin or eyes and keep it away from children.
• If this should happen, rinse immediately with plenty of water. Seek immediate medical help if necessary.

☐ **Job 7. Renew coolant.**

Anti-freeze should protect your vehicle from the dangers of freezing up. However, there is the danger that topping-up the coolant with plain water will weaken the mixture and weaken the beneficial 'all the year round' corrosion inhibitors built into the mixture. Therefore, the anti-freeze/coolant mixture should be changed at least every two years, while many motorists are happier to still regard the job as an annual pre-winter precaution.

If you decide to renew the mixture in your vehicle's cooling system, first consult your handbook to determine the cooling system's capacity - alongside that data the handbook might even recommend (as a percentage) what the anti-freeze content should be.

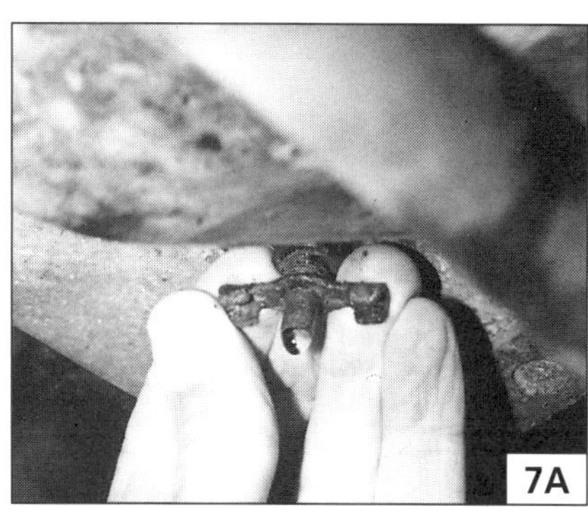

7A. On older vehicles, drain taps on both the radiator...

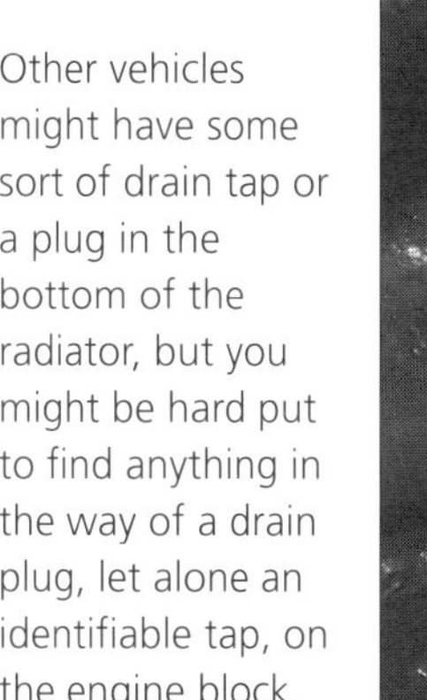

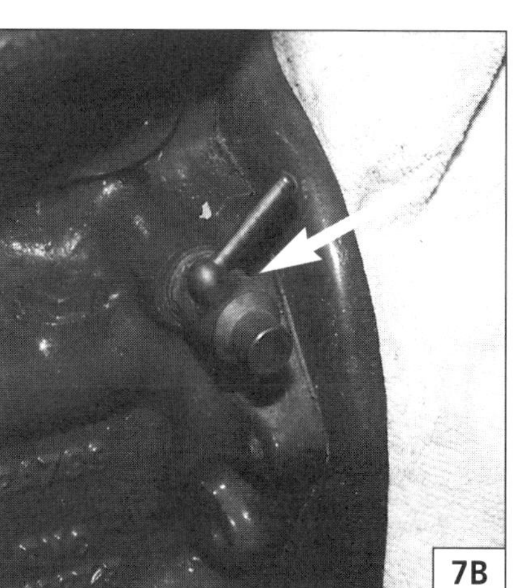

7B. ...and the engine cylinder block are easily identifiable and easily found.

Other vehicles might have some sort of drain tap or a plug in the bottom of the radiator, but you might be hard put to find anything in the way of a drain plug, let alone an identifiable tap, on the engine block.

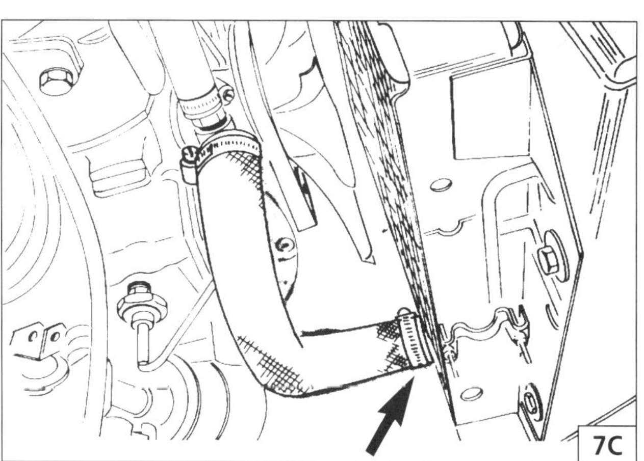

7C. For the vast majority of vehicles, the only way to let coolant out is to temporarily disconnect the bottom hose (arrowed) from the radiator. (Illustration, courtesy Ford)

INSIDE INFORMATION: Every few years, you may want to flush the system. Disconnect top and bottom hoses from the radiator. Insert the garden hose, first into the bottom of the radiator, then into the end of the bottom hose (heater taps open), stuffing the gap with a piece of rag. Then flush again from above. You'll be surprised by how much muck you'll shift and your heater could even work better afterwards!

Anyway, when you do drain, by whatever means, first remove the filler cap (from radiator or expansion tank, as appropriate) to aid the flow - and, of course, never attempt the job until the coolant has cooled sufficiently for there to be no danger of scalding. Heater controls should be set to 'Hot', incidentally, so that this part of the system is also open to coolant flow.

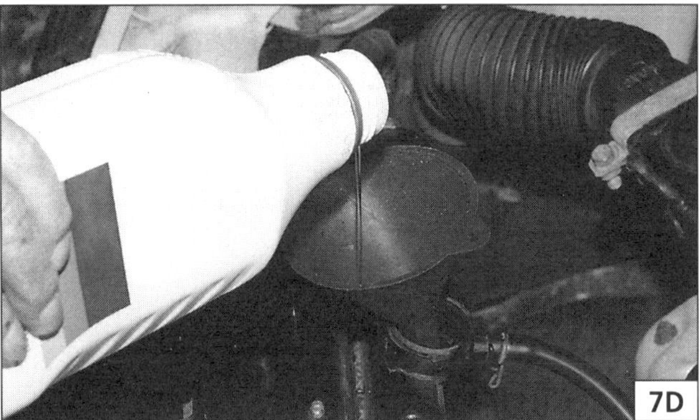

7D

7D. It is usually more sensible to first add the required quantity of neat anti-freeze, then top up with clean water as required to bring the coolant content to its correct level. If the radiator has a cap, pour the anti-freeze into the radiator...

7E

7E. ...if the radiator doesn't have a cap, pour the anti-freeze into the expansion tank.

Pour slowly and carefully, so that the system gradually fills without danger of air-locks building up anywhere. If the system is fitted with bleed valves, open them until no more air comes out. When the level appears to be correct, start the engine and let it run for a few minutes with the filler cap off. Note that as the thermostat starts to open (evidenced by the radiator top hose warming up) any minor air-locks may disperse, causing the level to drop back a bit.

Top up as required, stop the engine, and if all appears to be well, replace the cap.

In the unlikely event of a serious air-lock, however, this could cause the level to rise and threaten an overflow, so be ready to replace the cap and switch off immediately.

Such an air-lock is often betrayed by one or more of the heater hoses still feeling cold (or at best only luke warm) even when the engine has been run for a while - the heater hoses should warm up and, indeed, feel quite hot some while before that top hose will start to feel warm. Again, take all due precautions when feeling the hoses.

INSIDE INFORMATION: A crude, but effective way of dispersing this air-lock, having now stopped the engine, is first to loosen the heater return hose at its junction within the engine compartment - this is the one that probably leads to the radiator bottom hose stub or an adjacent stub at the water pump.

7F

7F. On some vehicles it might be easier to detach it at the heater unit connection, but make sure it is the return hose, and not the feed hose from the engine. And first, check for the presence of one - or more - of those bleed valves.

7G

7G. Now run the engine and retighten the hoses almost immediately in the hope that air has been expelled . Try raising the front of the vehicle and running the engine for a minute or two as another means of dislodging air. Also, try revving the engine several times.

Top up the coolant level now as required, and check it after every run for the next few days to ensure that it has settled down, and that no leaks are occurring anywhere.

INSIDE INFORMATION: DON'T allow the engine to run low on coolant, it could cause permanent damage. Take a 50/50 anti-freeze mixture with you on your first few runs after refilling with coolant. Check and top up after the first few miles - and after the first few journeys, until the level stabilises.

☐ Job 8. Renew engine oil.

Oil change intervals are usually more frequent on diesel engined motor caravans than on petrol engined ones. There is good reason for this, so don't be tempted to stretch the intervals! Owners of turbo diesel engines should use synthetic or at least semi-synthetic oil in their engines - in fact all engine types will benefit from this.

SAFETY FIRST!

• All used engine oil is carcinogenic (cancer inducing). This is why it is essential to work cleanly, to protect hands and wrists with barrier cream and polythene protective gloves, and to regularly wash clothing soiled with old oil.
• Refer to Chapter 1, Safety First!, for more information on used engine oil, and contact your local authority for details of your nearest oil disposal point.

Oil drain plugs are often overtightened. i) Take care that the spanner does not slip causing injury to hand or head. (Use a socket or ring spanner - never an open-ended spanner - with as little offset as possible, so that the spanner is near to the line of the bolt.) ii) Ensure that your spanner is positioned so that you pull downwards, if at all possible.

INSIDE INFORMATION: When buying your oil and filter, purchase a sump drain plug sealing washer. The cost will be negligible but it will help avoid those irritating oil drips on the drive.

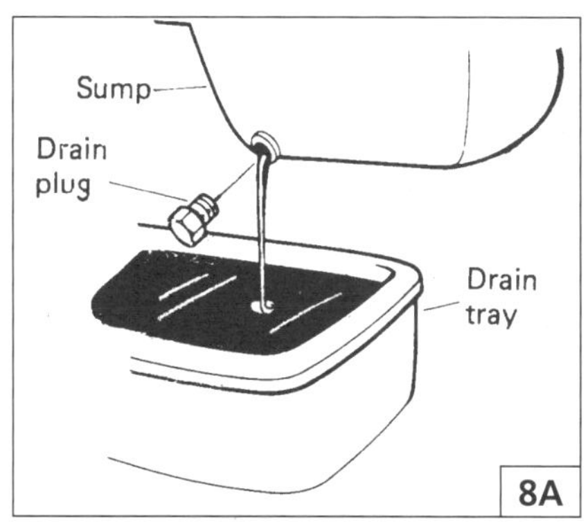

8A. Ensure that you have a container for draining the oil in - and make sure it is large enough! If you're not sure, find your 'van's sump capacity from the handbook and measure an equivalent quantity of water into the drain tray, to check it. This could prevent a terrible mess! Cover the ground with several layers of newspaper.

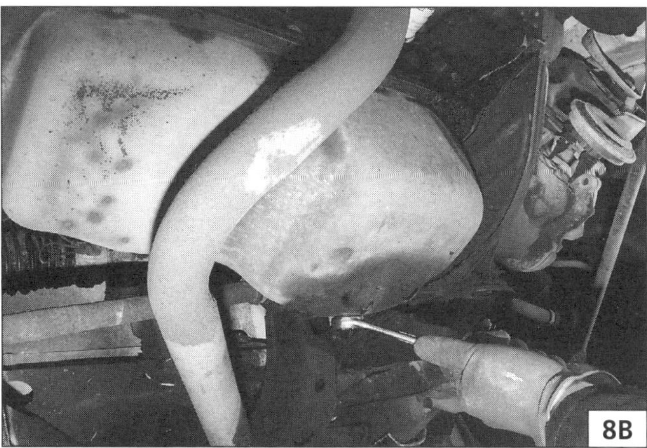

8B. Check whether the sump plug has a hexagon head which can be undone with a conventional ring spanner, or whether (perhaps recessed) it requires a special drain plug key. Do not attempt to 'make do' or you risk 'rounding' the drain plug, making it extremely difficult to grip with any tool.

IMPORTANT NOTE: If you have to raise the vehicle to obtain sufficient working room, it will need to be supported securely on heavy duty ramps or axle stands suitable for a commercial vehicle: make sure you have these to hand. See *Chapter 3, Using Your Motor Caravan*, for information on lifting the vehicle.

making it easy! *• The best time to drain the oil is after a short drive, when the oil will be warm and will flow more easily.*
• Before undoing the drain plug, take off the oil filler cap. This relieves any partial vacuum in the system - the faster the oil can drain from the sump the more debris it will drag out with it.
• If the drain plug is fitted into the side of the sump, bear in mind that the initial spurt of draining oil may carry some distance sideways.
• Position the drain tray (or bowl) accordingly, being ready to move it inwards as the spurt wanes and the oil falls vertically.

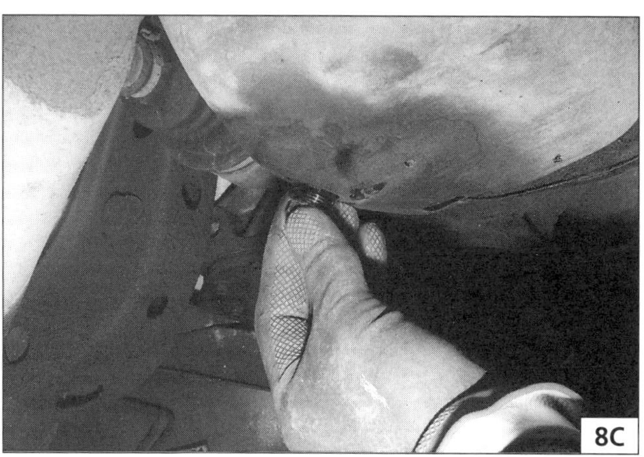

8C. Undo the last few turns of the drain plug by hand, giving yourself room to withdraw hand and plug quickly before the oil runs under your sleeve. Incidentally, check, by feeling the sump, that your short drive hasn't made the oil too hot to handle. If so, don't take any risks; let it cool a bit!

8D. Clean the drain plug thoroughly and (if it's not a taper-seat type) renew its sealing washer.

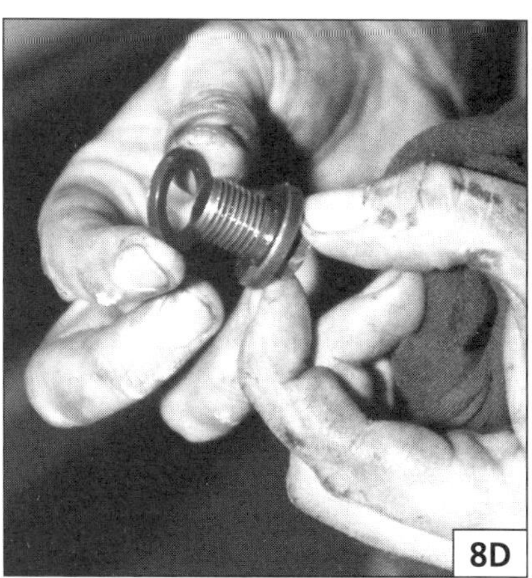

VW AIR-COOLED ONLY

8E

8E. If you have a VW air-cooled motor caravan, you'll need to clean the sump strainer as follows. Remove the dome nuts holding the surrounding plate to the crankcase and remove the strainer.

8F

8F. This collection is what you should end up with. Thoroughly clean the strainer screen and plate, as well as the drain plug, in paraffin or a suitable solvent. Take note of how clean the assembly in the picture is. Fit new gaskets when you replace the strainer and plate and use new copper washers for the dome nuts and, where required, for the drain plug. Reusing the old gaskets and/or washers is simply asking for an oily garage floor.

8G

8G. And this is the order in which they all go back together. (Illustration, courtesy Volkswagen).

The six nuts which hold the strainer in place are dome nuts, the important point being that they should only ever be torqued up to 6 lb ft - no more! If they are over-tightened, they will tend to pull the stud out next time the screen is cleaned.

When the sump has dripped its last drop, you can clean up the sealing face of the sump drain plug and refit the cleaned-up plug - it should be done up tight, but not 'murdered'!

ENVIRONMENT FIRST!

• DON'T pour the old oil down the drain - it's both illegal and irresponsible.
• Your local council waste disposal site will have special facilities for disposing of it safely.
• Don't mix anything else with the old oil, as this will prevent it from being recycled.

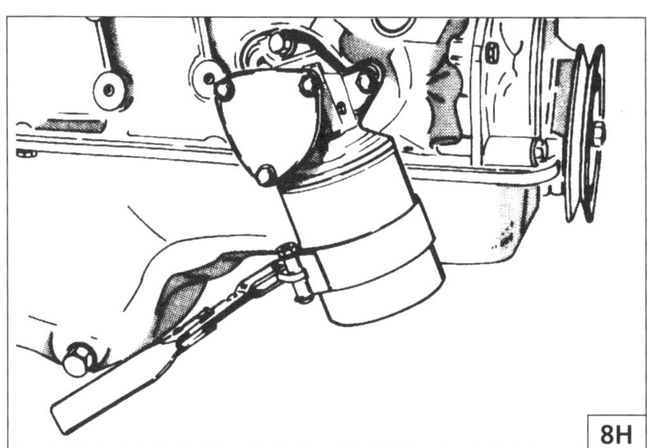
8H

8H. If you are going to change the oil filter at the same time as renewing the oil, now refer to **Job 9** before continuing. (Illustration, courtesy Ford)

8I

8I. Back up top, pour in the correct grade and quantity of fresh oil through the filler, almost always on the rocker cover or cam cover. Do so slowly, as some engines have a nasty habit of spewing back.

Having checked that the oil level corresponds with the correct mark on the dipstick, start the engine and run it for a few minutes while you check around for leaks. Satisfied that all is well, switch off and allow time for the oil to settle before re-checking the level, topping-up if necessary - the new filter will 'use up' some of the oil.

Pour the old oil into an empty can, ready for taking to your nearest disposal point (probably your local 'tip'). Clean out the drain tray.

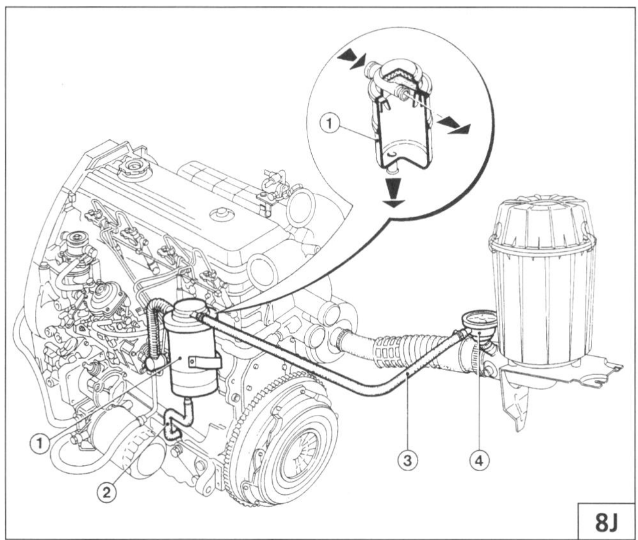

8J. More modern vehicles - those fitted with emission control equipment, in the main - also have a renewable crankcase breather filter. Many older ones have a washable one. Follow the pipework from crankcase to air inlet and inspect, replace or clean the filter, as necessary. (Illustration, courtesy FIAT Auto UK)

Filter Maintenance

☐ **Job 9. Renew engine oil filter.**

The oil filter is fitted on the side of the engine somewhere, sometimes low down, sometimes higher up. On an old vehicle it might be of the bowl-and-element type and on newer vehicles a one-piece canister unit.

Before removing the filter, provide for oil spillage with a drain tray.

On the face of it, the throw-away one-piece canister should be the most straightforward to deal with. But often the bowl-and-element type, secured to the engine with a long through-bolt with conventional hexagon head, is the easiest to remove.

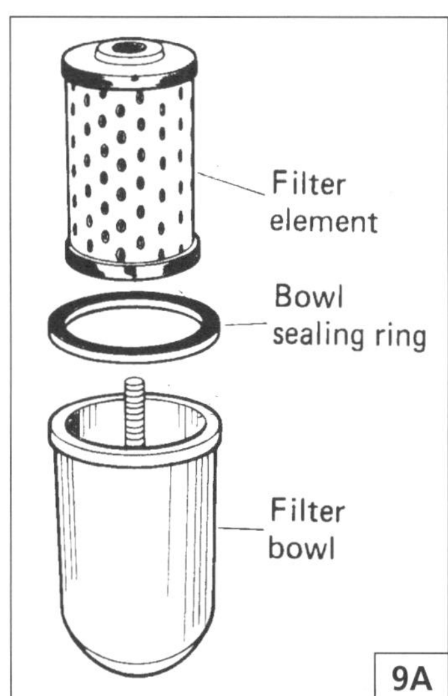

9A. With the latter, having unscrewed the through-bolt, you then lift the bowl away, preferably bringing with it the receptacle beneath to contain any dripping oil: the bolt should remain captive within the bowl. Upending the bowl should tip out the old cartridge filter element. Watch out for a metal base plate and spring beneath the element, restraining them should they try to slide down the bolt, although they should, in fact, also be captive. Discard the old filter element and swill out the bowl with paraffin, using a brush, if necessary, then dry the bowl inside and out with clean, lint-free cloth.

Inside the box containing your new filter element should also be a narrow sealing ring. You'll probably find it still stuck in the groove in the filter head on the engine (the part to which the bowl was bolted) - it has to be carefully prised out with the point of a dart or a slim screwdriver blade.

Once it's out, (and it's usually pretty inaccessible, or at least difficult to see!) make sure the groove and the face of the filter head are thoroughly clean and dry.

It can be quite difficult to get the new seal to stay in place while you offer up the bowl and new filter. You have to work against spring pressure and ensure the narrow rim of the bowl is seated evenly on the seal while you screw in and partially tighten the through-bolt.

making it easy! *Smearing the seal with grease before positioning it will help to retain it, but you must make sure that it doesn't 'escape' anywhere before you fully tighten up the bowl - tight, but not 'murdered'!*

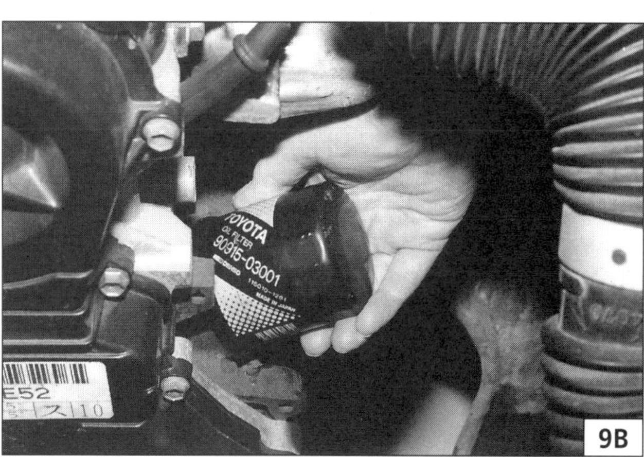

9B. The modern screw-on, screw-off, throw-away canister oil filter should be a much easier proposition. And it is - provided you can unscrew it! Although when fitted it is only screwed on hand-tight, it is amazing how tightly it sets in service. The problem is compounded when, as is so often the case, the filter is inaccessible.

9C. Hopefully there will be enough room to attack it with one of the various DIY filter straps, or wrenches that are on the market.

making it easy! *• If access is that bad, but you can get your hands to it, one trick that often works is to wipe clean the outside of the filter, wrap abrasive paper around it, grip it tightly and unscrew.*
• If all else fails, drive a screwdriver right through the filter and twist it loose, using the screwdriver as a lever/handle.

9D

9D. Once off, it's simply a case of cleaning up its mounting point, moistening the captive seal of the new canister with clean oil, then screwing on the new filter - hand tight only!

☐ **Job 10. Renew air filter/adjust**

10A

10A. Generally the element will be found beneath a lid on the air filter body, the lid held perhaps by a central nut, perhaps by plastic or wire clips (A and E), perhaps by both nuts and clips, perhaps by three or four nuts or bolts. You will invariably find out just by looking! (Illustration, courtesy FIAT Auto UK)

10B

10B. The disposable filter (F) just lifts out. Ensure that the new filter's seals locate properly. (Illustration, courtesy FIAT Auto UK)

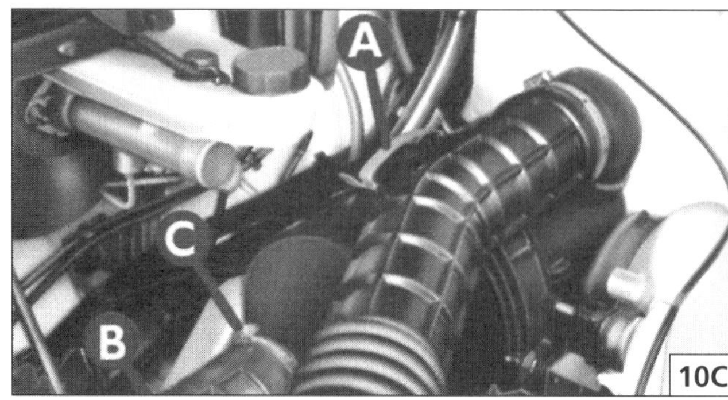

10C

10C. On some, usually larger and/or diesel vehicles, some trunking (B) may have to be removed by undoing clips (A and C)...

10D

10D. ...and the filter element is sometimes held in place (D) with a wing nut. (Illustrations, courtesy FIAT Auto UK)

10E

10E. Some really old, 'classic' models of motor caravan - those based on air-cooled VWs, for example - have an oil-bath type air filter instead of the dry paper element type. With these you should remove the top cover of the filter casing (similarly secured) remove the element then release the lower part of the casing from its mountings. Tip out the old oil (NOT down the drain!) and clean out the sludge in the bottom using white spirit or paraffin. While you're doing this, let the filter soak for a while in solvent, and when it's clean, let it drip dry. Reinstate the filter casing and fill it to the specified level with the correct grade of oil (usually engine oil) - refer to your specific handbook for details. Refit the element and reassemble the rest of the casing.

10F

10F. On older engines, the air intake to the lid or body may have a crude swivel adjustment for summer or winter running, the adjustment usually causing the air intake to be moved nearer to (winter) or further away from (summer) the exhaust manifold; sometimes an alternative position for a length of air intake hose has the same effect.

10G

10G. Sometimes (more sophisticatedly!) there may be an automatically operated flap such as the one shown here. Check that it closes the flap when the engine is started up in cold weather and opens the flap in warm weather when the engine is hot.

SAFETY FIRST!

Whenever you are dealing with diesel fuel, it's essential to protect your hands by wearing polythene gloves.

☐ **Job 11. Drain water from diesel fuel filter.**

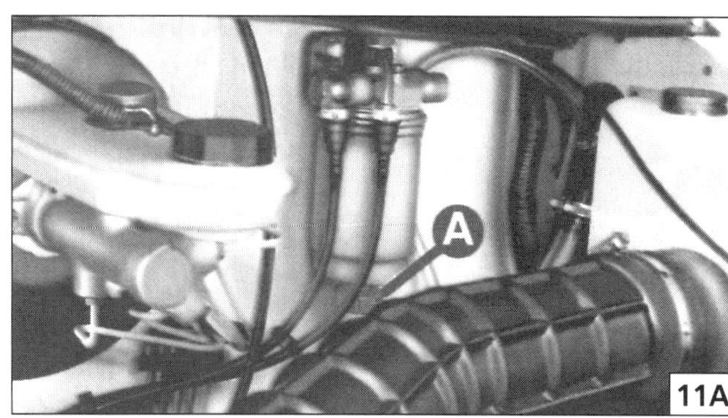

11A

11A. Draining is achieved simply by undoing the drain screw (A) by several turns (it may be necessary to remove it completely on some makes of filter) and refitting/tightening it when fuel emerges from the filter free of water. Water can be seen as large, colourless bubbles in the fuel. If you're not sure of what you're looking at, just evacuate a cupful of fluid and you can be sure you've rid yourself of trapped water. (Illustration, courtesy FIAT Auto UK)

FACT FILE: DIESEL FUEL FILTER

Water is damaging to the diesel injection system. Unfortunately, water is ever-present in diesel fuel, due to the natural condensation which occurs in filling station storage tanks, and the vehicle's own fuel tank.

1

1. A water trap or sedimenter is included in-line with the fuel supply to the injection pump, usually as an integral part of the fuel filter, but sometimes as a separate unit which may be remote from the fuel filter. On some vehicles it may even be mounted elsewhere on the vehicle. It is most usually in the form of a bowl below the filter element, fitted with a drain orifice and screw-plug at its lowest point. If it is a stand-alone unit, it is merely a bowl. Not only does it collect water but also the larger pieces of contaminant which may find their way into the system. Water draining is usually specified at every service.

2

2. If your car is fitted with a water level sensor in the filter though, wired to a tell-tale lamp at the facia panel, you can afford to leave water-draining for longer. Cars with a Lucas filter but no such sensor, can have one retrospectively fitted.

There are three main designs of diesel fuel filter. Pic 3. shows a removable canister (A) with a disposable inner element (B) and sealing ring (C); Pic 4. Has a disposable filter body (A) sandwiched between water bowl (B) and filter head (A). Pic 5. is a fully disposable filter cartridge (A), which is attached to the pump and oil cooler connections on this Ford unit.

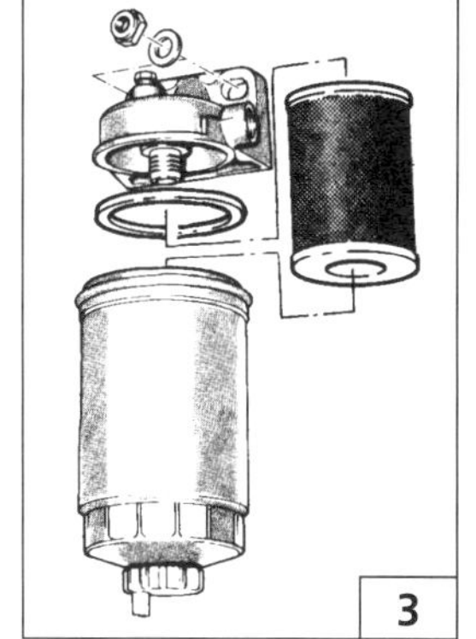
3

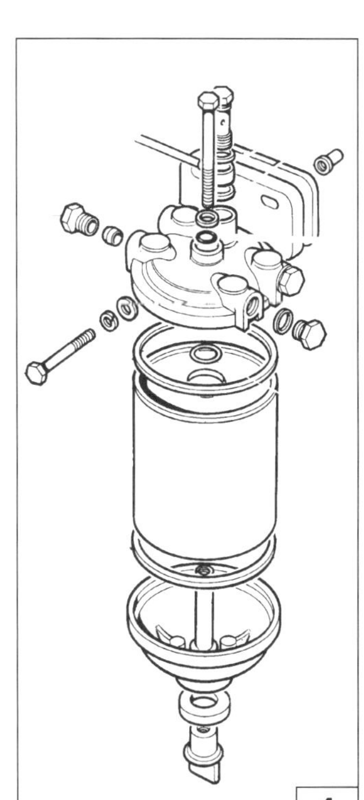
4

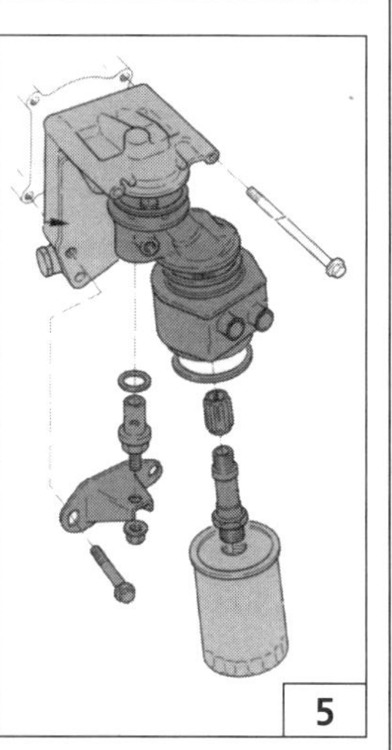
5

making it easy!
- *With some filter types you may find that fluid does not emerge when the drain tap is opened.*
- *This is because the fuel/water is retained in the filter by suction.*
- *You can break this suction by opening the vent screw at the filter head, or, if no such screw is present, by slackening the fuel outlet union at the head (the union of the fuel hose which connects with the injection pump).*
- *After opening the system in this way, it may be necessary to bleed the fuel system of air if you encounter engine-starting difficulties. See* ***Job 12****.*

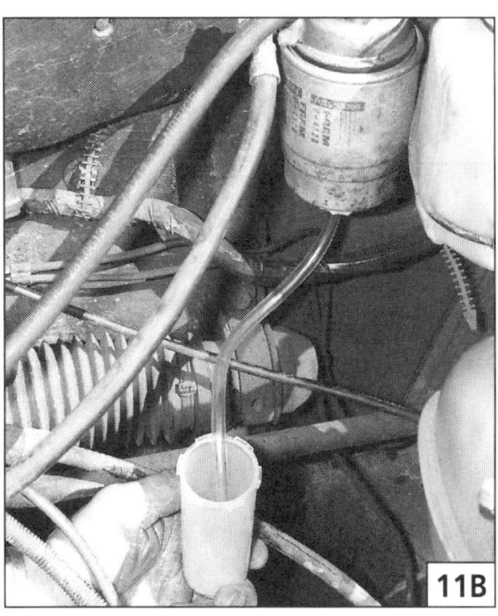

11B. Because diesel fuel is damaging to rubber components such as cooling system hoses and drive belts, it may be expedient to push a length of plastic piping onto the drain tap (nearly all have a stub for this purpose) to allow direction of the fluid into a suitable container. Some diesel vehicles are equipped as standard with a drain hose.

11C. Some Peugeot-Citroen diesel engines produced from 1992 are equipped with this unique design of fuel filter.

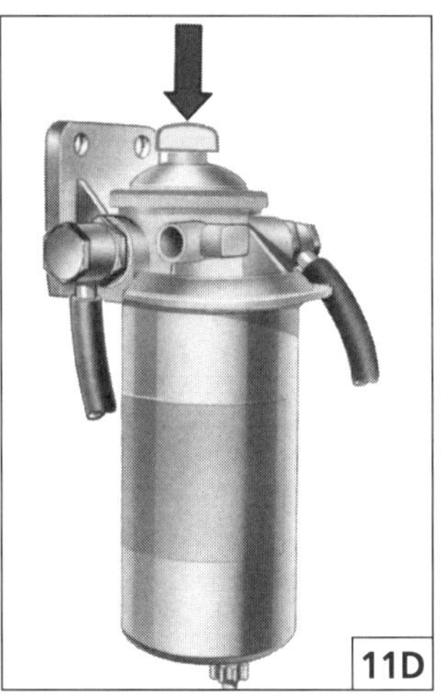

11D. The majority of diesel fuel filters on motor caravans are like this one. Drain by loosening the drain plug at the bottom of the filter, then pumping the plunger (arrowed) until no more water comes out.

Job 12. Renew diesel fuel filter.

Also, see *FACT FILE: DIESEL FUEL FILTERS* at the start of **Job 11**.

Like the conventional cartridge-type engine oil filter, most diesel fuel filters are disposable and screw hand-tight to a filter head, sealing by means of a rubber ring. Some are of a two-part design in which the filter base/water bowl or canister has a threaded centre tube running up through the filter element and bolting through the filter head.

Quite a few filter heads carry a hand-operated priming pump which allows the filter to be primed with fuel, and also facilitates the purging (bleeding) of air from the fuel system.

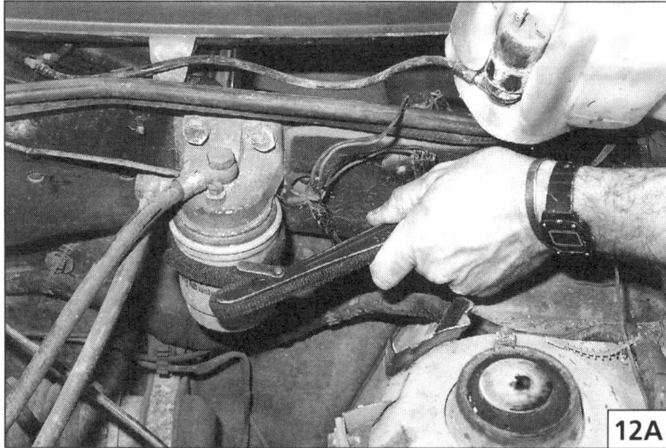

12A. The filter is removed by unscrewing by hand, or if too tight, with the aid of an oil filter wrench.

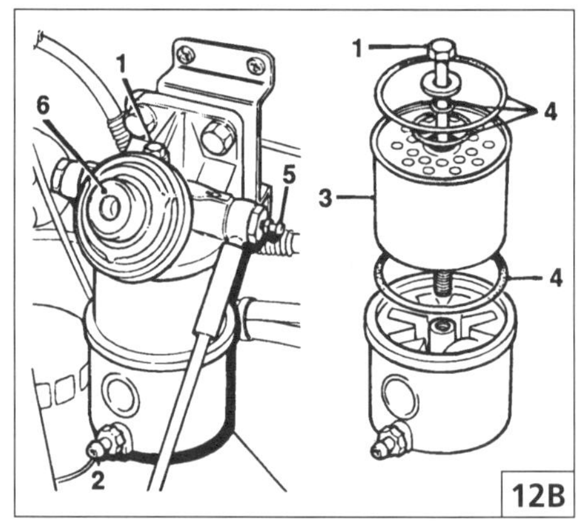

12B. Alternatively, removal is a question of undoing the centre nut/bolt (1). Note the sealing rings (4); ensure that the small one is in the filter box when you buy the replacement cartridge (3)! (Illustration, courtesy V.L. Churchill/LDV Limited).

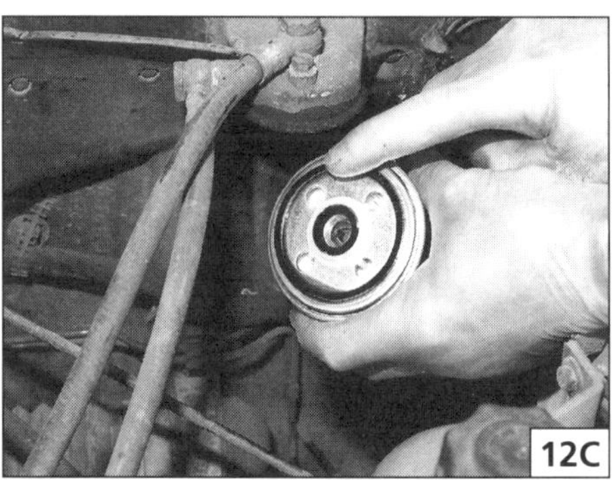

12C. The rubber sealing ring at the top of the filter element or cartridge should be smeared with diesel fuel prior to fitting so that it doesn't grip and prevent proper tightening.

12D. Note that certain designs of filter, such as the Delco type fitted to some Bedford models, and the Bosch type shown here, have a small diameter inner seal as well as a larger outer one, plus a plastic retainer to secure it prior to fitting the filter. (Illustration, courtesy V.L. Churchill/LDV Limited).

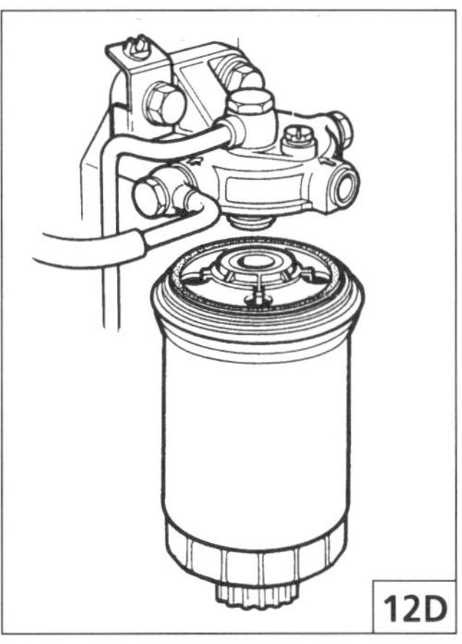

INSIDE INFORMATION: On some fuel systems, particularly those which are not provided with a hand priming pump, it is a good idea to fill the fuel filter assembly with diesel fuel before reassembling it. This will reduce the amount of air-bleeding required.

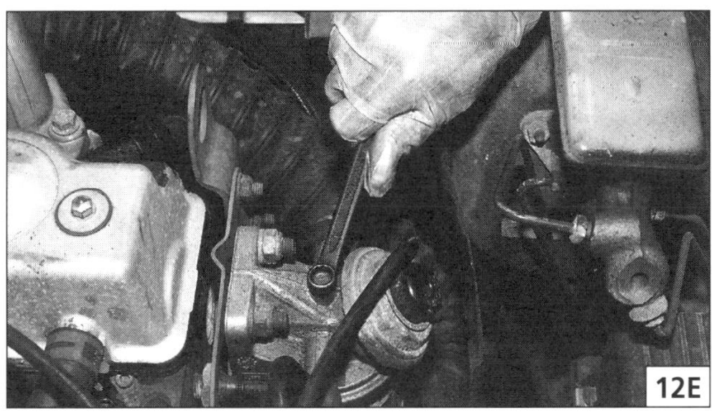

12E. The new filter is screwed firmly into place by hand only or, if it's of the bolt-retained type, tightened gently with a spanner.

When a diesel fuel filter has been replaced it is important to bleed air from the filter assembly before starting the engine. Air in the fuel system gives rise to difficult starting and erratic engine running, though if present in tiny bubbles only it eventually bleeds itself out via the injection pump return line as the engine runs.

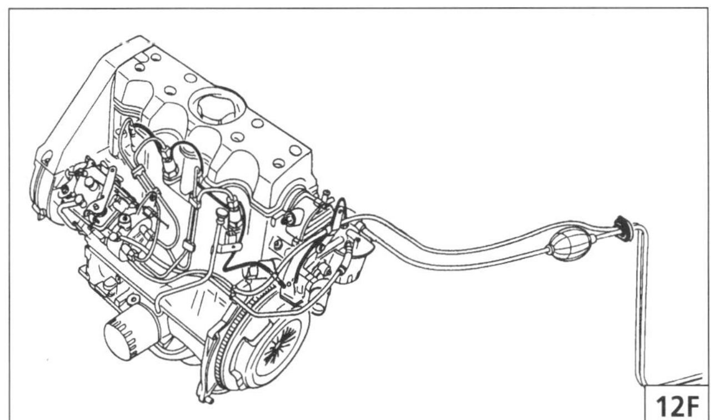

12F. If the vehicle has a priming bulb separate to the fuel pump, you prime the system by pumping the bulb, rather like the doctor taking your blood pressure!

12G. If the vehicle doesn't have a fuel supply pump external to the fuel injection pump it probably has a manual priming device either on the filter head, or somewhere in the engine bay, in-line with the fuel supply pipe or hose.

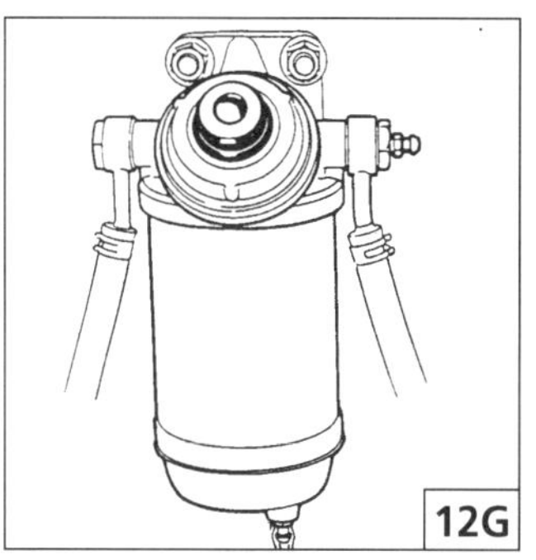

12H. An external fuel supply pump usually has its own priming lever (arrowed). (Illustration, courtesy V.L. Churchill/LDV Limited).

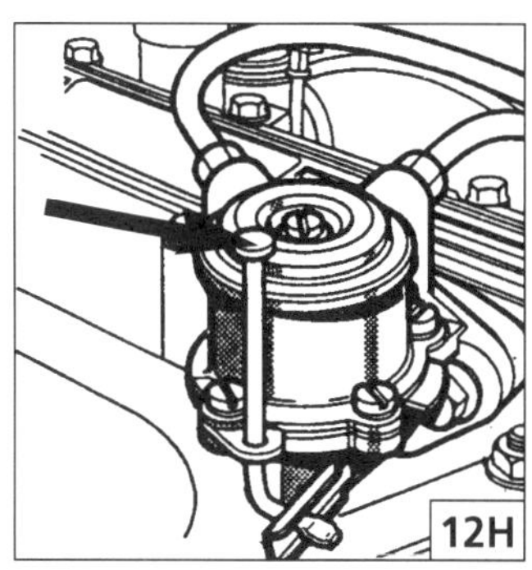

12I. A primer allows fuel to be drawn from the tank without the engine running, and there is usually an air bleed hole (with a screw plug in it) on the filter head to allow aerated fuel to emerge while priming by hand. (Illustration, courtesy Ford Europe Limited).

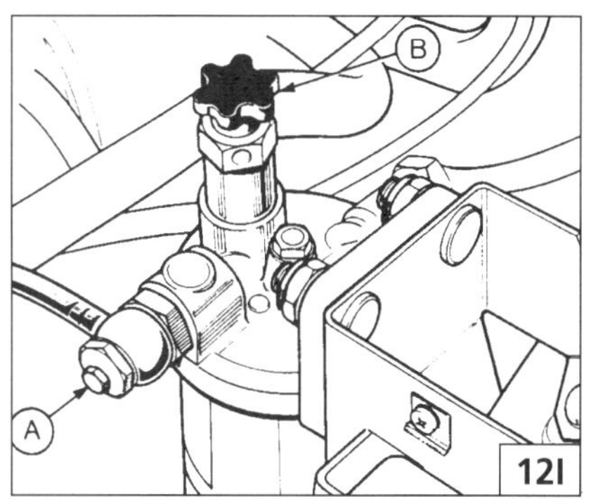

In rare cases where no primer is fitted, bleeding can be achieved by cranking the engine with the starter motor, though to prevent the engine from starting, the injector unions should first be slackened and surrounded with rags to absorb wasted fuel.

12J. In addition to bleeding air from the fuel filter vent, bleeding can also be carried out from the injection pump fuel inlet union and the injector unions if air has been absorbed that far into the system. As with water, air can be seen as bubbles in the fuel, and as soon as bubble-free fuel emerges, the vent screw or union can be retightened.

INSIDE INFORMATION: It is best to hold the primer on the downstroke (or compressed, depending on primer type) when retightening, to prevent air from being drawn back into the system.

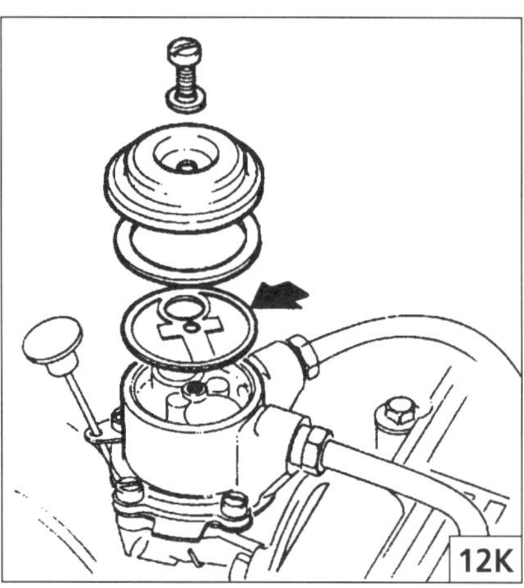

12K. Don't forget that certain lift pumps such as the AC and the Super Par have their own servicing requirement. At the specified intervals, remove the top cover, remove the wire mesh filter, wash it clean and refit.

Job 13. Renew petrol fuel filters.

SAFETY FIRST!

- ***Please read the Safety information in Chapter 1, especially that relating to the safety hazards surrounding petrol (gasoline).***
- ***Disconnect the vehicle's electrical supply before opening any part of the fuel system.***
- ***Have a suitable workshop-sized extinguisher to hand, in case the worst should happen.***
- ***If a fire should break out, turn off the ignition - and thus the engine and fuel pump - immediately so that no more petrol can be pumped through.***
- ***Because of the fire risk, however, slight, and because of the very strong danger from exhaust fumes, carry out the next part of the work outdoors.***

13A. Look in the engine compartment for a renewable in-line fuel filter - usually fitted in-line with the supply to the carburettor. Observe the fitted direction of the filter before removing it, and any fuel-flow direction arrows marked on the body of the replacement filter.

When renewing, contain fuel leakage with a rag. Renew hose clips if they are distorted or no longer tighten properly. Do not overtighten clips to the extent that they cut into the hosing.

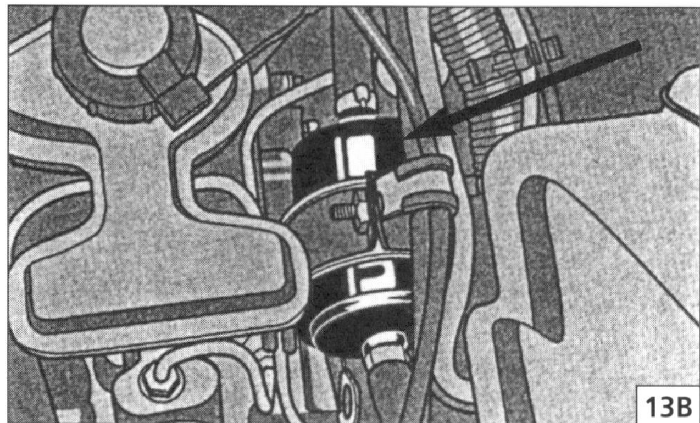

13B. Petrol engines with fuel injection MAY have a large fuel filter which only needs renewing at large-mileage intervals - refer to your specific vehicle information. Some of these fuel-injection system filters are connected in-line with the supply pipe by 'banjo' unions. These are undone using a spanner or socket, and taking care to collect the two copper washers either side of the union 'bolt'. Always observe any fuel-flow direction arrows on replacement fuel filters.

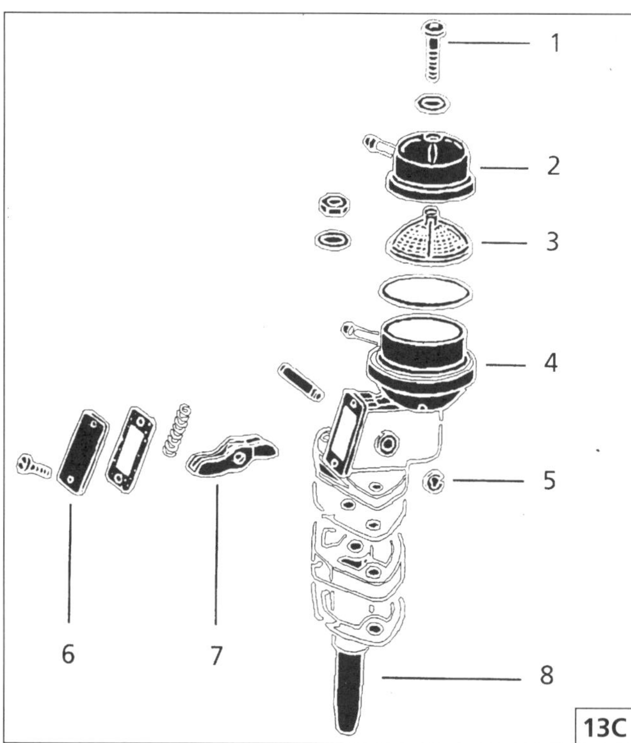

13C. Some earlier petrol-engined motor caravans, such as the VW Transporter, may have an engine-driven mechanical fuel supply pump with a removable filter screen inside it. This is inevitably mounted under the lid of the pump and at certain service intervals it should be removed and cleaned of debris.

The pump cover is usually removed by unscrewing a centre bolt or nut, and lifting off the cover to reveal the screen underneath. The screen can be lifted out and cleaned in petrol.

Check for the presence of any seals before refitting the cleaned screen and the pump cover. Run the engine and check for fuel leaks.

On all fuel filter types, run the engine and check for leaks around the filter unions.

Petrol Engine Spark Plugs

☐ **Job 14. Check/clean/renew spark plugs.**

making it easy!

14A.• Before detaching plug leads, mark them with numbered tags of masking tape, so that you can be sure to replace them in exactly the same order.

• Some engines have their plugs buried quite deeply and for these, extra long plug spanners are available.

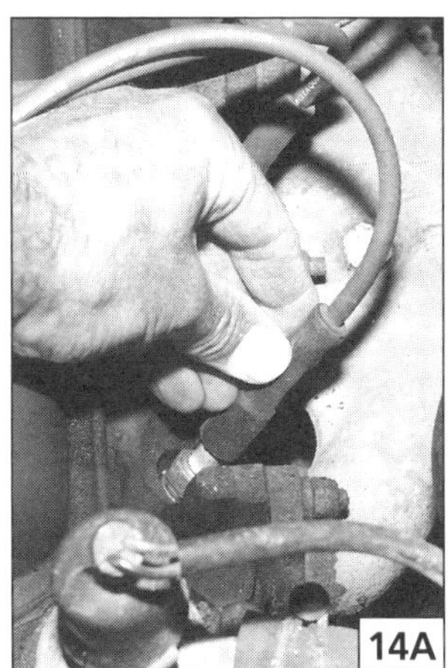

14A

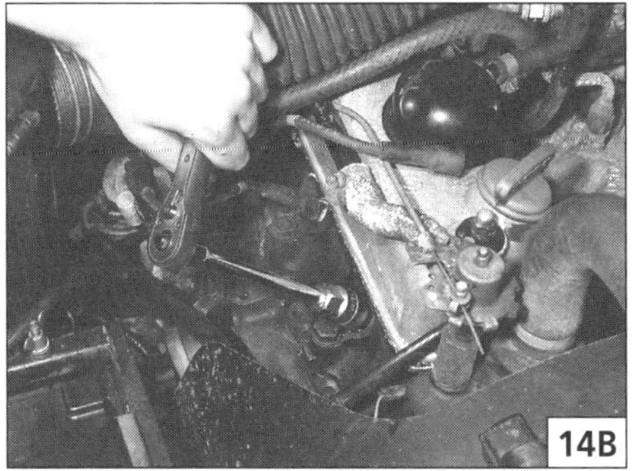

14B

14B. You will need a proper tubular spark plug removal tool which can be bought as a separate item, although it is normally included in a good quality socket set. It needs to be the correct size for the plugs used on your engine (predominantly 14mm, but sometimes 10mm thread diameter, with correspondingly larger or smaller bodies). Incidentally, you don't often see the actual spanner size quoted, but they are, respectively, 13/16 in. AF (21 mm) and 5/8 in. (16 mm).

Note that grime is apt to accumulate around the plug seating, and since much of this could be abrasive you don't want it getting into the cylinders. So, a simple precaution before removing a plug, is to brush away all the surrounding dirt.

Keep the plugs in cylinder order as you remove them and check their condition. The colouring at the business end of a spark plug in healthy condition is grey/brown and the plug tip should be dry.

Should any plug look unhealthy, it might be symptomatic of a tiring or failed plug, or it might indicate a fault with the engine, perhaps confined to just the one cylinder - and you know which cylinder because you kept the plugs in order of removal. Didn't you?

14C. If the plugs are definitely fit for further service, use a brass-bristled wire brush to spruce up their electrode end.

14C

14D. Now check the electrode gaps, bearing in mind that spark erosion widens the gap. Use a feeler gauge of the appropriate value according to the plug gap specified in your vehicle data (e.g., 0.025 in. or '25 thou', or, metrically, 0.60 mm).

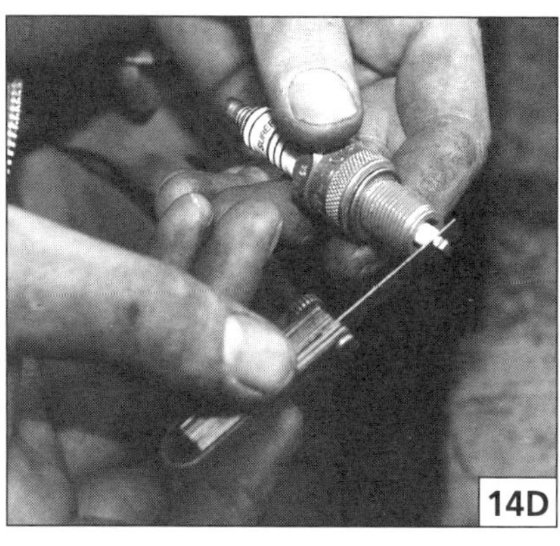

14D

If the gap does need altering, it's best to use the tool for the job. The slots in one of the blades can be used (carefully) to lever the plug's side (earth) electrode nearer to, or further from, the central electrode - NEVER attempt to bend the centre electrode.

14E. Before replacing the plugs, use pliers to ensure that the terminal nut at the HT lead end is tight (some engines, e.g., VW air-cooled, dispense with this nut) and that the plug stem is clean and dry - dirt here, particularly oily dirt, can encourage the HT current to 'track' to earth rather than continue on to the plug electrodes.

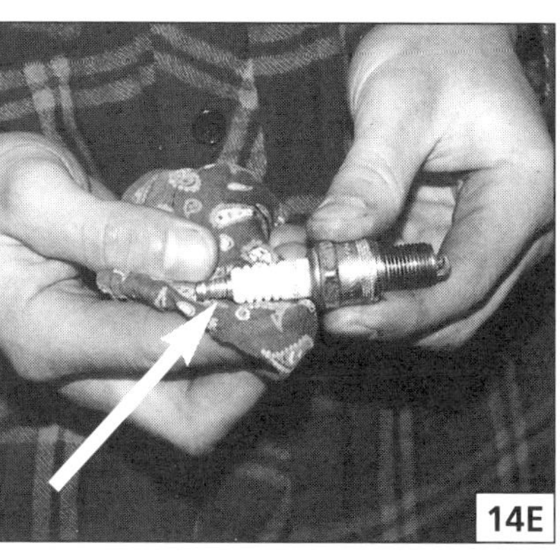

14E

making it easy!

• In our experience a smear of copper grease on the (cleaned up) spark plug threads helps them to screw in smoothly now and prevents them setting so tight in service as to make their removal difficult next time.

• We particularly like the smooth, positive, thread pick-up when dealing with those air-cooled VW engines, where, with the plug held in the tubular spanner, you have to 'feel' for a plug hole you can't see and pray that you don't cross-thread the plug - a potentially expensive nightmare on any aluminium-head engine!

Make sure, using rag and screwdriver blade as necessary, that the actual plug seating is absolutely clean before screwing-in the plug using your fingers first, then the spanner to initially do it up hand-tight. The 'rule-of-thumb' then is that, using the spanner, plugs with washers should be tightened a further quarter of a turn, and taper-seat plugs a further one-sixteenth of a turn.

Diesel Engine Glow Plugs

☐ **Job 15. Renew glow plugs.**

The glow plugs are vital to the diesel engine's ability to start from cold. If cold-starting is difficult, or the engine starts amid a lot of black exhaust smoke and won't run smoothly until it has warmed up, you can suspect glow plug problems. If that's the case, take the vehicle to a diesel specialist - you'll find at least one in every major town.

You'll rarely see glow plug renewal intervals specified in service schedules, but a general rule is that by 30,000 miles they are past their prime, so we, along with Lucas, recommend renewal at this mileage.

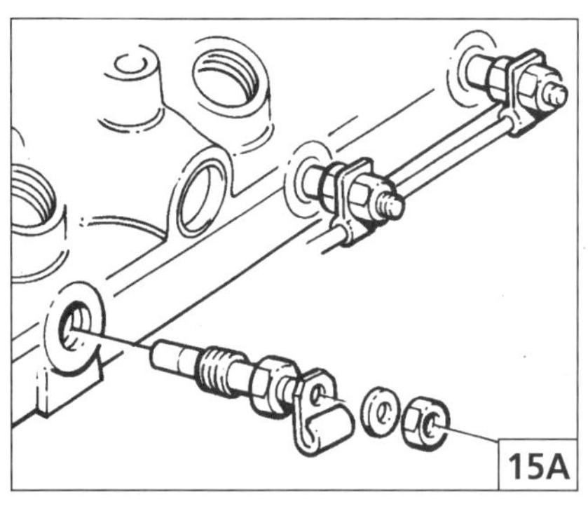

15A. Before removing a glow plug from the cylinder head, disconnect the battery earth lead. It is important that you first refer to FACT FILE: COMPUTER PROTECTION, at the start of the ENGINE BAY section previously, to avoid damaging electronic components. Next, disconnect the wire or connecting strap from the plug and unscrew it from the cylinder head by just a couple of turns using a ring spanner or socket. (Illustration, courtesy Ford Europe Limited).

15B. Clean away dirt from around the plug so that none finds its way into the engine once the plug is removed, then fully unscrew the plug (and its sealing washer, if fitted).

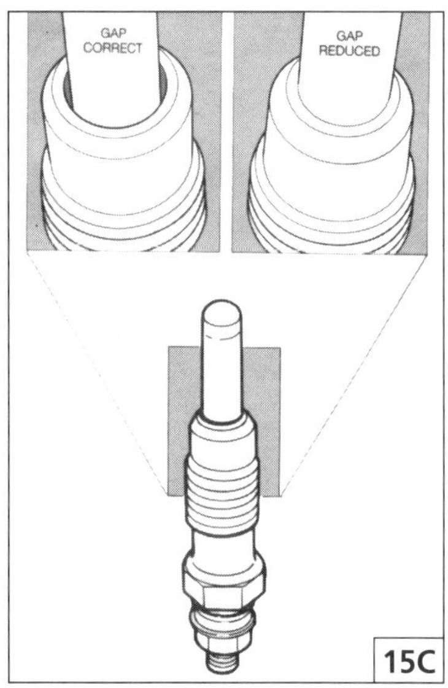

15C. Where a plug sealing washer is fitted this should be renewed before refitting the plug. If a plug tightening torque is specified, it is important to observe it, as overtightening can cause damage.

Make sure that the electrical connection to each plug is clean and corrosion-free, then refit the supply wire or strap before reconnecting the battery.

Generator Drive Belt

☐ **Job 16. Check/adjust/renew belt.**

> **SAFETY FIRST!**
>
> ***Always keep your fingers away from the blades of a thermo-electric cooling system fan unless the battery has been disconnected - it could surprise you by coming on suddenly when the engine is either running or not running!***

Still often referred to as the 'fan belt' because on older vehicles it drove the mechanical cooling fan (usually attached to the water pump) as well as the generator, this drive belt continues to be a vital component. On a modern vehicle, while the fan is usually thermostatically controlled and driven by an electric motor, the belt probably still drives the water pump, as well as the alternator. If it slips, or breaks, the vehicle will eventually grind to a halt, having run out of electricity, or overheated, or both.

16A. Even though diesel engines don't require electricity to operate an ignition system, they do require a continual voltage to the fuel pump shut-off solenoid, which otherwise closes under spring-pressure, shutting off fuel supply to the pump. The shut-off, and its supply wire (disconnected) are shown here. Also, some modern 'high-tech' diesel motor caravans now have an electronically controlled fuel injection system.

16B. In order to drive efficiently, as well as being in good condition, the belt must be reasonably tight - but not over-tight - around the drive pulleys. Look on the inside of the belt for a shiny surface, cracks or oil; look at the edges for fraying. Replace if there are any problems. Checking belt condition can be awkward, both from the point of view of restricted access and the difficulty of seeing enough of it in its fitted state: you really need to be able to rotate the engine (ignition off) using a spanner on the alternator or crankshaft pulley nut, bending and twisting each newly exposed length of belt to show up cracks or other damage.

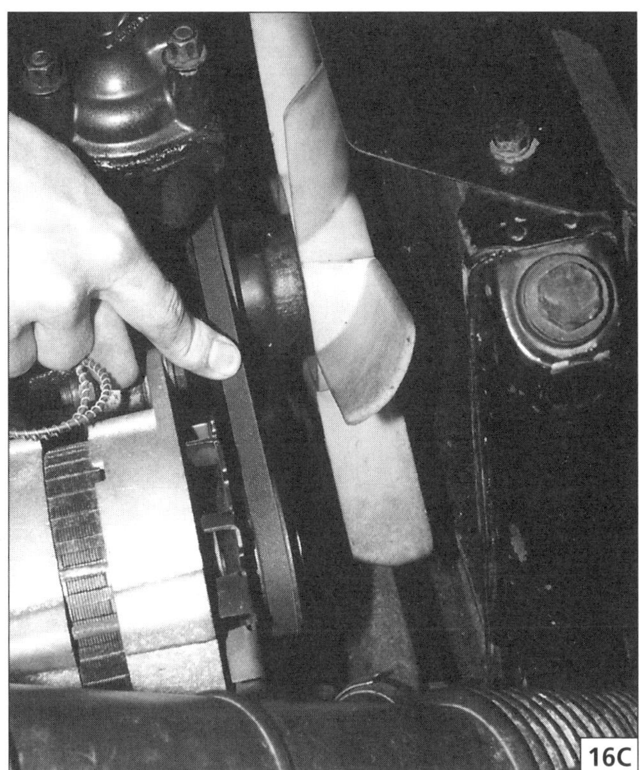

16C. For the belt tension check, a typical recommendation is that there should be approximately 12 mm (1/2 in.) deflection, but check with your vehicle's handbook. Do not overdo the belt tension, for this puts undue strain on the generator and water pump bearings. Test with firm thumb pressure midway on the belt's longest run between pulleys.

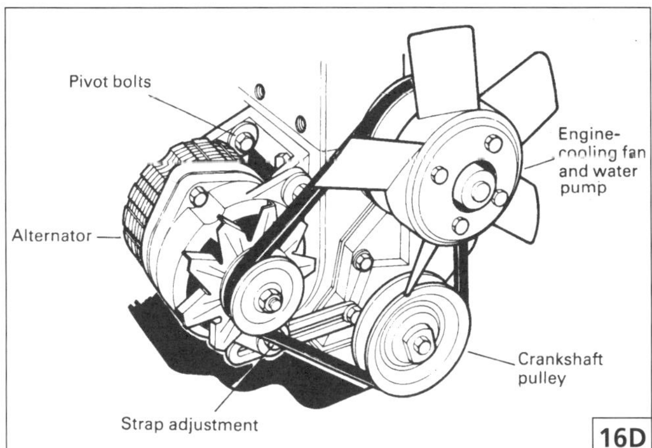

16D. If adjustment is required, the generator pivot bolt(s) and slotted adjustment strap bolts on engine and generator need to be slackened. The generator is then pivoted away from the engine until the belt is sufficiently taut, and the bolts are then re-tightened.

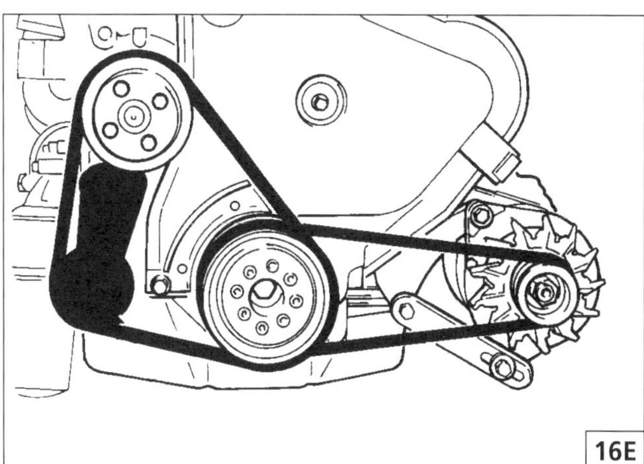

16E. There will often be small variations on the theme, but the principles of adjusting the belt by slackening the adjuster bolts are exactly the same. This engine has a separate water pump belt drive. Belts for power steering and air conditioning are more common, but all need checking. (Illustration, courtesy Ford Europe Limited).

making it easy! *• If necessary, a suitable piece of wood can used, carefully, as a lever between the engine and the generator drive end bracket to maintain the belt tension while the bolts are tightened.*

• But don't over tighten the belt - it will damage the alternator.

16F. Very occasionally, you may come across a simple threaded rod and bracket tension adjustment (16F.4). Simply tighten or undo the rod, as required.

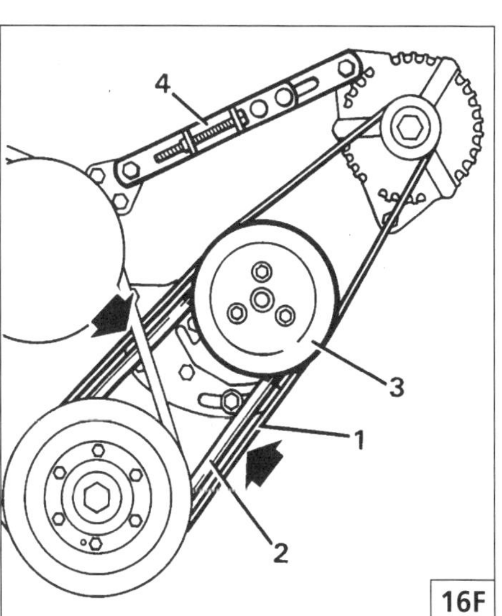

making it easy! *• Belt renewal is just a simple extension of the tensioning procedure.*

• In view of this drive belt's vital importance, you should always carry a spare and the right sized spanners to slacken the adjustment bolts. If, even when the generator is pushed tight to the engine, the new belt is difficult to get over the pulleys, follow the old bicycle chain and sprocket trick: push as much of the belt as possible onto the edge of the final pulley, then rotate this pulley to wind the rest of the belt into place.

AROUND THE VEHICLE

Wheels and Tyres

☐ **Job 17. Check tyre pressure/condition.**

Tyres that show uneven wear tell their own story. If any tyre is worn more on one side than another, consult your tyre specialist. It probably means that your suspension or steering is out of adjustment - probably a simple tracking job but conceivably symptomatic of suspension damage. If a tyre is worn more in the centre or on the edges, it could mean that your tyre pressures are wrong, but once again, have the vehicle checked. Incorrectly inflated tyres wear rapidly, can cause the vehicle's handling to become dangerous, and can worsen fuel consumption. When checking your tyres, don't forget to include the spare.

17A

17A. Check tyre pressures 'cold', if possible, for after any appreciable run the tyres will have warmed up and the air inside will have expanded, giving a higher pressure reading. Don't forget to check the pressure of the spare tyre at the same time - you never know when you'll need to use it! Remember that prolonged high-speed driving and/or carrying a full load of passengers or luggage requires the tyre pressures to be higher than normal.

Garage airline readings can be unreliable, so use a good quality gauge of your own to check that the tyre pressures accord with your handbook recommendations.

17B

17B. Check the tyres for tread depth, using a quality gauge. Current UK laws state that there should be a minimum of 1.6mm tread across the centre 3/4 of the outer circumference of the tyre. However, it should be regarded as an absolute minimum and safe drivers will want to replace their tyres well before this. Check the tread of the tyres for sharp stones and other foreign bodies which could cause a puncture.

Make a visual check on both sides of each tyre for uneven wear, cuts, bulges or other damage in the walls. Raise each wheel off the ground, using an axle stand, otherwise you won't be able to see the inside of each tyre properly, nor will you be able to check that part of the tyre that is in contact with the ground. If you find any splits or other damage, the tyre(s) should be inspected immediately by a tyre specialist who will advise whether repair is possible or replacement is the only answer.

17C

17C. Having checked the tyres, it's always a good idea to check the tightness of the wheel bolts or nuts. You need to make sure that the bolts are not loose, of course, but it's not necessary to apply huge amounts of torque - don't forget, if you have a flat tyre on the road, you'll need to be able to get the wheel off again! This last point needs particular attention if you have had new tyres fitted by a specialist where fitters with pneumatic wrenches can sometimes get a little over-enthusiastic.

Lights and Indicators

☐ **Job 18. Check all lights and horns.**

LIGHT BULBS

IMPORTANT NOTE: See *Chapter 4, Part I - Exterior Lights and Part II - Interior Lights* for information on replacing bulbs inside the motor caravan and on the outside of the coachbuilt body.

Even if the bulbs are sound, light output will be seriously reduced if the light lenses are dirty and this is an offence. On a long, 'dirty' journey, you should stop whenever possible and wipe the lenses clean.

18A

18A. If you need to change a headlight bulb, your handbook might be more specific, but this fitting is fairly typical. Here, working from within the engine compartment, behind the headlight unit, you first pull off the rubber boot (A) covering the terminal block which plugs onto the blade pins of the bulb.

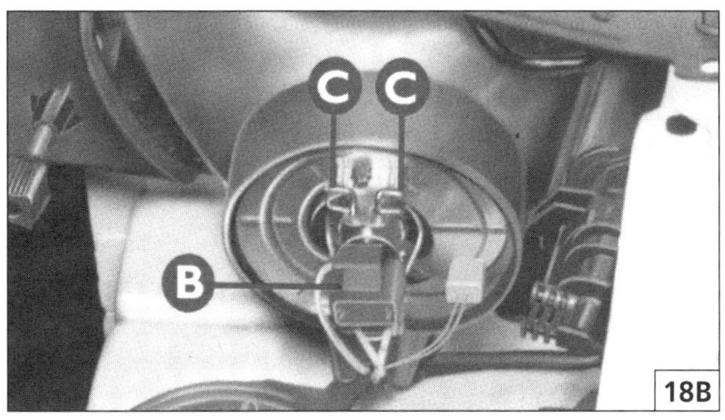

18B. You then pull away the terminal block (B), lift the securing spring arms (C) from their slots...

18C. ...and withdraw the headlight bulb. When fitting the new, you'll find that it will sit happily only in one position, steadied by different sized cut-outs and lugs.

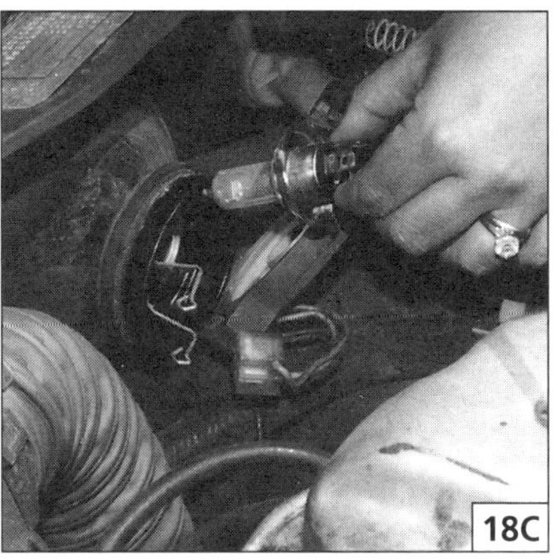

18D. The sidelight bulb (A) usually sits alongside the headlight bulb.

18E. Access to such as the tail light, stop light (or brake light) and direction indicator bulbs of modern rear light clusters varies. On this vehicle you undo the two triangular knobs (A)...

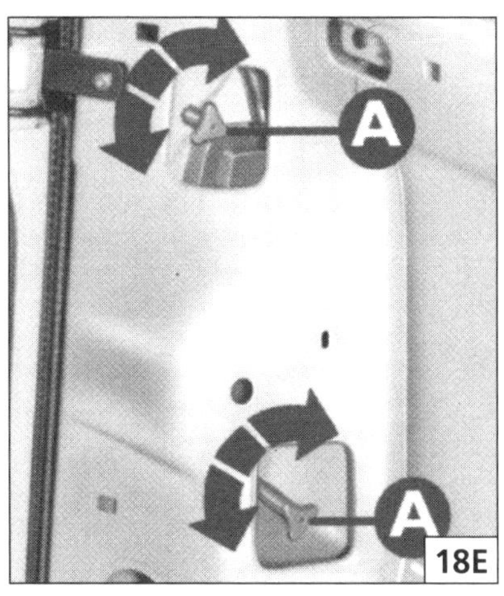

18F. ...then remove the light cluster. Other makes use clips to hold the cluster in place.

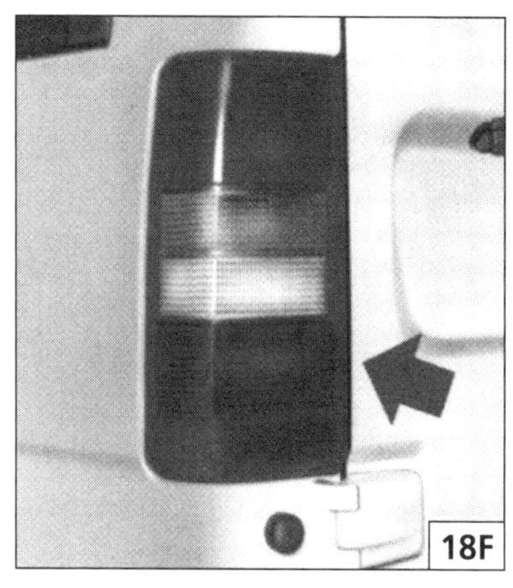

18G. The bulb assembly is usually held in with tabs (B)...

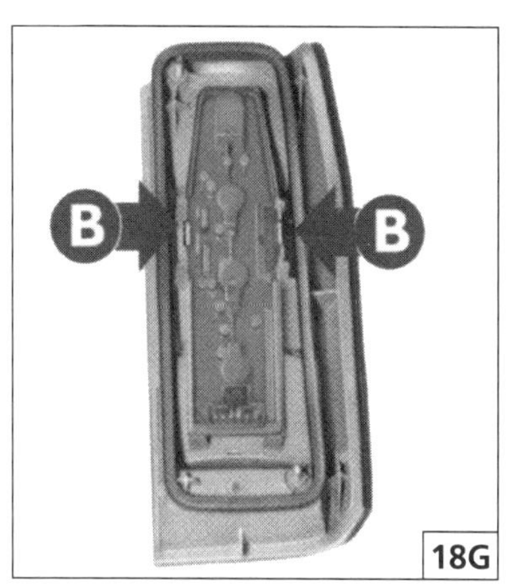

18H. ...after which the bulbs can be removed. On many older vehicles it is normal for access to the bulbs to be gained by first unscrewing the lens unit from the outside. (Illustrations, courtesy Fiat Auto UK)

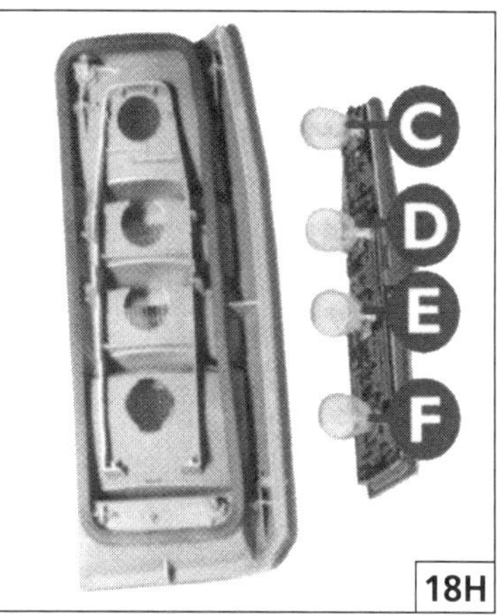

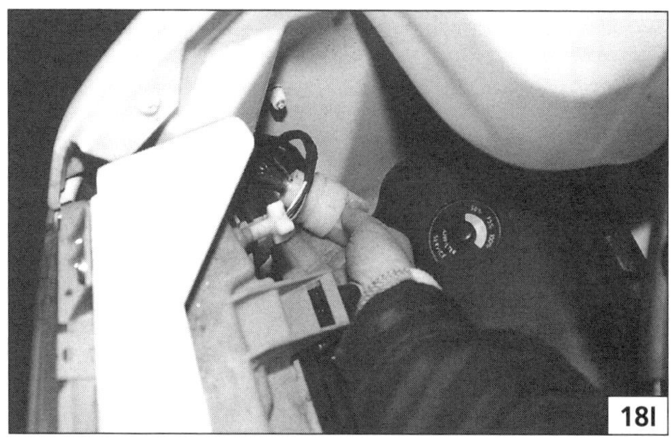

18I. On this Mercedes Sprinter, the indicator bulb housing is withdrawn from inside the engine bay by turning it 1/4 turn anti-clockwise...

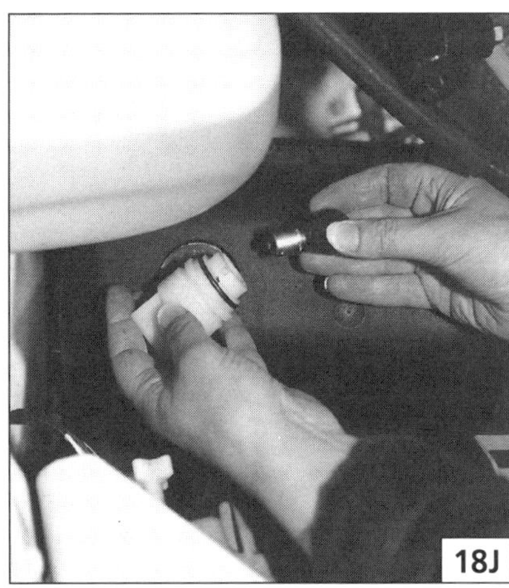

18J. ...and the (coloured!) bulb taken out of the bulb holder. On some vehicles, the bulb holder is held in with a spring clip.

SIDE INDICATOR BULBS

Several different types here: Some, such as FIAT, have a sealed unit. If the bulb goes, unclip it from inside the wing, pull off the wiring connector and fit a new unit from your dealer. Others are unclipped from the wing (either from behind or by turning the lens/unit 1/4 turn and pulling out) and then have replaceable bulbs inside.

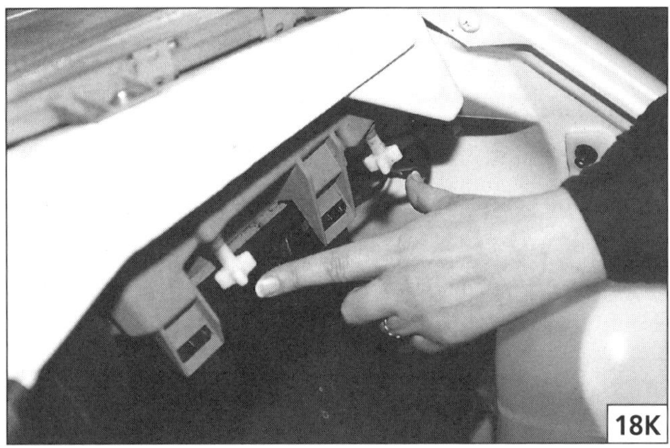

18K. Headlight beams should be reset after bulbs have been changed. If yours seem dangerously 'high' and you *have* to drive at night, you could lower them yourself. However, it is not possible to check or set headlight adjustment accurately at home, so it will have to be checked/set by a garage with proper headlight beam setting equipment.

18L. Ensure that, if your 'van has a beam setter, the level is set to 'O' before the headlight levels are checked by your garage - with the vehicle unladen - to give room for adjustment later.

FUSES

If the bulb of a 'failed light' proves to be sound, the problem may be a 'blown' fuse, in which case a whole set of other electrical components may stop working at the same time. If you have a blown fuse (you'll need your handbook to tell you which is which), on an older vehicle the fuse will probably be a strip-type, with the fuse wire either enclosed in a metal-capped glass tube (as here) or the wire could be exposed, wrapped round a ceramic strip. Either type is simply held by spring clips in the 'fuse box'. Once again, look in your handbook to see where the makers have hidden it.

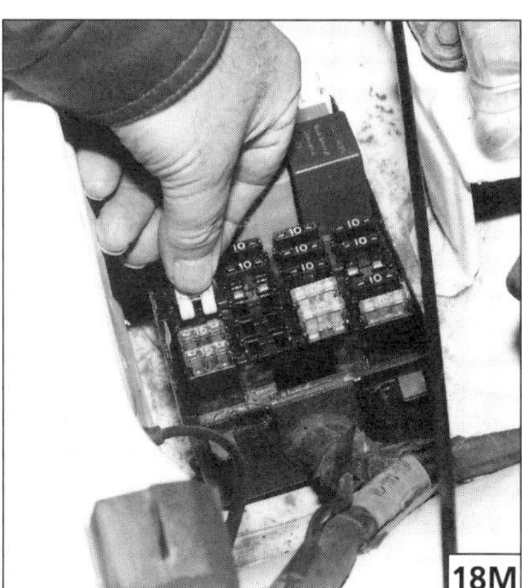

18M. A typical modern type of fuse is the plug-in 'blade' type, as shown here. You can buy replacements from any auto accessory store.

SAFETY FIRST!

- ***If a fuse blows again, after you have replaced it, DON'T be tempted to 'cure' the problem by using a fuse of a higher rating than the one specified, or worse still, using something to bridge the gap where the fuse goes.***
- ***The fuse will have blown (if more than once) because of an electrical problem.***
- ***Vehicle fires can start in seconds and are normally caused by electrical problems, so have an auto-electrician check it out.***

THE HORN

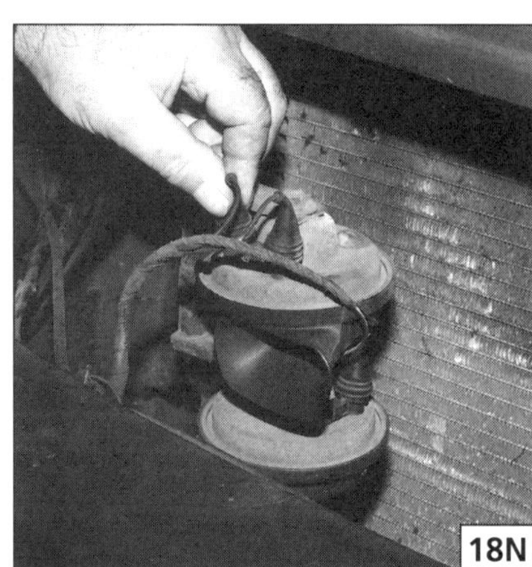

18N. Try the horn button. If the horns fail to work, examine the wiring to the horns themselves. Horn wiring and connections are more complex than they appear at first. For instance, both terminals at the horn should be 'live'! If there is no obvious problem with the wiring connections, have the horn circuitry and switches checked over by a specialist.

Wipers and Washers

☐ Job 19. Check/clear washers.

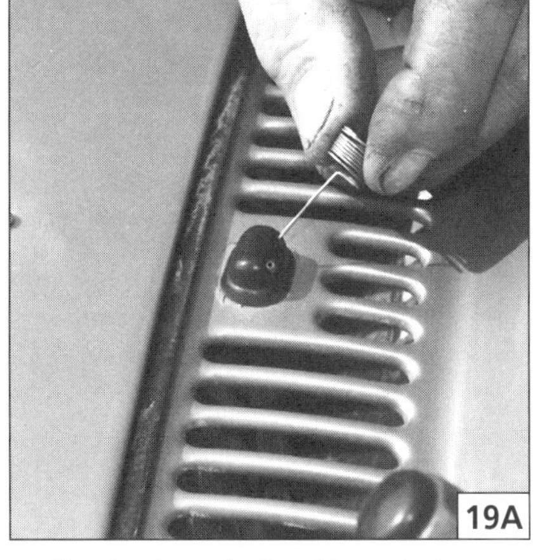

19A. If the spray from one of the screenwash or headlight-wash jets seems uncertain or is non-existent, and you're sure the feed tube to the jet is secure, try poking the jet with a pin to clear possible blockage. Note that on 'ball' type jets, you can use the pin also to swivel the jet to adjust both vertical and lateral aim.

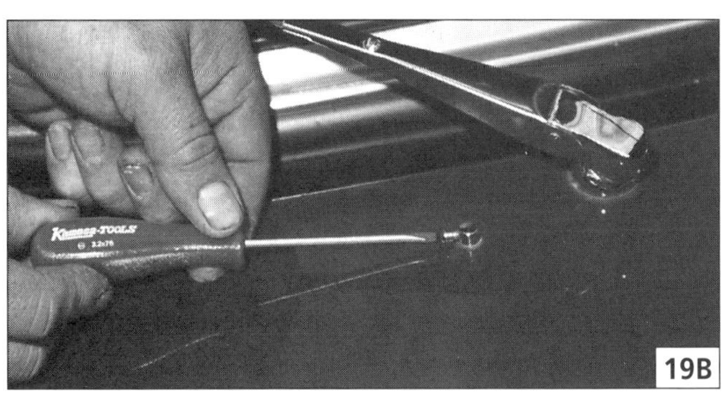

19B. Older types may have a slot in the jet head so you can use a screwdriver blade to adjust the vertical aim, while you may need a small spanner on the jet base to alter lateral aim.

☐ Job 20. Renew wiper blades.

If your wipers are smearing, streaking or juddering, a good accessory shop will be able to advise you as to whether you need complete replacement blades, or whether new rubber 'refills' can be fitted to your existing blades - fitting instructions will come with the pack.

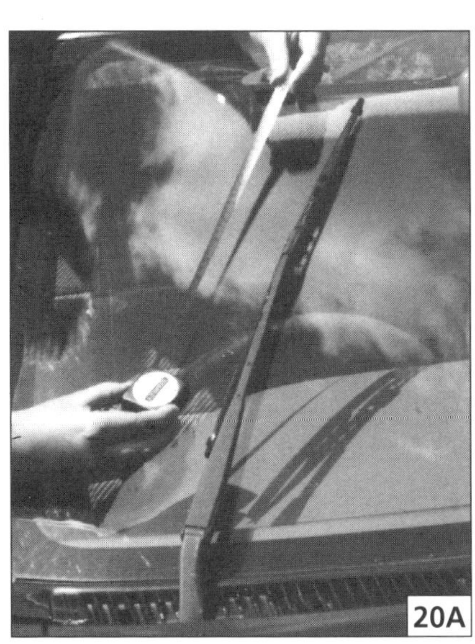

20A. You will need to know the length of your wiper blades, and it is advisable to measure both driver's and passenger's side, since sometimes they are of unequal length. Don't forget, also, to check the rear wiper, where fitted.

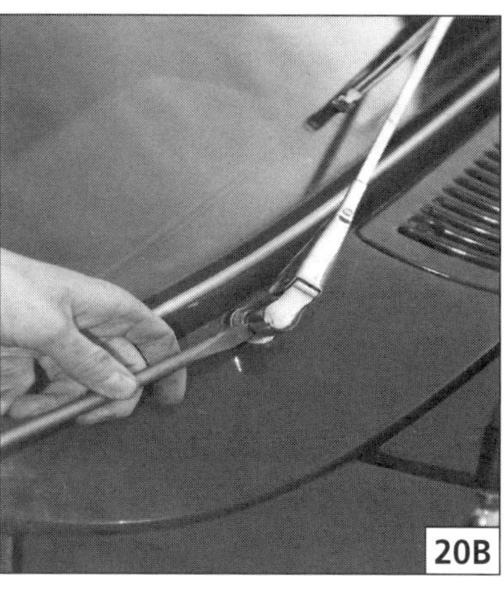

20B. Should a wiper arm need to be removed (perhaps for re-positioning on its splines to obtain a better sweep of the screen), some can just be pulled or levered off, perhaps after removing a locking screw, or lifting the arm to relieve spring tension, while others...

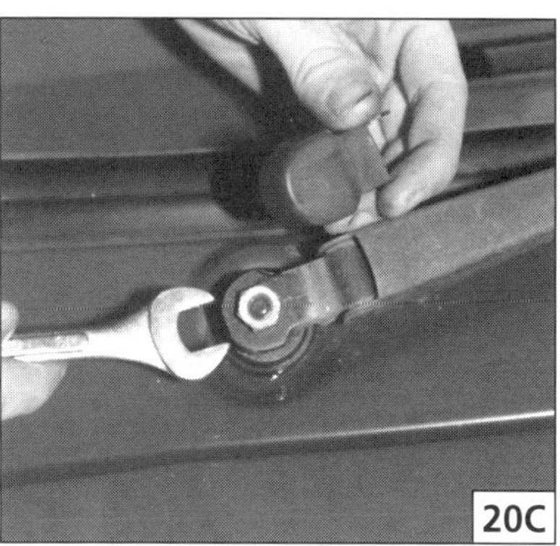

20C. ...will be secured by a nut, having first pulled off its protective cover.

Brakes

☐ Job 21. Check brake pads and discs.

As well as the 'low fluid' warning light on your brake hydraulic system, some brake systems have an electrical sensor built into the disc pad mounting that will illuminate another warning light on the facia to alert the driver to the fact that the pad friction material has worn to the point where it would be prudent to renew the pads.

(Sometimes one warning light serves several possible brake system malfunctions, plus reminding you that the handbrake is applied).

Where no pad wear warning system exists, the vehicle handbook should at least specify a minimum permissible friction material thickness and will normally recommend that the pads are inspected every 6000 miles.

Minimum pad thickness recommendations may vary from, say, 1/16 in. (1.5 mm) to double this, 1/8 in. (3 mm). It is wiser to work to the higher figure, since it can be a relatively short step from 1/16 in. to the 'warning squeal' that tells you that a pad metal backing plate is now rubbing on the disc! Not only will the brakes be dangerously ineffective, but also expensive disc damage will be taking place.

On older vehicles, where the disc brake unit is fairly well exposed, you might be able to see the pads quite clearly. On more modern vehicles, with deeply dished road wheels, the brake unit may be almost totally enclosed by the wheel.

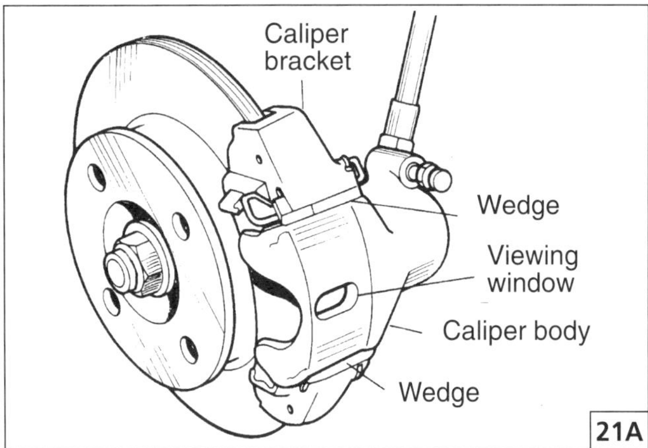

21A. Sometimes the cut-outs of the wheel design allow viewing of the pads through a 'window' let into the brake calliper - although you may need to first remove any wheel trim and you may also need a pencil-beam torch for a clear view. Often, even just for checking, you will need to remove the road wheel. And even then the pads may still be visible only through a window as just described, with maybe the torch still required as well.

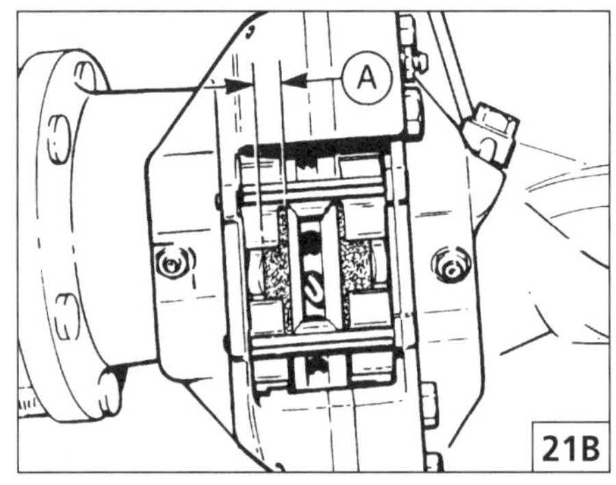

21B. **Remember** that it is the friction material thickness you are checking, not the total pad thickness. (That said, some manufacturers have been known to give a total friction material/backing plate thickness - e.g., 7mm).

If the pads need renewing, they must be renewed in 'axle sets' - i.e., new pads on both offside and nearside wheels of the same axle. Get this job done by the professionals!

While you're down at brake level, take a look at the brake disc surfaces. Check that they are not unduly scored or so badly worn as to leave a prominent ridge around the disc circumference. Very mild annular scoring is normal on older vehicles and can be ignored. Badly scored or badly ridged discs will seriously reduce braking efficiency even with fully bedded-in pads. New pads would take for ever to bed-in on them and meanwhile braking efficiency could be virtually nil!

If you're in any doubt about the condition of your discs, get a mechanic to give his opinion, and if disc renewal is recommended, don't hesitate!

☐ Job 22. Check/adjust brake shoes.

Whereas disc brakes are generally self-adjusting, some drum brake installations, front and rear, will have provision for manual adjustment of the brake shoes to compensate for the friction lining wear which can lead to increased brake pedal travel and (potentially dangerous) unbalanced braking. However, the majority of motor caravans built in the last ten years have disc-type front brakes and automatically-adjusting rear drum brakes.

22A. On those that are manually adjustable, look for a squared protrusion on the drum backplate (arrowed): on front brakes there will normally be two such adjusters, diametrically opposed, one for each shoe; on rear brakes there will normally be just the one.

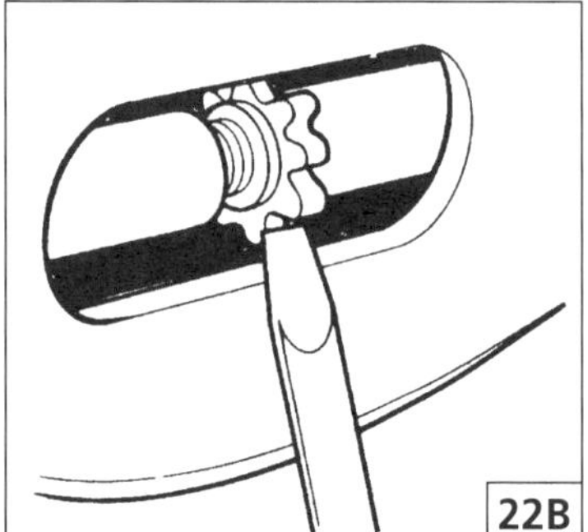

22B. An unusual exception to the squared adjuster on rear brakes is a toothed wheel adjuster, normally accessible through a plugged aperture on the backplate, sometimes through an aperture in the drum face. Often such an adjuster will have two toothed wheels, set close together, so each shoe is adjusted separately. The wheels can be turned by using a screwdriver blade, levering between the wheel teeth and the edge of the access aperture.

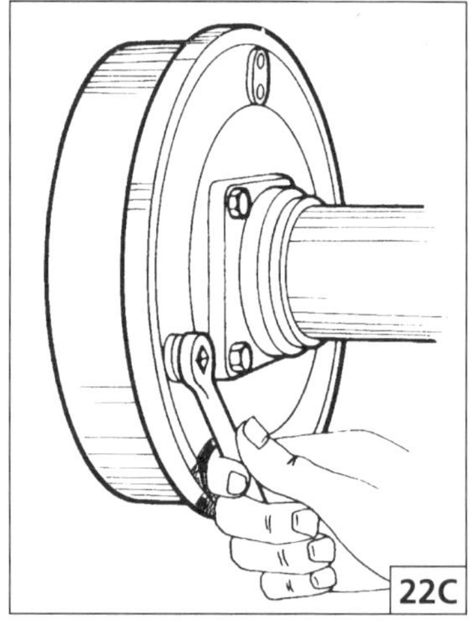

22C. After long service, the squared adjuster may be difficult to turn, and it's always advisable to buy a proper brake spanner for the job. This will be a sturdy item, whereas a 'make do' spanner is likely to slip and round off the adjuster.

It is also advisable to give these adjusters a squirt of releasing fluid before attempting to turn them.

Looking at the brake backplate, generally squared adjusters should be turned clockwise to tighten the adjustment, anti-clockwise to slacken it. A twin toothed wheel adjuster normally requires the teeth on the right-hand wheel to be levered upwards to tighten its shoe, and vice versa on the left-hand adjuster wheel. Obviously, then, turning either the opposite way will slacken the adjustment.

To adjust, first slacken each adjuster until the wheel spins freely. Next, working on one adjuster at a time, turn it until the wheel locks up; now slacken off until the wheel just spins freely again - it is permissible for the shoes to be heard just rubbing slightly. After adjustment, operate the brake pedal and handbrake a few times to settle the shoes, then re-check the adjustment, altering it as necessary.

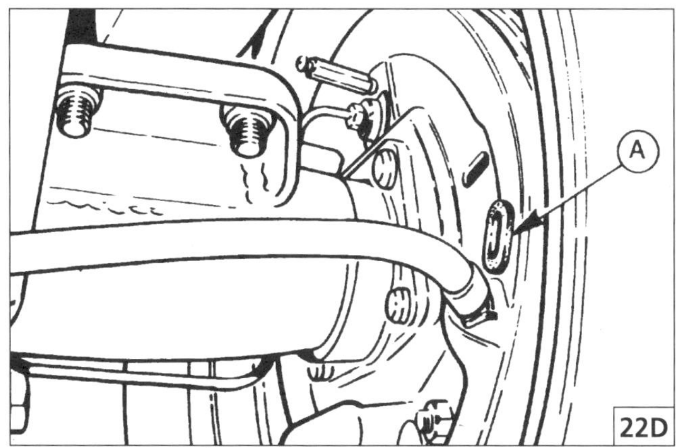

22D. Most modern motor caravans have plugged 'peepholes' (A) in their brake drums to allow a fuss-free check of remaining brake shoe lining thickness. Pull the plug (situated, usually, practically on the circumference of the drum backplate) and you can peer in to the shoe lining with the aid of a torch and perhaps a small mirror too. Admittedly only one shoe can be seen, but that is generally representative of wear on all the shoes of that axle.

As with the pads, the average recommended minimum thickness for brake shoe linings is 1.5 mm (1/16 in.). Again, we suggest that that's too little, and that it would be safer to double the recommendation.

Rear drum brake shoes (less highly stressed than front disc pads) will cover many thousands of miles before they need renewing, and will probably continue to work quite adequately down to that sixteenth of an inch.

If possible, it is best to inspect the brake shoe assemblies with the drums off, and we strongly recommend you have a professional mechanic do this for you.

Locks, Latches, Hinges and Cable Releases

☐ **Job 23. Lubricate.**

It doesn't always figure highly, if at all, in service schedules, but there are a fair few moving parts on the motor caravan which would benefit from occasional oil-can lubrication. They will then work more smoothly, probably more quietly, and will certainly last longer. Here are just a few examples - we have already touched on some earlier in the text, but if you get into the habit of regularly 'carrying the can' around your vehicle, you'll probably spot a few more!

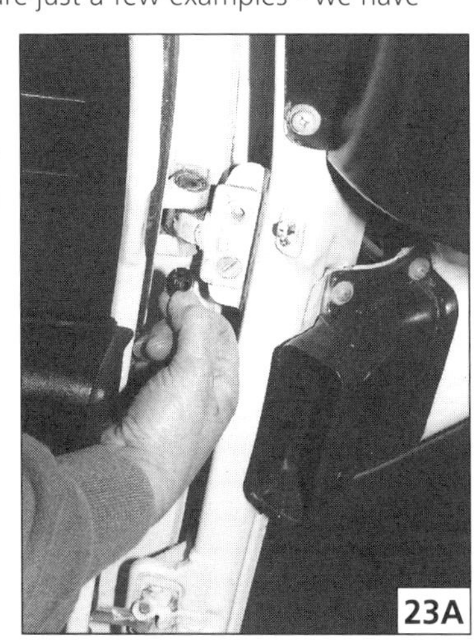

23A. Prime areas for neglect are the door hinges. On this well thought out design (actually on an elderly VW motor caravan!)...

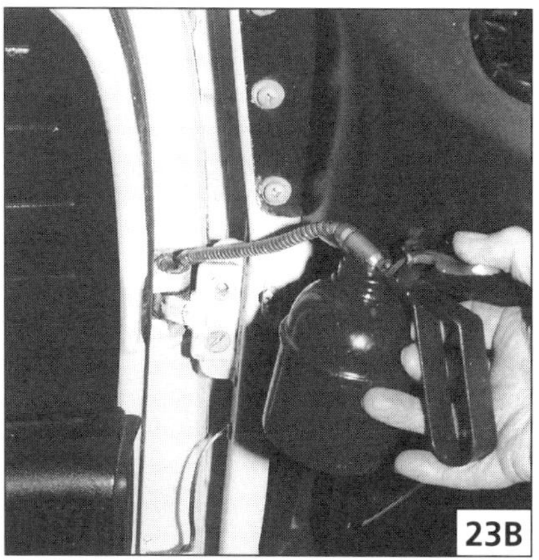

23B. ...you first prise out a plastic cap from the top of the hinge, then direct the oil can nozzle into the hollow beneath.

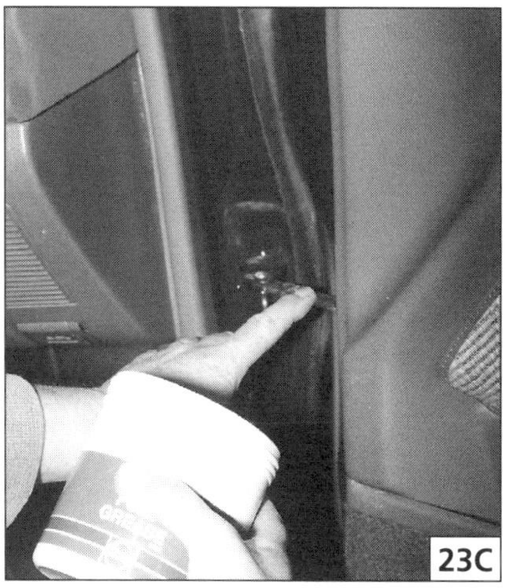

23C. Actually a can of grease, rather than oil, but here a door check strap which, if left unlubricated, dries out, rusts up, and not only retards smooth door opening and closing, but also causes those strident 'graunching' noises which are always an embarrassment! An occasional smear of grease works wonders.

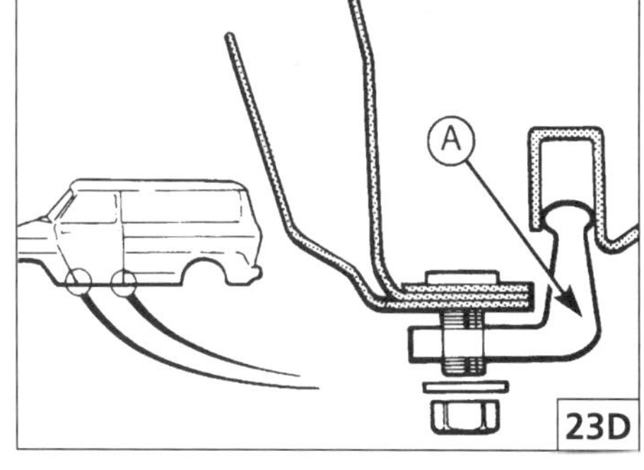

23D. As indeed it does in the side-channel of the sliding side doors used on many motor caravans. Apply grease on these open channels sparingly, as the more is applied, the more road-dirt is attracted to the greased parts.

23E. Another variation on the type of can: on older, or previously neglected door hinges, it could be beneficial to first douse them with penetrating fluid, following up with the oil can a little later, when the penetrating stuff has done its work.

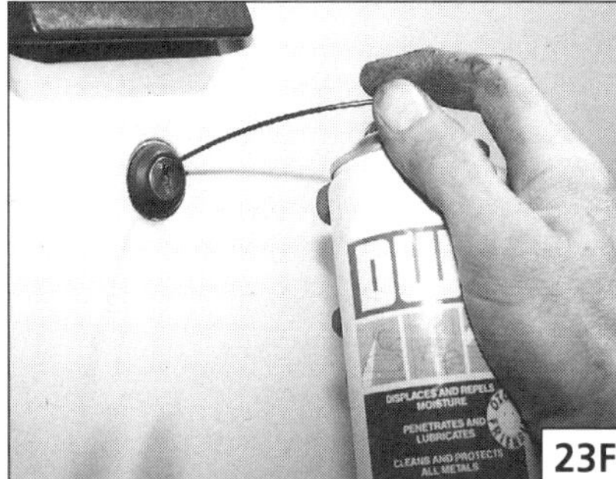

23F

23F. The penetrating fluid, using the can's slim 'accessory tube', is handy for penetrating key lock mechanisms, or door lock push-buttons.

23G

23G. Don't forget the door latch mechanisms, too, for, as with the hinges, lack of lubrication here soon leads to wear and noise, and the door drops out of alignment and has to be slammed shut - more noise, more wear!

23H

23H. While you've got the oil can or tin of grease to hand, go back under the bonnet. If the bonnet latch is not kept lubricated one day you may find you can't, in fact, get under the bonnet, because the latch has rusted and seized. There are possible 'emergencies' that could arise from this, but even more horrific is when a bonnet that has not closed securely flies open when you are driving! Lubricate the bonnet release and safety catch using clean silicone grease so that you won't soil clothes when leaning into the engine bay.

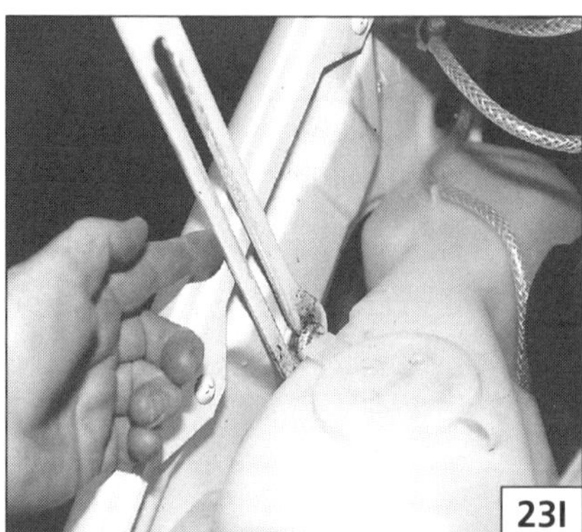

23I

23I. The bonnet stay - more substantial, usually, than on cars - needs lubricating, if of the sliding-type.

Lubricate the bonnet hinges too.

23J

23J. Also lubricate the boot or tailgate lock, and petrol filler flap latch and hinges. If they have a remote release inside the vehicle, lubricate the release cable - if you can get at it! But note that many remote releases on motor caravans are electrically operated, in which case, DON'T APPLY OIL! A case in point is a remote operated petrol filler flap, but at least lubricate the flap hinge and catch, and keep the area clean.

NB Do not lubricate the steering lock, except with the tiniest drop of oil on the end of a key to prevent the lock barrel from seizing.

UNDER THE CAR

Steering and Suspension

☐ Job 24. Check shock absorbers.

If your is a smaller-type of motor caravan, bounce each corner of the vehicle in turn in order to check the efficiency of the shock absorbers. If it 'bounces' at all, the shock absorbers have had it. They should be replaced in pairs and efficient shock absorbers can make an enormous difference to your vehicle's safety and handling.

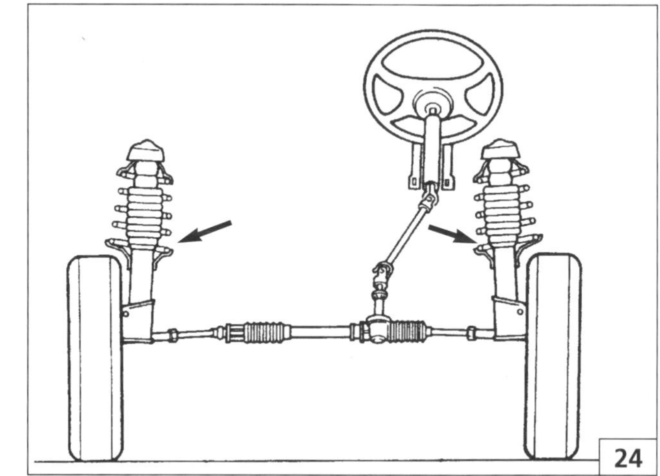

24

24. Check for fluid leaks from the telescopic shock absorbers. If they are seeping, fluid leaks will first show from the top shroud (arrowed) - often semi-hidden behind coil springs. Faulty shock absorbers must be replaced, always in pairs. (Illustration, courtesy FIAT Auto UK)

Job 25. Check mountings.

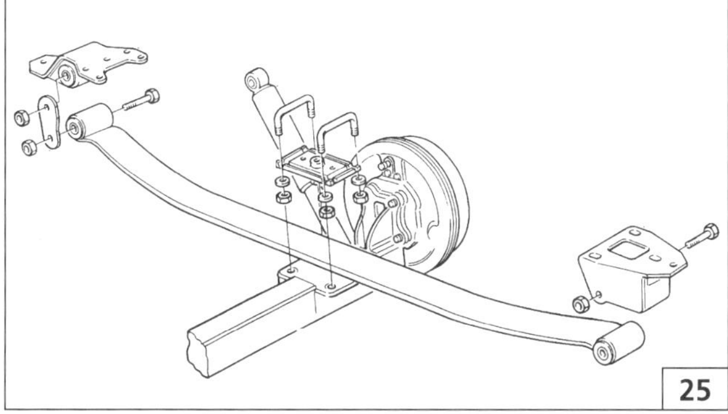

25. All of the suspension mounting, and especially the U-bolts on leaf spring rear suspension, should regularly be checked for tightness. (Illustration, courtesy FIAT Auto UK)

Job 26. Check/lubricate steering and suspension.

Steering and suspension grease points are unusual on all but the oldest motor caravans. Use the grease specified by your manufacturer - in most cases a multipurpose grease.

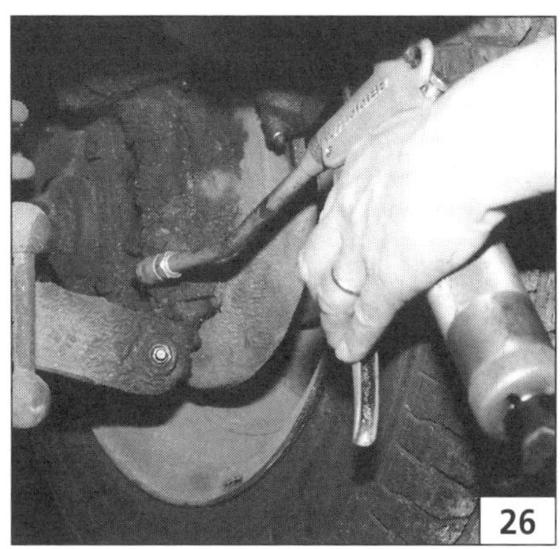

26. Clean off the grease nipple before pushing the grease gun nozzle onto the nipple. Three or four 'pumps' on the grease gun should be enough. You'll get used to the 'feel' if grease is entering the joint satisfactorily and, indeed, you might hear or see some old grease escaping (forced out by the new). Clean surplus grease away thoroughly.

In some cases it might be advantageous to raise the vehicle, allowing wheels and suspension to hang free, whereupon the grease may enter joints more readily.

STEERING RACK GAITERS

Be sure to check both gaiters, on the ends of the steering rack - unless your vehicle has a steering box, in which case this doesn't apply. Check them both with the steering on full lock in each direction. Replace damaged or split gaiters IMMEDIATELY! The rack will very rapidly wear out if there's a split to let the 'weather' in.

TRACK ROD ENDS (TREs)

With the wheels on the ground, reach underneath and wrap your hand around each TRE while an assistant lightly works the steering wheel an inch or two in each direction. If ANY wear can be felt or seen, or if the rubber shroud is split, have the TRE replaced straight away.

General

Job 27. Clean mud traps & body drain holes.

Hose the underside of the vehicle (if particularly muddy) and allow to dry before putting in the garage, or scrape off dry mud. Also, clean out the main mud traps behind the headlights and under the wings.

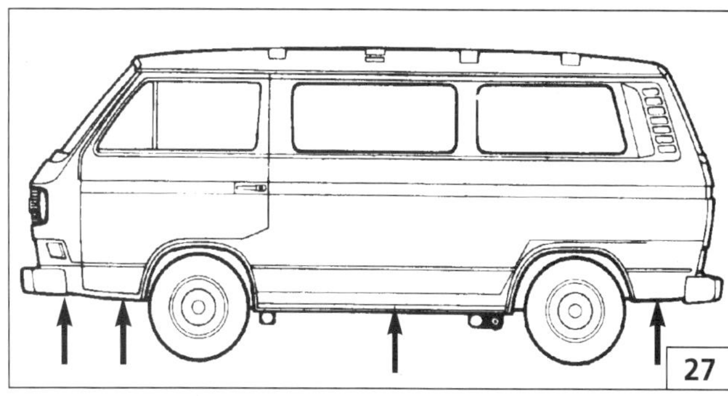

27. Check and clear the drain holes in sills, doors, and around the rear of the vehicle. (Illustration, courtesy Volkswagen)

Transmission

Job 28. Check/top-up/renew manual gearbox oil.

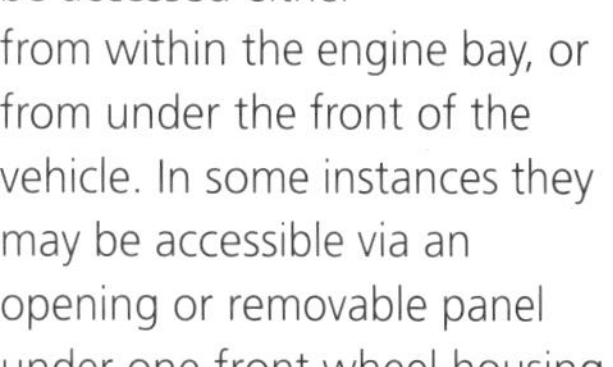

28A. Most modern, front-wheel drive vehicles feature a 'transmission' unit that houses both the gearbox and the final drive in close proximity, sharing a common supply of oil. On these the filler/level plugs may be accessed either from within the engine bay, or from under the front of the vehicle. In some instances they may be accessible via an opening or removable panel under one front wheel housing.

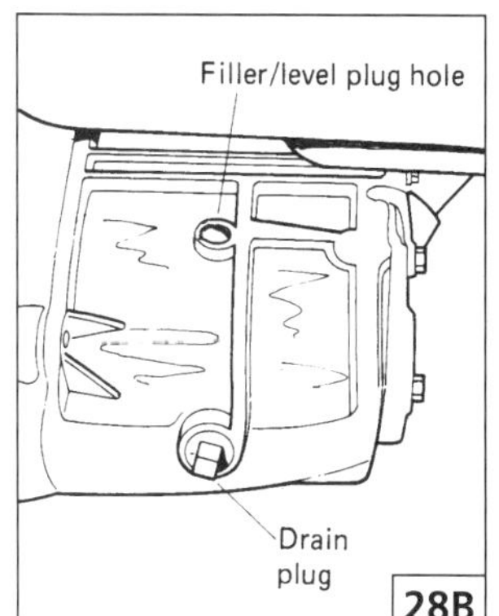

28B. However, most rear-wheel drive and 4WD motor caravans have a separate gearbox beneath the floor, with final drive housed in the rear axle. In the case of four-wheel-drive, there is, of course, a final drive in the front axle too, and an additional 'gearbox' known as the 'transfer' box. These units are accessed from beneath the vehicle, which should be raised and safely supported for the purpose.

Some modern transmission units do not have a drain plug; on these an oil change is not considered ever to be necessary, and so is not catered for. On these all you need do is check and top-up the oil level at the specified intervals.

Clean away dirt from the filler/level plug area before unscrewing and removing the plug: check with a finger that oil is up to the level of the plug hole. You can use a length of bent wire as a dipstick for this purpose.

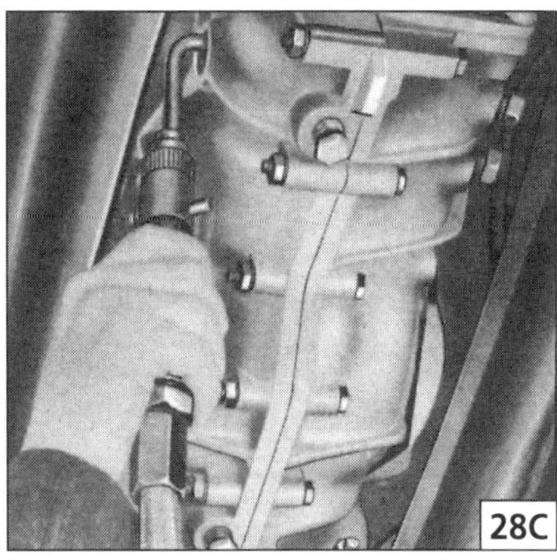

28C. If necessary, add gear oil. You'll be using a 'squeezy' type bottle with a flexible spout to get the oil in, unlike the VW mechanic in this picture, who is using a special pump-type filler to get oil into this air-cooled VW Transporter gearbox. Replace the plug when the oil has finished overflowing from the plug hole, and mop up any spillage.

To renew the gearbox oil, undo the drain plug, and allow the oil to drain (preferably when it's hot). Note that with some front-drive 'transaxle' gearboxes (those housed within the engine bay) there is sometimes a separate drain plug for the final drive unit - so check for this. Clean the plug hole and plug, check the condition of any sealing washer which may be fitted (and renew the washer if necessary). Refit the plug and tighten firmly with an average-length spanner or socket-driver handle, but no more. Then, fill with new oil.

☐ **Job 29. Renew automatic transmission fluid.**

You will find a sump-type drain plug at the bottom or the lower part of one side of the auto. transmission unit. Drain when the oil is still hot, and check the condition of any sealing washer that may be present with the drain plug.

There may also be a transmission filter or filters to wash out in white spirit, which is rarely a difficult thing to do. You'll find it after removing the transmission sump in most cases. Also, you usually have to buy new washers for the drain and filter plugs. And remember SCRUPULOUS CLEANLINESS is vital! If the work becomes too involved, leave it to the professionals! (Illustration, courtesy Ford)

☐ **Job 30. Lubricate grease points.**

REAR WHEEL DRIVE AND 4WD ONLY

30. Some propshaft universal joints and propshaft centre support bearings need occasion greasing via nipples. Follow the advice given in **Job 26** for this.

☐ **Job 31. Check/top-up/renew axle oil.**

REAR WHEEL DRIVE AND 4WD ONLY

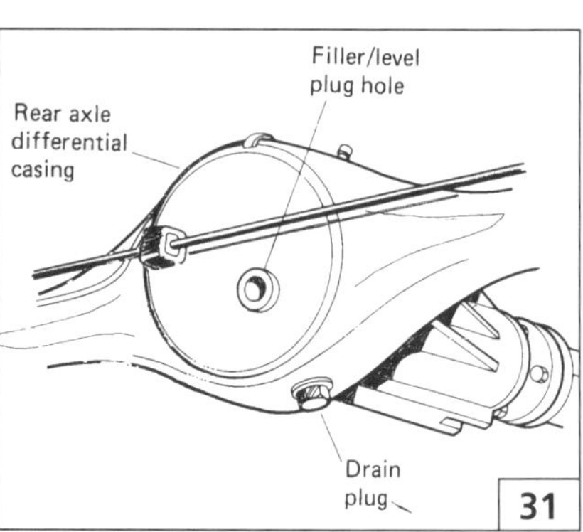

31. Look for the filler/level plug on the differential casing. Generally, transmission oils are sold in plastic 'squeezy' bottles, supplied with a flexible extension tube, and topping-up (particularly where access is restricted) is easiest using these bottles and tubes. Squeeze in oil until the level overflows, then replace the plug and mop up as necessary.

making it easy / *Stand the (sealed!) bottle in a bowl of hot water for fifteen minutes before topping-up: It will go in **much** more easily!*

An 'EP' (extreme pressure) or Hypoid gear oil may be recommended - typically 'EP90'. As with the engine oil, draining, when required, is best done after a short run, when the warmed-up oil will flow more easily.

☐ **Job 32. Check driveshaft gaiters.**

FRONT WHEEL DRIVE ONLY

Driveshafts are very expensive to replace but they will wear out VERY rapidly if a split gaiter lets the oil or grease out and water in. Check inner and outer gaiters on both driveshafts and have them replaced as soon as is necessary if split.

LONGER TERM SERVICING

These are Jobs that need to be carried out at higher mileages. In most cases, you'll probably ask your local specialist or main dealer to carry them out for you. Check handbook or main dealer for your vehicle's recommended service intervals.

Every Two Years

☐ **Job 33. Replace brake fluid.**

☐ **Job 34. Remove and clean diesel glow plugs.**

Every 60,000 Miles

☐ **Job 35. Replace camshaft timing belt, where applicable.**

IMPORTANT NOTE: Some vehicles have a shorter recommended replacement period - check your handbook.

☐ **Job 36. Change gearbox oil.**

☐ **Job 37. Change rear axle oil, if applicable.**

☐ **Job 38. Check, replace if necessary, diesel glow plugs and injectors.**

APPENDIX 1
SPECIALISTS AND SUPPLIERS FEATURED IN THIS BOOK

All of the products and specialists listed below have contributed in various ways to this book. All of the consumer products used are available through regular high street outlets or by mail order from specialist suppliers.

APACHE Awnings, (CGI Camping), P O Box 373, Newcastle, Staffs, ST5 3TD. Tel: 01782 713099

Auto Camping Club Membership, 8 Beaconsfield Road, Woodbridge, Suffolk, IP12 1EQ. Tel: 01394 384431

Auto-Sleepers Ltd., Orchard Works, Willersey, Broadway, Worcs, WR12 7PT. Tel: 01386 853338

Auto-Trail Ltd., (part of ABI Leisure plc), Unit 1A, Pelham Road Industrial Estate, Manby Road, Immingham, South Humberside, DN40 2DW. Tel: 01469 577944

Belling Appliances Ltd., Talbot Road, Mexborough, S Yorkshire, S64 8AJ. Tel: 01709 579902

Bilbo's Trading Co., Marlfield, Eastbourne Road, South Godstone, Surrey, RH9 8JQ. Tel: 01342 892499

Calor Gas Ltd., Appleton Park, Riding Court Road, Datchet, Slough, SL3 9JG. Tel: 01753 540000

Camping Gaz (GB) Ltd., 9 Albert Street, Slough, Berks, SL1 2BH. Tel: 01753 691707

Car-a-Tow, The Haven, Arrowsmith Road, Wimborne, Dorset, BH21 3BG. Tel: 01202 672500

Carver plc, Engine Lane, Coppice Side Industrial Estate, Brownhills, Walsall, W Midlands, WS8 7ES. Tel: 01543 452122

Compass Caravans Ltd., Riverside Industrial Estate, Langley Park, Durham, DH7 6TY. Tel: 0191 373 0899

Electrolux Ltd., Oakley Road, Luton, Beds, LU4 9QQ. Tel: 01582 494111

Fiat Auto (UK) Ltd., Fiat House, 266 Bath Road, Slough, Berks, SL1 4HJ. Tel: 01753 511431

Ford Motor Company Ltd., Eagle Way, Warley, Brentwood, Essex, CM13 3BW. Tel: 01277 253000

Hayes (Leisure) Ltd., Walsall Road, Darlaston, West Midlands, WS10 8UL. Tel: 0121 526 3433

Motor Caravan Information Services, SMMT, Forbes House, Halkin Street, London, SW1X 7DS. Tel: 0171 235 7000.

MURVI Motorcaravans Ltd., 4 East Way, Lee Mill Industrial Estate, Ivybridge, Devon, PL21 9PE. Tel: 01752 892200

Perkson Ltd., The Hayes, Lye, Stourbridge, W Midlands, DY9 8NS. Tel: 01384 424984

Simpsons Motor Caravans, Suffolk Road, Great Yarmouth, NR31 0LN. Tel: 01493 601696

Spinflo Ltd., 4-6 Welland Close, Parkwood Industrial Estate, Rutland Road, Sheffield, S3 9QY. Tel: 0114 273 8157

Swift Motorhomes Ltd., Dunswell Road, Cottingham, Hull, HU16 4JS. Tel: 01482 847332

The Caravan Club, East Grinstead House, East Grinstead, West Sussex, RH19 1UA. Tel: 01342 326944

The Motor Caravanners' Club, 22 Evelyn Close, Twickenham, Middx. TW2 7BN. Tel: 0181 893 3883

The National Caravan Council, Catherine House, Victoria Road, Aldershot, Hants, GU11 1SS. Tel: 01252 318251

Thetford Ltd., Unit 6, Centrovell Estate, Caldwell Road, Nuneaton, Warks, CV11 4UD. Tel: 01203 341941

Volkswagen, V.A.G. (UK) Ltd., Yeomans Drive, Blakelands, Milton Keynes, MK14 5AN. Tel: 01908 601777

Persons Authorised to Sign and Issue Inspection and Completion Certificates.

The 'competent person' who signs your certificate should be one of the following:

- a member of the Electrical Contractors Association (ECA) or a member of the Electrical Contractors Association of Scotland;
- an approved contractor of the National Inspection Council for Electrical Installation Contracting (NICEIC);
- a qualified person acting on behalf of the above (in which case he should state for whom he is acting).
- The names and addresses of Approved Contractors in any locality (there are over 8,000 in the UK) can be obtained from Electricity Board Shops, or from NICEIC (Tel: 0171 582 7746).
- Members of the ECA can be obtained from ECA (Tel: 0171 229 1266) or ECA Scotland (Tel: 0131 225 7221).

APPENDIX 2 - WHAT TO TAKE

However good your memory may be, you would be hard pushed to remember all of the thousand and one things you'll need to take on a caravanning holiday. Use the list shown below, adding your own personal requirements in the spaces provided under each category and we guarantee - you'll still forget something!

FORWARD PLANNING

- ☐ Cancel milk and papers.
- ☐ Check household insurance policy is up to date.
- ☐ Disconnect TV aerial from set and electrical equipment.
- ☐ Inform neighbours, relatives, Neighbourhood Watch, Police (if interested).
- ☐ Lock house, doors/windows and shed. Leave key with neighbour?
- ☐ Turn off gas/water/electricity. (N.B. Freezer, central heating froststat and alarm need power!)
- ☐ ....
- ☐ ....

PAPERWORK

- ☐ Bank and Credit Cards.
- ☐ Cash, cheques and foreign currency.
- ☐ Cheque Books/Travellers Cheques.
- ☐ Club Membership Cards.
- ☐ Contact telephone numbers.
- ☐ Driving Licence.
- ☐ Green card and card documents if touring abroad.
- ☐ Insurance Certificate.
- ☐ Log Books.
- ☐ Maps and guides.
- ☐ Pens/paper/stamps etc.
- ☐ ....
- ☐ ....

BASE VEHICLE

- ☐ First Aid Kit.
- ☐ Foot pump.
- ☐ Fuel can.
- ☐ Overseas requirements, e.g. spare bulbs, snow chains, fire extinguisher, according to country.
- ☐ Levelling ramps.
- ☐ Tyre pressure gauge.
- ☐ Warning triangle.
- ☐ ....
- ☐ ....

LIVING ACCOMMODATION

- ☐ 240v mains lead and adaptor.
- ☐ Awning and fittings.
- ☐ Chemical fluid/sachets.
- ☐ Chemical toilet.
- ☐ Corner steady brace.
- ☐ Corner steady pads.
- ☐ Fire blanket.
- ☐ Fire extinguisher.
- ☐ First Aid Kit.
- ☐ Fresh water hoses.
- ☐ Gas cylinders and spanner.
- ☐ Gas hose - spare.
- ☐ Insect screens.
- ☐ Lamps.
- ☐ Mains polarity tester.
- ☐ Spare fuses/bulbs.
- ☐ Spirit level.
- ☐ Step.
- ☐ Submersible pump.
- ☐ Toilet tent (if applicable).
- ☐ Waste water container(s).
- ☐ Waster water hoses.
- ☐ Wheel chocks.
- ☐ Wheel lock.
- ☐ ....
- ☐ ....
- ☐ ....

TOOLS & EQUIPMENT

- ☐ Jack.
- ☐ Spare keys.
- ☐ Spare wheel/tyre.
- ☐ Tools.
- ☐ Wheelbrace.
- ☐ Torch and batteries.
- ☐ ....
- ☐ ....

HOUSEHOLD

- ☐ Adhesive tape.
- ☐ Air freshener.
- ☐ Aluminium foil.
- ☐ Ant killer/powder.
- ☐ Ashtrays.
- ☐ Barbecue/accessories.
- ☐ Beach 'gear'.
- ☐ Biscuit tin.
- ☐ Bread bin.
- ☐ Breadboard/knife.
- ☐ Broom.
- ☐ Butter dish.
- ☐ Can/bottle opener.
- ☐ Cheese grater.
- ☐ Cleaning cloths.
- ☐ Clock.
- ☐ Clothes brush.
- ☐ Clothes line/rack/pegs.
- ☐ Coat hangers.
- ☐ Colander.
- ☐ Coolbox/freezer packs.
- ☐ Corkscrew.
- ☐ Crockery.
- ☐ Cruet.
- ☐ Cutlery.
- ☐ Drinks.
- ☐ Dusters.
- ☐ Dustpan and brush.
- ☐ Egg Cups.
- ☐ Fish slice.
- ☐ Folding chair.
- ☐ Folding table.
- ☐ Food.
- ☐ Glasses/tumblers.
- ☐ Grill pan.
- ☐ Insect spray.
- ☐ Kettle.
- ☐ Kitchen knives/tools.
- ☐ Kitchen rolls.
- ☐ Matches/lighter.
- ☐ Measuring jug.
- ☐ Mixing bowl.
- ☐ Mop and bucket.
- ☐ Needles/thread.
- ☐ Polythene bags/food wrap.
- ☐ Rubbish bags.
- ☐ Saucepans.
- ☐ Scissors.
- ☐ Seal top containers.
- ☐ Shoe cleaning kit.
- ☐ Shopping bags.
- ☐ Sieve.
- ☐ Soap powder.
- ☐ String.
- ☐ Sunlounger.
- ☐ Table cloths.
- ☐ Tablemats.
- ☐ Tea/coffee pot.
- ☐ Tea strainer.
- ☐ Tissues.
- ☐ Toilet paper.
- ☐ Towels.
- ☐ Tray(s).
- ☐ Vacuum flask.
- ☐ Washing-up bowl/scourer.
- ☐ Washing-up liquid.
- ☐ Whisk.
- ☐ ....
- ☐ ....
- ☐ ....
- ☐ ....
- ☐ ....
- ☐ ....

BEDDING

- ☐ Air bed pump.
- ☐ Blankets.
- ☐ Camp bed(s) - awning.
- ☐ Hot water bottles.
- ☐ Pillows/cases.
- ☐ Sheets/liners.
- ☐ Sleeping bags/duvets.
- ☐ ....
- ☐ ....
- ☐ ....

PERSONAL

- ☐ Clothing.
- ☐ Flannel.
- ☐ Footwear.
- ☐ Hairbrush/comb.
- ☐ Handcleanser (Swarfega).
- ☐ Insect repellent.
- ☐ Make-up etc.
- ☐ Medicines etc.
- ☐ Nail scissors.
- ☐ Rainwear.
- ☐ Shaving kit/mirror.
- ☐ Soap/soapbox.
- ☐ Sun glasses.
- ☐ Sun hats.
- ☐ Suntan oil.
- ☐ Swimwear.
- ☐ Toilet bag.
- ☐ Toothbrush/paste.
- ☐ Umbrella.
- ☐ Wellington boots.
- ☐ ....
- ☐ ....
- ☐ ....

RECREATION

- ☐ Binoculars.
- ☐ Books.
- ☐ Camera/films, video tapes.
- ☐ Playing cards.
- ☐ Radio/cassette player and tapes.
- ☐ Toys and games for journey.
- ☐ TV/aerial.
- ☐ ....
- ☐ ....

APPENDIX 3 - SERVICE SCHEDULE

SERVICING THE BASE VEHICLE

Note that the following are our own recommendations, and they're worth sticking to if you have, for example, an older motor caravan for which servicing information is scarce.

However, where the vehicle manufacturer's service schedule is available, we urge you to stick with that, and to give it priority over these following recommendations.

EVERY 500 MILES, WEEKLY OR BEFORE A LONG JOURNEY

The Engine Bay

- ☐ Job 1. Check/top-up engine oil.
- ☐ Job 2. Check/top-up coolant.
- ☐ Job 3. Check/top-up battery.
- ☐ Job 5. Check/top-up automatic transmission fluid.
- ☐ Job 6. Check/top-up brake/clutch fluid.

Around the Car

- ☐ Job 17. Check tyre pressure/condition.
- ☐ Job 18. Check all lights and horns.
- ☐ Job 19. Check/clear washers.
- ☐ Job 20. Renew wiper blades.

EVERY 6,000 MILES - OR EVERY SIX MONTHS, WHICHEVER COMES FIRST

The Engine Bay

- ☐ Job 4. Check/top-up power steering fluid/steering box oil.
- ☐ Job 8. Renew engine oil.
- ☐ Job 9. Renew engine oil filter.
- ☐ Job 11. Drain water from diesel fuel filter.
- ☐ Job 14. Check/clean/renew petrol spark plugs.
- ☐ Job 16. Check/adjust/renew generator drive belt.

Around the Car

- ☐ Job 21. Check brake pads and discs.
- ☐ Job 22. Check/adjust brake shoes.
- ☐ Job 23. Lubricate locks, latches, hinges and cable releases.

Under the Car

- ☐ Job 30. Lubricate transmission grease points.
- ☐ Job 32. Check driveshaft gaiters.

General

- ☐ Job 27. Clean mud traps and body drain holes.

EVERY 12,000 MILES - OR EVERY TWELVE MONTHS, WHICHEVER COMES FIRST

The Engine Bay

- ☐ Job 7. Renew coolant.
- ☐ Job 12. Renew diesel fuel filter.
- ☐ Job 13. Renew petrol fuel filters.

Under the Car

- ☐ Job 24. Check shock absorbers.
- ☐ Job 25. Check mountings.
- ☐ Job 26. Check/lubricate steering and suspension.
- ☐ Job 28. Check/top-up/renew manual gearbox oil.
- ☐ Job 31. Check/top-up axle oil (RWD & 4WD ONLY).

EVERY 24,000 MILES - OR EVERY TWO YEARS, WHICHEVER COMES FIRST

The Engine Bay

- ☐ Job 10. Renew air filter/adjust air intake.
- ☐ Job 34. Remove and clean diesel glow plugs.

Under the Car

- ☐ Job 33. Replace brake fluid.

LONGER TERM SERVICING

Every 30,000 Miles

- ☐ Job 15. Renew glow plugs.

Every 36,000 Miles

- ☐ Job 29. Renew automatic transmission fluid.

Every 60,000 Miles

- ☐ Job 35. Replace camshaft timing belt, where applicable.
- ☐ Job 36. Change gearbox oil.
- ☐ Job 37. Change rear axle oil, if applicable.
- ☐ Job 38. Check, replace if necessary, diesel injectors.

SERVICING THE LIVING ACCOMMODATION

PREPARING FOR THE START OF THE SEASON

- [ ] Job 1. Check all hinges and brackets.
- [ ] Job 2. Check beds and seats.
- [ ] Job 3. Check upper bunks.
- [ ] Job 4. Check curtains, blinds and nets.
- [ ] Job 5. Have gas system inspected.
- [ ] Job 6. Check vents and flues.
- [ ] Job 7. Check flexible gas hoses and regulator.
- [ ] Job 8. Carry out leak test.
- [ ] Job 9. Check gas appliances.
- [ ] Job 10. Replace CO and smoke detector batteries.
- [ ] Job 11. Prepare refrigerator.
- [ ] Job 12. Check fresh water system.
- [ ] Job 13. Renew water filter.
- [ ] Job 14. Check waste water system.
- [ ] Job 15. Clean out waste water system.
- [ ] Job 16. Check level indicators.
- [ ] Job 17. Prepare w.c..
- [ ] Job 18. Prepare heating system/s.
- [ ] Job 19. Check extractor fans and air conditioning.
- [ ] Job 20. Remove portable heater.
- [ ] Job 21. Check compatibility of cylinders and regulators.
- [ ] Job 22. Check 12 volt system.
- [ ] Job 23. Check wiring and connections.
- [ ] Job 24. Have mains electrics inspected.
- [ ] Job 25. Check hook-ups.
- [ ] Job 26. Check mains voltage system.
- [ ] Job 27. Check external low-level vents.
- [ ] Job 28. Check awning rail seal.
- [ ] Job 29. Check/lubricate cornder steadies.
- [ ] Job 30. Check/lubricate folding step.
- [ ] Job 31. Check underfloor tank moutings.
- [ ] Job 32. Check wheelarches/wheelboxes.
- [ ] Job 33. Clean bodywork.
- [ ] Job 34. Check awning.
- [ ] Job 35. Prepare generator.
- [ ] Job 36. Check audible and visual warning systems.
- [ ] Job 37. Check cycle rack.
- [ ] Job 38. Check towing equipment.

BEFORE EVERY LONG JOURNEY

- [ ] Job 39. Check auxiliary battery fixings.
- [ ] Job 40. Clean/out prepare cassette w.c.
- [ ] Job 41. Replenish fresh water system.
- [ ] Job 42. Check roof vents.
- [ ] Job 43. Check for flammable surfaces.
- [ ] Job 44. Check bedding arrangements.
- [ ] Job 45. Check inventory.

REGULAR CHECKS

- [ ] Job 46. EVERY WEEK - Check electrical trip unit.
- [ ] Job 47. EVERY WEEK - Check fire extinguisher.
- [ ] Job 48. EVERY 2 - 4 WEEKS - Service w.c. flushing mechanism.
- [ ] Job 49. ONCE A MONTH - Check accessible gas pipes and connections.
- [ ] Job 50. ONCE A MONTH - Check auxiliary battery.

EVERY THREE MONTHS

- [ ] Job 51. Check all gas pipes/connections.
- [ ] Job 52. Check flame failure device.
- [ ] Job 53. Check appliance security.

ONCE A YEAR

- [ ] Job 54. Check interior for damp/leaks.
- [ ] Job 55. Check fire blanket.
- [ ] Job 56. Adjust water pressure.
- [ ] Job 57. Replacing a microswitch.
- [ ] Job 58. Clean folding wash basin.
- [ ] Job 59. Check body/chassis mountings.
- [ ] Job 60. Check body retention.
- [ ] Job 61. Remove window and body scratches.
- [ ] Job 62. Check windows.
- [ ] Job 63. Check/lubricate external doors.
- [ ] Job 64. Check/lubricate locker doors.
- [ ] Job 65. Check/lubricate filler caps.
- [ ] Job 66. Check elevating roof.
- [ ] Job 67. Check roof vents.
- [ ] Job 68. Check roof racks and ladders.
- [ ] Job 69. Check/clean furniture.
- [ ] Job 70. Lubricate hinges and catches.
- [ ] Job 71. Check internal doors.
- [ ] Job 72. Check 'advice' notices.
- [ ] Job 73. Check fluid couplings.

PREPARING FOR STORAGE AT END OF SEASON

- [ ] Job 74. Check insurance policy!
- [ ] Job 75. Prepare storage site.
- [ ] Job 76. Check security.
- [ ] Job 77. Drain fresh water system.
- [ ] Job 78. Remove/drain water filter.
- [ ] Job 79. Drain waste water system.
- [ ] Job 80. Service w.c. and shower.
- [ ] Job 81. 'Winterise' the w.c..
- [ ] Job 82. Clean out refrigerator.
- [ ] Job 83. Prepare curtains, blinds and screens.
- [ ] Job 84. Remove/clean upholstery.
- [ ] Job 85. Prepare interior.
- [ ] Job 86. Maintain auxiliary battery.
- [ ] Job 87. Store gas cylinders.
- [ ] Job 88. Dry and store awning.
- [ ] Job 89. Drain generator fuel.
- [ ] Job 90. Maintain air conditioning.
- [ ] Job 91. Check seams and seals.
- [ ] Job 92. Check body/cab joints.
- [ ] Job 93. Check top box mountings and seals.
- [ ] Job 94. Clean bodywork.
- [ ] Job 95. Lubricate cycle rack.
- [ ] Job 96. Maintain tyres.

A

A-Class 10
Air conditioning 67, 91
Air filter 106
Alternator, drivebelt 112
Automatic transmission fluid 99, 122
Awning 27, 70, 91
  rail seal 68

B

Battery
  auxiliary 72, 75, 91
  electrolyte 98
  specific gravity 98
  topping up 97
Bedding 55, 58, 72
  slatted beds 55
  bunks 56, 58
Blinds and Flyscreens 59, 90
Bodycab Joints 93
Bodywork 70, 94,
  drain holes 121
Brakes
  discs 117, 118
  fluid 100
  pads 117, 118
  shoes 118, 119
Bulb renewal (see 'Lights')
Brakes and Asbestos, safety 7
Buying Guide .... 9 to 20
  what to consider 12

C

Clutch fluid 100
Coachbuilt 10
Connecting Up .... 28 to 30
Contents 4
Cooking equipment 53
Coolant
  check specific gravity 97
  drain and replace 101, 102
  top-up 97
Corner steadies 26, 69
Couplings 86
Curtains and blinds 59, 90
Cycle rack 70

D

Data-base 1
Dismountables 12
Doors
  lubricate 82
  locker 83
  internal 86
  exterior 82
Drainage
  taps 25
Drivebelts
  alternator 112
Driveshaft
  gaiter 122
Driving 21, 26

E

Electrical
  12-volt 37, 67
  connecting up on site .... 28 to 30
  connections 68
  Continental european connections 29
  disconnecting 30
Electrical system .... 37 to 39
  site connections 29
  site supplies 29
Electricity
  mains 39, 68
  mains, safety 68
  mains, voltage 68
  trip unit 72
Elevating roof 11, 84
Extractor fans 67

F

Filler cap 84
Fire blanket 79
Fire extinguisher 73
Fixed roof 12
Flame failure device 53, 64, 77
Folding step 26, 69
Folding table 25
Fuel Filter
  drain water, diesel 107
  renew, diesel .... 108 to 110
Furniture
  clean 85
Fuses 60, 63

G

Gas cylinders 24, 37, 67, 91
Gas regulator and hose 60, 67
Gas system .... 37 to 37, 59
  appliances 61
  flame structure 62
  lubricate controls 62
  pipes and connections 74, 76, 77
  safety 78
Gearbox, oil
  manual 121, 122
Generators 70
  drain fuel 91
Glowplugs, diesel 112

H

Heaters 41, 67
  blown air central heating 41
  Fanmaster system 41
  flued 39, 40
  portable 67
  propex 42, 43
High-top 11
Hinges and catches 57, 58, 85
Hinges and locks
  external 82, 119
Horn 116

I

Insurance
  policy 87
Interior 81

L

Leaks 60, 78
Level indicators 67
Levelling 27
Lights
  bulb replacement 34, 114
  exterior 34
  indicators 116
  interior 35

M

Micro-Motor caravans 12
Microswitch 79
Mountings 80, 121

O

Oil change
axle oil 122
petrol engines ..... 102 to 105
Oil filter
petrol 105
Oil level
topping up 96
Operating Instructions ..... 31 to 56

P

Parking 23, 26
Pitching 27
Power steering
fluid 98

R

Refrigerator 25, 54, 55, 65, 90
Reversing 23
Roof
elevating 84
racks and ladders 85

S

Safety First ..... 5 to 8
Seams and seals ..... 91 to 93
Seats 58
Security 87
Service History 125, 126
Servicing the Base Vehicle ..... 95 to 122
Servicing the Living Accommodation ..... 57 to 94
Shock absorbers, ... 120
Shower 89
Smoke detector 64
Spark plugs 111
Specialists and Suppliers 123
Steering 121
rack gaiters 121
track rod ends 121
Storage 87
Superpitch 30
Suspension 121

T

Toilet 67, 89
cassette ..... 49 to 52, 72
flushing mechanism 74
Thetford Porta Potti 48, 49
Top box
mountings 94
seals 94
Towball 71
Towing 30, 71
Tyres
maintain 94
pressures 114

U

Upholstery 91
safety 72
Using Your Motor Caravan ..... 21 to 30

V

Vents 60, 68, 72, 85

W

Warning notices 86
Warning systems 70
Wash basin 80
Waste system 44, 45, 66
Water
clean 66
drain 88
filter 66, 88
heaters 46, 47
pressure 79
system 44, 45, 65, 66
tank mountings 69
topping up 72
Weight limits 23
calculating payloads 23
What to take 124
Wheel
changing ..... 31 to 34
clamps 87
Windows
scratches 81
top-hinged 25
Windscreen washers 117
Windscreen wipers 117